THE ONSET OF GLOBAL GOVERNANCE

Dedicated to the memory of my mother, Claire K. Leonard

The Onset of Global Governance

International Relations Theory and the International Criminal Court

ERIC K. LEONARD
Shenandoah University, USA

ASHGATE

Published by
Ashgate Publishing Limited
Gower House
Croft Road
Aldershot
Hampshire GU11 3HR
England

Ashgate Publishing Company
Suite 420
101 Cherry Street
Burlington, VT 05401-4405
USA

Ashgate website: http://www.ashgate.com

British Library Cataloguing in Publication Data
Leonard, Eric K.
The onset of global governance : international relations theory and the International Criminal Court
1.International Criminal Court 2.International relations - Philosophy 3.Humanitarian law 4.Globalization - Social aspects
I.Title
327.1'01

Library of Congress Cataloging-in-Publication Data
Leonard, Eric K.
The onset of global governance : international relations theory and the International Criminal Court / by Eric K. Leonard.
p. cm.
Includes bibliographical references and index.
ISBN 0-7546-4531-2
1. International Criminal Court--History. 2. International criminal courts--History. 3. International relations. 4. World organization. I. Title.

KZ6311.L46 2005
345'.01--dc22

2005018435

ISBN-10: 0 7546 4531 2

Printed and bound in Great Britain by MPG Books Ltd, Bodmin, Cornwall

Contents

Acknowledgements

This text owes a great deal to the criticism and suggestions of the many individuals who read earlier drafts. I would like to thank Yale Ferguson, Kenneth Campbell, and Mark Huddleston for their insightful comments and scathing criticism. I would especially like to thank James Oliver and Kurt Burch for both their professional expertise and personal friendship. Their intellectual guidance, patience, and encouragement helped me shape this text and continue on the correct path until its completion. To them I owe a great debt and eternal gratitude. I would also like to thank Mary McGlynn, Cindy Waksmonski, and Ramona Wilson. Not only did they supply me with the technical advice necessary to complete this project, but their constant words of encouragement and enduring guidance kept me on track and progressing towards my goal. Finally, I would like to thank all of my students at Shenandoah University and the University of Delaware. Your intellectual curiosity is infectious and for that I am forever grateful.

In addition, I would like to thank my family, who provided me with the emotional support system necessary to complete such a lengthy and arduous endeavor. First I would like to thank my in-laws, Rose Ann and Anthony Mennella, for believing in my ability and always holding out hope for the best. The support you provided me was immeasurable. A resounding thank you goes to my father, Edward Leonard, and my stepmother, Marie Hoffmann. They believed in me when no one else did and it was their "encouragement" that resulted in me going back to school and pursuing a career in academia. Thank you for the unending support and faith in my ability. Thank you also to my three young children Nicolas, Stefani, and Mathieu. Your unending supply of hugs and tireless laughter were a greater benefit then you could ever imagine. Finally, I owe the largest amount of gratitude to my wife, Lisa Marie Mennella. Her love, support, extensive patience, and companionship have made this long road not only bearable, but also delightful. She has made the long days and sleepless nights worthwhile. Without her by my side I would never have been able to accomplish all that I have.

This manuscript is dedicated to the memory of my mother, Claire K. Leonard, who taught me that with hard work and perseverance I could accomplish anything. Thank you for everything. You are always in my thoughts.

List of Abbreviations

CICC	Coalition for the International Criminal Court
IASC	United Nations Inter-Agency Standing Committee
ICC	International Criminal Court
ICJ	International Court of Justice
ICRC	International Committee of the Red Cross
ICTR	International Criminal Tribunal for Rwanda
ICTY	International Criminal Tribunal for the former Yugoslavia
IFOR	Humanitarian Intervention Force for the former Yugoslavia
IGO	International Governmental Organization
ILC	International Law Commission
IMT	International Military Tribunal
IMTFE	International Military Tribunal for the Far East
MNC	Multinational Corporation
NATO	North Atlantic Treaty Organization
NGO	Non-Governmental Organization
NLI	Neoliberal Institutionalism
P-2	China and the United States
P-5	United Nations Permanent Security Council Members
PrepCom	Preparatory Committee for the Establishment of an ICC
SOA	Spheres of Authority
SOFA	Status of Forces Agreements
TAN	Transnational Advocacy Network
TNC	Transnational Corporation
UN	United Nations
UNGA	United Nations General Assembly
UNSC	United Nations Security Council
US	United States of America
WTO	World Trade Organization

Chapter 1

The Need for Analysis

> Trials never end, of course. Unhappiness and misfortune are bound to occur as long as people live, but there is a feeling now, that was not here before, and is not just on the surface of things, but penetrates all the way through: We've won it. It's going to get better now. You can sort of tell these things.
>
> Robert M. Pirsig[1]

Introduction

In his 1993 article, Stephen Krasner, reflecting a mainstream neorealist understanding of international relations, asserts that the confrontation between state sovereignty and human rights makes the formation of a viable human rights regime unlikely. According to Krasner, "States have been reluctant to accuse other states of human rights violations because of the danger that their own sovereign control would be undermined."[2]

As a result of this statement, one could presume that Krasner regards the establishment of a permanent international criminal court as problematic, subject to manipulation by certain states, and simply an implausible solution to violations of humanitarian law. According to Krasner, nation-states will not relinquish their sovereignty to a transnational court and in regards to the issue of humanitarian law states will continue to set the agenda. From this perspective, the establishment of a permanent international human rights regime is unlikely because it challenges the core constitutive principle of the global system—that is state sovereignty.

Counter to Krasner's argument is the current reality surrounding the establishment of a permanent International Criminal Court (ICC). At the time of writing this text, the Rome Statute for an International Criminal Court has one hundred and thirty-seven signatories and ninety-nine ratifying states.[3] The establishment of such an institution creates a tension in which either Krasner's

---

1 Robert M. Pirsig, *Zen and the Art of Motorcycle Maintenance* (New York, NY: Bantam Books, 1981), 372-373.

2 Stephen D. Krasner, "Sovereignty, Regimes, and Human Rights," in *Regime Theory and International Relations,* ed. Volker Rittberger (Oxford: Clarendon Press, 1993), 164.

3 The Rome Statute of the International Criminal Court is the result of the United Nations Diplomatic Conference of Plenopotentiaries on the Establishment of an International Criminal Court, Rome, Italy, June 15-July 17, 1998. As of June 1, 2005, ninety-nine nation-states have ratified the Statute. See the Appendix for a complete listing of ratifications and signatories. The number of signatories did stand at one hundred and thirty nine, but the United States and Israel withdrew their signatures.

depiction of humanitarian law as an issue-area is incorrect or the mainstream understanding of international relations is inadequate, or both. Thus, the central research questions contained in this text are as follows: 1) what does the formation of a permanent International Criminal Court represent in terms of governance in the contemporary world? 2) What does this suggest about the way in which international relations scholars analyze world politics?

In addressing these questions, this text will first and foremost assess the formation of the International Criminal Court as established during the Rome Conference. Second, through an analysis of this case and its formation process, I will draw some conclusions about the changing nature of world politics in terms of the primacy of state actors, authority, governance, and norm construction.

In order to accomplish these goals, this text will analyze the ICC formation process from three different analytical approaches: neoliberal institutionalism, regime theory, and global governance. This method of analysis provides my audience with three different readings of the ICC, thus revealing different aspects of this case. The primary purpose of this exercise is not to test the different perspectives in order to ascertain the "best" one, but to employ these three different perspectives in order to ascertain a fuller and richer understanding of this novel institution. With that said, it would be naïve of me to think that this method does not provide any test of these perspectives and their relevancy. By employing them to understand the formation of the ICC, I am judging their ability to understand this particular case. Thus, a secondary accomplishment of this discourse is an elementary form of theory testing at least as these perspectives pertain to this case and this issue-area.

The Current Global Context

> During the 1980s and 1990s, theorists recognized that something deeper was happening, something more fundamental than a mere interconnectedness among states and between states and individuals…Spurred by technological change and the globalization of economic life, the state is challenged, its sovereignty undermined and constrained, its structures unable to provide the necessary public goods.[4]

> No longer is the world organized into a set of discrete sovereign states exercising a large (though never complete) degree of control over their domestic economies. Globalizing

[4] Karen A. Mingst, "Global Governance: The American Perspective," in *Globalization and Global Governance,* ed. Raimo Vayrynen (Lanham, MD: Rowman & Littlefield, 1999), 89. One public good that the state is unable to provide is protection from violations of humanitarian law. This is one of the reasons why the formation of the ICC is so important.

> patterns add new complexity to what is quaintly called international relations; they transcend, blur, and even redefine territorial boundaries.[5]

These two statements succinctly capture the changing nature of the current global system. The system is no longer constructed solely of Westphalian polities, but is instead a system of multiple actors concerned with multiple issues. As the Commission on Global Governance stated:

> What is new today is that the interdependence of nations is wider and deeper. What is also new is the role of people and the shift of focus from states to people. An aspect of this change is the growth of international civil society. These changes call for reforms in the modes of international cooperation…[6]

The common term for this transformative process is globalization. One could assert that the past two decades have entailed an intensification of this globalization process. Therefore, it is necessary to begin this text with a brief analysis of the globalization process in order to understand the environment within which the ICC is forming.

Martin Shaw defines globalization as: "[a] complex set of distinct but related processes—economic, cultural, social and also political and military—through which social relations have developed toward a global scale and with global reach, over a long historical period."[7]

Arguably, the intensification of this process over the past decades has initiated a global system in which the interaction between actors has also intensified, along with an increase in the actual number of influential actors.[8] The global system now consists of not only states, but also non-state actors who are operating in and across a system of culturally and economically permeable boundaries. As a result, a multiplicity of actors, including, but not limited to nation-states, appear to be embodying the idea of international authority and the level of interdependence

---

5 James H. Mittelman, "How Does Globalization Really Work?" in *Globalization: Critical Reflections,* ed. James H. Mittelman (Boulder, CO: Lynne Rienner Publishers, 1997), 229.

6 Commission on Global Governance, *Our Global Neighborhood: The Report of the Commission on Global Governance* (Oxford: Oxford University Press, 1995), XIV.

7 Shaw, "State of Globalization," 498.

8 As Yale H. Ferguson and Richard W. Mansbach, "Global Politics at the Turn of the Millenium: Changing Bases of 'Us' and Them," *International Studies Review* 2 (1999): 77-108, explain, globalization has to some extent been going on for centuries, but contemporary globalization is distinct in its intensification of this process. Quoting from Jan Aart Scholte, "Beyond the Buzzword: Toward a Critical Theory of Globalization," in *Globalization: Theory and Practice,* ed. Eleonore Kofmon and Gillian Youngs (New York: Pinter, 1997), 432, "[today] Borders are not so much crossed as *transcended."*

between actors and issues appears on the rise. It is from this type of environment that the formation of an ICC becomes plausible.

This brief description of the current global context is crucial because globalization is not simply about the rise of transnational entities and the interdependence of states. Globalization is also a process of localization that often takes the form of ethnic violence and the reassertion of "nested polities."[9] James Rosenau terms this process "fragmegration", in order to capture the fragmenting and integrating aspects of globalization. Because the ICC is a transnational entity that deals with the results of the fragmentation of nation-states and the localization of international politics, one could argue that the ICC is an institution that arose in part from this fragmegration process. The need for such an institution appears to stem from the increased rise in intra-state violence and the rise in prominence of ethnic, religious, and cultural polities across the globe.[10] These issues have always been at play in global politics, but now appear more prominent in the eyes of both decision-makers and scholars. The approval of the Rome Statute captures the prominence of these issues and exemplifies the importance of this case in light of the current global order.

Importance of the International Criminal Court

On April 11, 2002, a group of state representatives, along with a coalition of non-governmental organizations (CICC), International Criminal Court supporters, and media personnel, gathered at the United Nations headquarters in New York. The

---

9 Rosenau, *Domestic-Foreign Frontier,* 78-98, explains the dualistic nature of the globalization process. But it is Yale H. Ferguson and Richard W. Mansbach, *Polities: Authority, Identities and Change* (Columbia, SC: University of South Carolina Press, 1996) and Yale H. Ferguson and Richard W. Mansbach, "History's Revenge and Future Shock," in *Approaches to Global Governance,* ed. Martin Hewson and Timothy J. Sinclair (Albany, NY: State University of New York Press, 1999), 197-238, that describe the localizing effect of globalization. They discuss the idea of "nested polities" or subnational loyalties that are now gaining increased prominence among certain populations. This tends to undercut the established Westphalian borders because these nested polities exist within the Westphalian state but pledge their loyalty to a nation, not a Westphalian state. As Ferguson and Mansbach, "History's Revenge, Future Shock," 210, state, "the revival of nested precolonial identities…increasingly challenge the Westphalian structures imposed by conquering Europeans."

10 As the UN's Inter-Agency Standing Committee (IASC) stated on June 14, 1999, the nature of conflict today is not international conflict, but intra-state conflict. Since the ICC will have the power to address such conflicts in a legal manner, the UN IASC publicly supports the ratification process of this institution. Karen Berg, "A Permanent International Criminal Court," *UN Chronicle* 34 (1997): 2, also points to the need for the ICC because crimes today are often "not committed by a group of persons from the same State, nor within the borders of one State or against the civilians of one State."

purpose of this gathering was to celebrate the establishment of a permanent International Criminal Court. At this event, the Rome Statute for an International Criminal Court received its sixtieth ratification, establishing it as a functioning organization. For many states, non-governmental organizations (NGOs), and other human rights advocates, this marked a joyous moment in the struggle to uphold international humanitarian law and the principles of global justice. As Persig's epigram at the beginning of this chapter describes, there is a feeling amongst advocates of an ICC that things are getting better and that advances are occurring in the fight for global justice.

The fight to construct an International Criminal Court is not simply the product of the past fifteen years and all its turmoil. The international community first discussed the idea of a permanent international criminal court after World War I with the unsuccessful attempt to establish an international tribunal on war crimes. After World War II, the victorious governments established the Nuremberg and Tokyo war crime tribunals, thus setting the precedent for an international criminal court. In 1948, many members of the United Nations General Assembly called specifically for the establishment of an international criminal court, but in 1954 the UN abandoned this effort due to strong opposition from the world's most powerful states. It was not until 1989 that Trinidad and Tobago re-introduced the idea of forming an ICC. At that time, the United Nations General Assembly requested that the International Law Commission (ILC) prepare a draft statute on the ICC. In 1994, the ILC submitted its final draft statute and the General Assembly recommended that a conference convene to try to negotiate a treaty that would enact an ICC. From this process the Rome Statute was born and the resultant ICC gained international legitimacy.[11]

The establishment of a permanent International Criminal Court is an important and novel development in contemporary international relations for several reasons. First, as stated earlier, the formation of an International Criminal Court institutionalizes important elements of the international human rights regime. More specifically, it results in the protection of individuals against the crime of genocide, crimes against humanity, war crimes, and crimes of aggression.[12] In the past, certain countries and institutions have offered protection against some of these crimes. The post-World War II Nuremberg and Tokyo international military tribunals, the 1948 Genocide Convention, the 1948 Universal Declaration of Human Rights, the International Court of Justice, and the ad hoc tribunals for the former Yugoslavia and Rwanda each represent attempts to institutionalize, to some extent, the human rights regime. However, none of these institutions and/or conventions provides for the same protections found in the Rome Statute.

---

[11] Chapter two contains a more detailed discussion of the history of the ICC formation process.

[12] Rome Statute of the ICC, Article 4 (2).

Second, the formation of the ICC is an important and novel development in international relations because of the court's *a priori* presumptive authority to act. Along with this, the Rome Statute holds individuals responsible for their actions. This premise of individual responsibility allows the ICC to accept cases that are beyond the scope of the International Court of Justice (ICJ).[13] Finally, the ability of the prosecutor to initiate an investigation *proprio motu* is crucial because of the independence that this will grant the court.[14] Simply put, no other convention, declaration or institution has had the legal authority to uphold humanitarian law as broadly and as fully as this institution. The ICC truly is the institutionalization of an international humanitarian law regime.

Another novel feature of this case is the fact that the establishment of an ICC initiates a global judicial mechanism of the humanitarian law regime that resides outside of the authority of nation-states. Signatories of the Rome Statute are nation-states, and the convention does call for a complementary relationship between the states' judicial systems and the ICC, but this does not mean that states control the actions of the Court.[15] States play a part, but it is the ICC and its third party arbitration system that has the ability to exercise its authority "on the territory of any State Party and, by special agreement, on the territory of any other State."[16] Therefore, the ICC appears to be an example of transnational authority, or authority that exists beyond the borders of the Westphalian state. This is not to imply that the role of nation-states in the formation process is insignificant. The role of states within this process is crucial and must maintain a high priority throughout this narrative.

This brings us to the sixth reason why the ICC is such an important international development—the drafting process of the Rome Statute differed in many ways from previous international treaty negotiations. Traditionally, an institutional bargaining process involved nation-states negotiating amongst themselves. The regime formation process surrounding the ICC was very different. It involved not only nation-states, but also numerous non-state actors.

---

13 The ICJ only rules on cases whose plaintiffs and defendants are states. Thus, the idea of individual responsibility is not part of the ICJ's jurisdiction. The ICC has taken a step forward in terms of international justice because the Rome Statute of the ICC specifically calls for the prosecution of individuals not states.

14 Berg, "Permanent International Criminal Court," and *Human Rights Watch 1998*, 1-4, assert these points in their argument for an international criminal court and why this court must be permanent and independent.

15 Rome Statute of the ICC, Article 1, states that the court "shall be complementary to national criminal jurisdiction." However, this does not mean that the ICC must act as the States demand. The ICC can prosecute individuals if the State does not take appropriate action or cannot take appropriate action to prosecute the individual in question.

16 Rome Statute of the ICC, Article 4 (2).

Therefore, the role of different NGOs in drafting the Rome Statute was crucial.[17] These NGOs drafted proposals, lobbied government delegates, and as Kirsch and Holmes explain, appear to have greatly influenced the creation of the final Rome Statute. In addition, their role does not end with the approval of the Statute. NGOs continue to play a role in obtaining ratifications of the Rome Statute. One example is Human Rights Watch's "Action Alert" document for NGOs concerning the necessary role of these organizations in moving the ratification process along.[18]

Along with the need to analyze the role of NGOs, this analysis must also account for the role of individual leadership. Many analysts assert that without the type of individual leadership that existed, both prior to and during the Rome Conference, the Statute would never have reached a final vote much less the approval status the Court holds today.[19] Thus, multiple channels (states, NGOs, and individual leadership) now at work within the international system require us to look beyond the nation-state. A proper analysis of the ICC will need to take into account not only the role of the state, but also the role of these non-state entities. The three analytical perspectives that this text engages will allow for this type of inclusive analysis. This is crucial because not only are new actors influencing regime formation, but also new "spheres of authority" are emerging within the global environment.[20]

The formation of the ICC is also an example of states ceding their authority to newly forming institutions. This process is acting to transform the Cold War pattern of governance that Krasner described earlier as bound up in the state sovereignty norm. With the formation of such institutions as the ICC, it appears as if new spheres of authority are arising. The question that this text must answer is why? Why would states form such institutions if they act to undermine their authority? An understanding of the ICC may illuminate an answer.

In sum, the formation of the ICC is clearly an important event for international relations and the global community. The goal of this project is to understand the formation of the ICC in order to draw some conclusions concerning regime formation processes, primary actors in the system, current spheres of authority, and the status of current governance structures. As stated earlier, in order to adequately address this goal, the text will analyze the ICC formation process through the lenses of three analytical perspectives, each of which rests on the underlying

---

[17] Philippe Kirsch and John T. Holmes, "The Rome Conference on an International Criminal Court: The Negotiating Process," *The American Journal of International Law* 93 (1999): 4-5, discuss the influential role of NGOs in the negotiations on the Rome Statute. NGOs such as Human Rights Watch, Amnesty International, Lawyers Committee for Human Rights, and others have played an important role in the drafting process.

[18] The following website made this Action Alert public in May 1999: <http://www.hrw.org>.

[19] One example is Bendetti and Washburn, "Drafting the ICC," 8-12.

[20] Rosenau, *Domestic-Foreign Frontier,* introduces the term "spheres of authority" to the field. I will discuss this term at length in chapter eight.

foundation that international actors have the ability to cooperate and will use this ability to better both their own position and the global community.

Analytical Framework

The Rome Statute is the result of massive amounts of international cooperation or conflict management; therefore, we can only understand this institution by invoking perspectives that presume that the construct of the international system is one of cooperation as well as conflict.[21] The three analytical approaches employed in this endeavor are: neoliberal institutionalism, regime theory, and global governance theory. All three perspectives have the ability to add to our understanding of the ICC and therefore will act in a complementary, not competitive, manner. In fact, one could assert that these approaches actually tend to nest within one another. Although each perspective tells its own distinct story, the approaches also overlap. Thus, the analysis tends to broaden and become more inclusive as we progress through this project, from the narrowest perspective of neoliberal institutionalism, to the broadest in global governance. By employing this type of methodology, this text bolsters the richness of the analysis and allows for a fuller understanding of the ICC and its effect on global politics.

Neoliberal Institutionalism

The first analytical perspective this narrative will employ is neoliberal institutionalism.[22] This theory arose from the idealist tradition. Neoliberal institutionalists attempted to build on the foundation of the idealist tradition in order to adequately explain and understand the global system of the 1980s. Scholars often consider this theory the mainstream theory concerning regime formation.[23] The main proponents of this theory are Robert Keohane, Robert Axelrod and Arthur Stein. These scholars espoused this theory as a retort to

---

[21] It is important to note that cooperation does not mean harmony. Robert Keohane, *After Hegemony: Cooperation and Discord in the World Political Economy* (Princeton, NJ: Princeton University Press, 1984), 12, states that we need to "define cooperation as mutual adjustments rather than to view it simply as reflecting a situation in which common interests outweigh conflicting ones. In other words, we need to distinguish between cooperation and the mere fact of common interests."

[22] Throughout this text, I will use the terms neoliberal institutionalist, neoliberalism, and neoliberal synonymously to refer to the neoliberal institutionalist's school of thought.

[23] Andreas Hasenclever, Peter Mayer and Volker Rittberger, *Theories of International Regimes* (Cambridge: Cambridge University Press, 1997), 23, state that neoliberalism "has come to represent the mainstream approach to analyzing international regimes, and the other two schools [power-based or realism and knowledge-based]…regularly make reference to its arguments in order to give their own positions a clear profile."

Kenneth Waltz's neorealist claims, although they accepted some of the core realist premises.[24] Six core principles frame the neoliberal institutionalist theory:

1. The global system is anarchical in its structure.
2. States are the primary actors in international relations, although international non-state institutions and actors do play a significant role.
3. States are rational-unitary actors, but they also share complementary interests with other states.
4. As far as these complementary interests exist, cooperation among states is possible and this cooperation often occurs under the auspices of international institutions in order to diminish cheating, create iterativeness, and reduce costs of transactions.
5. Hegemony is not a necessary factor for the formation or maintenance of cooperative regimes.
6. In pursuing their interests, states seek absolute, not relative, gains.[25]

This text will use the above framework to begin our understanding of the formation of the Rome Statute and the ICC. The analysis will center on states (although some discussion of non-state actors occurs) and on the absolute gains these states achieve by signing and ratifying the Rome Statute. What emerges from this analysis is an understanding of the actors involved and the ability of cooperation to occur between these sovereignty-bound actors despite the anarchical nature of the system. The neoliberal institutionalist perspective centers on states' interests and the cooperation that can arise from the existence of complementary interests among these actors—for it is from complementary interests that states often forge an international institution.

However, neoliberal institutionalism is still predicated on the notion of sovereign states as the primary actors of the anarchical system. Such a foundation is necessary but not sufficient for understanding the ICC's formation. This is due to the fact that such a perspective fails to account for the role of non-state actors. In order to complement the state-centered neoliberal institutionalist approach, one must engage a broader and more inclusive analytical perspective. This will result

---

24 Neoliberalism accepts many of the realist principles. These include: acceptance that the system is anarchical and that states are the primary actors of global politics, but not the only actors. A reading of Robert Keohane's, *After Hegemony: Cooperation and Discord in the World Political Economy* (Princeton, NJ: Princeton University Press, 1984) and David A. Baldwin, ed., *Neorealism and Neoliberalism: The Contemporary Debate* (New York: Columbia University Press, 1993) confirms such an assertion.

25 This list is a compilation of numerous core works of neoliberal institutionalist theory. These works include: Keohane, *After Hegemony;* Robert Axelrod and Robert O. Keohane, "Achieving Cooperation Under Anarchy: Strategies and Institutions," *World Politics* 38 (1985); and Robert Keohane, "Institutional Theory and the Realist Challenge After the Cold War," in *Neorealism and Neoliberalism,* ed. Baldwin, 269-300.

in a richer understanding of the ICC and its entire novel features. Thus, we now turn to an introductory discussion of the next analytical perspective—regime theory.

Regime Theory

Most international relations scholars define an international regime as, "[a] set of implicit or explicit principles, norms, rules, and decision-making procedures around which actors' expectations converge in a given area of international relations."[26] Despite this concise and widely accepted definition of a regime, the field has not constructed a parsimonious theory of regime formation. Regime theory is actually constructed of three schools of thought within the study of international regimes: (1) realism or power-based approaches, which obviously focus on power relations; (2) neoliberal institutionalist or interest-based approaches, which center on bargaining; (3) cognitivist or knowledge-based approaches, whose primary focus is ideational aspects of regime formation.[27]

If I am to employ an analysis based on regime theory, then one question that this text must address is how does the use of an interest-based perspective take us beyond our earlier analysis of the ICC from a neoliberal institutionalist's perspective. Along the same lines, although an analysis of either the power-based or the knowledge-based positions would introduce something novel to our study, isn't it also true that these types of analyses appear somewhat narrow in their focus? In fact, one could argue that employing any one of these alternative analyses might simply alter the central variable from one single factor (interest-based) to another (either power-based or knowledge-based). This may give us a different perspective from which to analyze the ICC, but it probably will not broaden our understanding of the formation process.

If this narrative is to adequately employ a regime theory analysis of the ICC, then it must first move beyond the traditional schools of thought concerning regime formation (as defined above). The problem with examining the ICC from one of these traditional schools of thought is their exclusivity. In general, the traditional approaches to regime theory fail to acknowledge the other schools of thought.[28] According to this traditional composite of regime theory, the central variable in the formation of a regime is power, interests, *or* knowledge.[29]

---

[26] Stephen D. Krasner, *International Regimes* (Ithaca, NY: Cornell University Press, 1983), 2.

[27] Hasenclever, Mayer and Rittberger, *Theories of International Regimes,* 6, provide us with this composite of regime theory and I will continue to use it throughout this study to address the prospect of regime formation.

[28] As stated above, traditionally scholars have studied regime formation from one of the single-factor models—power-based, interest-based, or knowledge-based. Hasenclever, Mayer and Rittberger, *Theories of International Regimes* clearly show this point.

[29] Hasenclever, Mayer and Rittberger, *Theories of International Regimes,* 6.

However, do any of these individual variables adequately explain regime formation? They do not, because they all fail to account for more than one causal factor.

As a result, this analysis employs a multivariate model of regime.[30] This model will not restrict itself to a power-based, interest-based, or knowledge-based account of the ICC. A multivariate model allows for an examination of all three of these factors, as well as engaging the concepts of leadership and context as crosscutting variables.[31] Thus, this form of analysis provides readers with a much more inclusive understanding of the ICC. As Young and Osherenko state:

> We have concluded that those interested in regime formation should accord high priority to what we have labeled multivariate analysis. No doubt, there is much still to be gained from efforts to clarify the role of individual factors, like leadership and context. But it now seems apparent that regime formation is a complex process that does not lend itself well to analyses that focus on single factors and seek to formulate propositions taking the form of necessary conditions.[32]

This inclusive method moves us beyond the neoliberal understanding of the ICC and yet embodies this perspective as well. In short, neoliberal institutionalism is an element of the multivariate model of regime theory thus it forms a piece of the foundation for an expanded analysis of the ICC. The multivariate model of regime theory subsumes the neoliberal perspective and acts as a complement to this approach. This type of analysis brings us closer to the richer and fuller understanding of the ICC that this text seeks.

Global Governance

The third and final perspective from which this text analyzes the ICC is global governance. Arguably, this perspective is the broadest approach employed. In many ways, as regime theory encompassed neoliberalism, global governance encompasses regime theory and institutes a "nesting" of one approach within another.[33] However, before analyzing the ICC from this perspective it is necessary that I first establish a working definition of global governance.

---

[30] Oran R. Young and Gail Osherenko, "Testing Theories of Regime Formation: Findings from a Large Collaborative Research Program," in *Regime Theory and International Relations,* ed. Volker Rittberger (Oxford: Oxford University Press, 1993), 238-243, show the inadequacy of a single-factor model and implore international relations scholars to use a multivariate model that is more inclusive of seemingly opposing factors.

[31] Both of these factors are part of Young and Osherenko's model.

[32] Young and Osherenko, "Testing Theories," 247.

[33] Nesting is defined as the phenomenon in which one perspective is embedded in another but neither loses their principle attributes.

International relations scholars identify numerous definitions of global governance including: a system of rule at all levels of human activity[34]; the sum of ways in which individuals and institutions manage their common affairs via cooperative action[35]; and the establishment and operation of a set of rules that guide interaction.[36] However, these definitions are all too exclusive. They tend to center on one particular aspect of the governance system; whether that aspect is rules, institutions, or cooperation. To better conceptualize the broad nature of this analytical approach, a viable definition of global governance must take into account all of these factors. Thus, this narrative defines global governance as: an intersubjectively accepted, global system of norms and rules that influence and guide the actions of international actors.[37]

By engaging the ICC using this definition, I am better able to examine not only the actors involved and the actions taken to initiate a cooperative arrangement, but also the norms and rules of the current order and their bearing on the formation of the ICC. This type of analysis essentially encompasses regime theory and neoliberal institutionalism, and uses them as nested perspectives within this analytical approach. A comparison of regime theory and global governance may enlighten this argument.

Regime theorists' assert a definition of a regime that is quite similar to the definition of global governance outlined above. Both definitions discuss rules, norms, and their bearing on international relations. However, a crucial difference is the breadth of their analysis. Regime theory attempts to analyze a particular issue-area, but according to global governance scholars, the analytical object is global order and the norms, rules, and actors that constitute that larger concept. Thus, the use of a global governance approach entails a study of change. Change within the international governance structure and subsequently, how the formation

---

34 James N. Rosenau, "Governance in the Twenty-First Century," *Global Governance* 1 (1995): 13.

35 Commission on Global Governance, *Our Global Neighborhood,* 2.

36 Olav Schram Stokke, "Regimes as Governance Systems," in *Global Governance: Drawing Insights for the Environmental Experience,* ed. Oran R. Young (Cambridge, MA: The MIT Press, 1997), 28.

37 This definition of global governance derives from several different sources. Two of the most crucial are James N. Rosenau, "Governance, Order, and Change in World Politics," in *Governance Without Government: Order and Change in World Politics,* ed. James N. Rosenau and Ernst-Otto Czempiel (Cambridge: Cambridge University Press, 1992), 1-29; and Lawrence S. Finkelstein, "What is Global Governance?" *Global Governance* 1 (1995): 367-372. However, despite the fact that the origins of this definition are found in numerous scholarly works, the final definition given here is this author's own. Also, note that this is a definition of the concept, not the theoretical perspective. As chapter eight will show, there is a difference between the two.

of the ICC has and will affect this emerging governance system.[38] In other words, global governance is the study of patterns of governance and the changes that occur within these patterns. Therefore, this perspective assists us in examining why Krasner's earlier depiction of this issue-area does not hold anymore and why state sovereignty may no longer be the guiding principle of international relations.

Instead of centering on the ICC and its implications on the global system, the use of a global governance approach requires that we look more at the international system and explore both the role of the ICC within the order of that system and as a manifestation of the system. This type of analysis allows me to draw some broader conclusions about the novel factors of the ICC. In other words, a global governance perspective not only analyzes the formation of the ICC, but it also broadens the analysis to include a study of the implications of the ICC and its features for the emerging governance structure.

Methodology

I feel it is important to mention the methodology of this text, both as a caveat and as a recommendation for future researchers. The primary objective of this text is not an attempt to test the different theories of international relations. Instead, it is an attempt to understand the formation of the ICC and then employ this understanding to further our knowledge of the current actors, regimes, and authority structures of the global system.[39] To accomplish this goal, I use a historically rich, qualitative methodology. As shown above, this approach entails the use of several different analytical perspectives to analyze a novel case study. This normative and qualitative method is similar to Graham Allison's method in his classic 1971 work, *Essence of Decision.* In this work, Allison analyzed the events surrounding the Cuban missile crisis from three conceptual models in order to gain a more complete understanding of the crisis itself. This text proceeds in a similar manner by using three analytical models in order to understand the events of an important case study—the ICC.

Although some may view this method as less "academic" then more quantitative assessments, Alexander George and Harry Eckstein defend the use of

---

[38] Martin Hewson and Timothy J. Sinclair, "The Emergence of Global Governance Theory," in *Approaches to Global Governance*, ed. Martin Hewson and Timothy J. Sinclair (Albany, NY: State University of New York Press, 1999), 3-22, assert that global governance may be the tool needed to explain global change in the post-Cold War era. If such a statement is true, then this analytical perspective should give international relations scholars a truer understanding of the role of the ICC in the emerging global order.

[39] As stated earlier, this does not mean that some form of testing does not occur. By engaging this case through three analytical approaches, there will be some inevitable comparisons made that take the form of an elementary theory testing exercise.

such a qualitative case study analysis.[40] Alexander George points out: "Even among behaviorally oriented political scientists, the single case study and the method of 'controlled comparison' of a few cases has become respectable, legitimate research strategy that can contribute to theory development."[41]

A sound case study requires three conditions. First, the researcher must employ a general variable for both description and explanation. This will allow for future comparisons and an accumulation of findings. In this case, that variable is the changing nature of global politics. Second, the researcher must clearly define the class of events that they are analyzing or the phenomenon that they are trying to understand. This will allow the researcher to develop an explanatory theory from this case study. Obviously, the formation of the ICC is that phenomenon. Third, the researcher must focus the analysis and be selective in their approach so that irrelevant or tangential analysis will not cloud their conclusion.[42] This is the reason for employing three specific analytical perspectives to guide my analysis.

Harry Eckstein proposes several forms of case study, including the disciplined-configurative study, the critical case study, the plausibility probe, and the heuristic case study. In this text, I employ the latter. According to Eckstein a heuristic case study represents: "an opportunity to learn more about the complexity of the problem studied, to develop further the existing explanatory framework, and to refine and elaborate the initially available theory employed by the investigator in order to provide an explanation of the particular case examined."[43]

Because one can view the ICC as a critical institution within world politics, analysis of this institution allows international relations scholars the opportunity to learn more about not only the institution itself and its formation process, but also the broader governance structures of the international system in general. Earlier in this chapter, I noted that international relations scholars could view the formation of the ICC as unprecedented because: (1) The ICC institutionalizes the international humanitarian law regime; (2) the Court is a permanent institution; (3) the Court will try individuals, not states; (4) the prosecutor has the ability to initiate an investigation on his/her own authority (*proprio motu);* (5) the ICC establishes an enforcement mechanism that resides outside of the borders of nation-states; and (6) the formation process shows the prominence of non-state actors.

In addition, if one considers the challenge that an international humanitarian law regime poses to state sovereignty, then this case becomes even more significant because it documents the undermining of the dominant norm in mainstream international relations theory. As Stephen Krasner and other scholars

---

40 Alexander L. George, "Case Studies and Theory Development: The Method of Structured, Focused Comparison," in ed. P.G. Luanan (New York: Free Press, 1979), 43-56, discusses five different types of case studies that Harry Eckstein emphasizes in his work.

41 George, "Case Studies," 49.

42 George, "Case Studies," 50.

43 George, "Case Studies," 52.

have shown us, the idea of state sovereignty has dominated the study of international relations for centuries.[44] However, the formation of the ICC does not appear to uphold this norm. Its primary function is to transcend the jurisdiction of states when necessary. Thus, the formation of this institution may represent an example of a new global governance pattern.

Conclusion

The goal of this text is to answer prominent questions about the formation of a permanent International Criminal Court; questions that go to the root of authority and governance in the current global system. The events of Rome 1998 indicate a new era of conflict management that involves both state and non-state actors. By analyzing the formation of this institution, we may better understand the influence of actors on global politics, the current governance pattern of the global system, and the process by which the global community will form future global institutions. Although one case study can provide us with only a limited amount of knowledge, it does present scholars with "a means of stimulating the imagination in order to discern important new problems, identify possible theoretical solutions, and formulate potentially generalizable relations that were not previously apparent."[45] And in many ways, shouldn't this serve as the goal of all academic literature?

---

[44] Heidi H. Hobbs, ed., *Pondering Postinternationalism: A Paradigm for the Twenty-First Century?* (Albany, NY: State University of New York Press, 2000), discusses the hold that state-centered theory has had on the field of international relations.

[45] George, "Case Studies," 51.

Chapter 2

Historical Rise of the ICC

> For nearly a half a century—almost as long as the United Nations has been in existence—the General Assembly has recognized the need to establish such a court to prosecute and punish persons responsible for crimes such as genocide. Many thought…that the horrors of the Second World War—the camps, the cruelty, the exterminations, the Holocaust—could never happen again. And yet they have. In Cambodia, in Bosnia and Herzegovina, in Rwanda. Our time—this decade even—has shown us that man's capacity for evil knows no limits. Genocide…is now a word of our time, too, a heinous reality that calls for a historic response.
>
> Koffi-Annan, United Nations Secretary-General

Introduction

On July 17, 1998, a conference of plenipotentiaries approved the Rome Statute of the International Criminal Court (ICC) by a count of one hundred and twenty nation-states in favor, seven opposed, and twenty-one abstentions.[1] This dramatic show of support was soon followed up with the sixtieth ratification of the Statute on April 1, 2001, thus bringing the Court into force on July 1, 2002.

This overwhelming approval of the International Criminal Court was the culmination of almost a century's worth of work. From the attempt to implement a criminal tribunal to try the Kaiser after World War I, to the International Military Tribunals of World War II, to the current ad hoc tribunals in the former Yugoslavia and Rwanda, the formation process surrounding the ICC has been a complicated one. The road to Rome is full of many twists and turns, but with the support of a large portion of the international community, the long journey towards international justice has passed a milestone of significance. Ultimately, the Rome Statute of the International Criminal Court may result in an international organization that will enforce some ideal of universal justice.[2]

Due to the long history behind the formation of the ICC, this narrative cannot simply pursue this topic as if its formation is solely the product of post-Cold War events. Although the overwhelming support expressed in Rome owes a great deal

---

[1] Cassel, "Why We Need the ICC," explains that no recorded vote was taken, but most observers accept that seven or eight nation-states voted in opposition. The eight possible opposition votes were cast by: the United States, Israel, China, Iran, Iraq, Libya, Sudan and Yemen.

[2] "Universal justice" as it is pertains to the areas of war crimes, genocide, crimes against humanity, and crimes of aggression.

to the ad hoc tribunals of the 1990s, these are not the only factors that led to the drafting and approval of the Rome Statute. The ICC has its roots in early twentieth century international law and to some extent, pre-twentieth century international law. If one is to fully understand the ICC, then this discussion must begin with an understanding of where the ICC came from, why its implementation stalled at certain points in history, and finally, why Rome was the moment at which the legal process that underpins humanitarian law finally became institutionalized, not just codified. Once the historical context is firmly in place, this narrative can move on to a more detailed analysis of the Court itself and its possible implications for the field of international relations and world politics in general.

Pre-World War II Era

When analyzing the foundations of the International Criminal Court, it is necessary to engage a historical analysis that takes into account events prior to World War II. As some scholars have shown, it is even beneficial to look at pre-twentieth century international law and how it impacted the formation of the current ICC.[3]

Pre-World War I Period

The history of the ICC has its roots in several major pre-twentieth century events. Two events in particular appear to be the most prominent because of their centrality to current understandings of humanitarian law, crimes against humanity, and war crimes. The first is the trial of Peter von Hagenbach in 1474.[4] Von Hagenbach was tried for, what is currently considered, a primitive form of crimes against humanity. Specifically, the charges brought against von Hagenbach included the crimes of murder, rape, and perjury.

---

[3] This is especially true in regards to war crimes and the prosecution of individuals for war crimes. Some examples of scholarly work that discusses pre-twentieth century cases of war crimes are: Christopher L. Blakesley, "Obstacles to the Creation of a Permanent War Crimes Tribunal," in *International Law: Classic and Contemporary Readings,* ed. Charlotte Ku and Paul F. Diehl (Boulder, CO: Lynne Rienner Publishers, 1998), 285, discusses the Hague Convention of 1899; Edoardo Greppi, "The Evolution of Individual Criminal Responsibility Under International Law," *International Review of the Red Cross* 835 (1999): 531-553, discusses the trial of Peter von Hagenbach in 1474.

[4] See George Schwarzenberger, *International Law as Applied by International Courts and Tribunals, vol. II: The Law of Armed Conflict* (London: Stevens, 1968), 462, and Jules Deschenes, "Toward International Criminal Justice," in *The Prosecution of International Crimes: A Critical Study of the International Tribunal for the Former Yugoslavia,* ed. Roger S. Clark and Madeline Sann (Somerset, NJ: Transaction Publishers, 1996), 30-32, for a detailed account of this trial.

In the mid-fifteenth century, Charles the Bold, Duke of Burgundy appointed von Hagenbach governor of the city of Breisach, which is situated in the Upper Rhine region of Germany. In von Hagenbach's attempt to please the Duke, he instituted a reign of terror over both the residents of Breisach and anyone who passed through his town on their way to the Frankfurt fair. Normal occurrences included arbitrary murder and rape, illegal taxation, and the confiscation of private property from the Breisach inhabitants. With the defeat of the Duke of Burgundy in 1474, von Hagenbach's reign of terror also came to an end. Von Hagenbach was arrested and tried before an ad hoc tribunal established by the Archduke of Austria.

This ad hoc tribunal consisted of twenty-eight judges from the coalition of towns and states that had defeated the Duke of Burgundy.[5] Von Hagenbach was accused of murder, rape, and perjury. His defense centered on the argument that von Hagenbach was simply complying with superior orders, a defense that would become very crucial to the International Military Tribunals concerning atrocities committed during World War II. This defense did not resonate with the ad hoc tribunal. As the court perceived the situation, even if von Hagenbach was given such orders, he did not have an obligation to carry them out. In fact, the court found that von Hagenbach had a duty to disobey those orders because of their atrocious nature. As a result of the court's decision, von Hagenbach was found guilty and sentenced to death.

This case is important to the history of the ICC because as George Schwarzenberger explains, the state of international law at this point in time was one in which "a state of de facto equality [existed] in which entities conduct their mutual relations as if they were subjects of international law." This is due to the fact that, "the Holy Roman Empire had degenerated to such an extent that relations between its members were conducted on a footing that is hard to distinguish from international relations."[6] The result is that many international law scholars consider the trial of Peter von Hagenbach the first ad hoc international criminal court.[7]

Approximately four centuries later, Gustave Moynier presented the international community with the first draft convention for the establishment of an international criminal court.[8] In 1872, Moynier proposed the formation of an

---

5 Christopher Keith Hall, "The First Proposal For A Permanent International Court," *International Review of the Red Cross* 322 (1998): 57, details the fact that the judges in this case came from towns in Alsace, Austria, Germany and Switzerland. This shows that the trial of von Hagenbach truly was an international one.

6 Schwarzenberger, *International Law,* 464

7 Greppi, "Evolution of Criminal Responsibility," and Deschenes, "Toward International Criminal Justice," share this opinion.

8 Gustave Moynier is one of the founders of the International Committee of the Red Cross (ICRC) and a longtime President of that organization. Prior to the formation of the ICRC, Moynier was President of the Geneva Public Welfare Society (the forerunner to the ICRC).

international judicial body that would prevent violations of the 1864 Geneva Convention. This Convention dealt specifically with the humane treatment of the sick and injured during periods of war. According to Moynier, although the Geneva Convention served a purpose as an international agreement, it lacked the ability to impose criminal responsibility on violators of this document. In an attempt to enforce this Convention, Moynier drafted the first proposal for a permanent international court. As Moynier stated in this proposal, the purpose of this proposed court is to:

> [E]nsure the implementation of the Geneva Convention of 22 August 1864, and of its additional articles, there will be established, in the event of war between two or more Contracting Powers, a tribunal to which may be addressed complaints concerning breaches of the aforementioned Convention.[9]

The ten-article proposal was the first draft for the establishment of a permanent international criminal court. Moynier understood that the Geneva Convention was virtually unenforceable without the establishment of such an institution. Thus, the primary role of the court, as conceived by Moynier, was to uphold the Geneva Convention via a permanent institution and guarantee that resulting judgments of the court would be impartial. Moynier finally brought to light that simply establishing another treaty was not sufficient and that if the international community wished to uphold international humanitarian law, then it was necessary to establish a permanent international criminal court.

Unfortunately, Moynier's proposal was not met with any widespread enthusiasm. Most international law experts of Moynier's time saw his proposal as ineffective, ambiguous, and unenforceable.[10] These scholars may have been correct, but this does not diminish the fact that much of Moynier's ideas found their way into the 1998 Rome Statute, thus showing their impact on the current state of humanitarian law.[11]

The year 1899 marked a third watershed event for humanitarian international law. It was during this year that the establishment of the Hague Conventions for the Pacific Settlement of International Disputes occurs. This conference, along with the subsequent 1907 Hague Convention, established a set of laws concerning conduct during wartime. As Howard Ball describes it:

---

9 Gustave Moynier, *Draft Convention for the Establishment of an International Judicial Body Suitable for the Prevention and Punishment of Violations of the Geneva Convention,* 1872 Article 1. Reprinted in Hall, "First Proposal."

10 Hall, "First Proposal."

11 These ideas would include the permanency of an international tribunal, the need to try individuals for their actions, and the issue of how the international court and national governments should interact.

> A fundamental principle was born at these meetings: the individual, irrespective of nationality, had rights and duties inherent in human nature and was both a subject and a member of an international community... These two Hague treaties codified certain actions in wartime as war crimes.[12]

The Hague Conventions established a list of war crimes that the international community could cite when prosecuting individual violators. These war crimes include: bombarding undefended towns or villages, wantonly destroying enemy cities or towns, mistreatment of prisoners of war, violating a nation's neutrality and others.[13] All twenty-six nation-states in attendance agreed to the categorization of war crimes, but failed to agree on its institutionalization. This was the second failed attempt to establish an international criminal court however it would certainly not be the last.

Despite the failure to form an international court, the codification of war crimes in an international treaty was certainly a huge step forward for international law. This type of action laid the groundwork for future treaties and conventions concerning major human rights violations. It is the first real movement towards a human rights regime within the area of war crimes, and the strength of this newly formed regime would soon be put to the test with the outbreak of World War I.

World War I and the Inter-War Period

The First World War was wrought with accusations of war crimes and even genocide. The Allied Powers (specifically Great Britain, France and Belgium) accused the Central Powers (Germany and Turkey) of atrocities such as: the deportation of Belgian civilians to Germany for slave labor, executing civilians who opposed German advances, sinking the *Lusitania* which resulted in the death of over two thousand civilians, and the killing of over a million ethnic Armenians by Turkish forces.[14] With the signing of The Hague Conventions, the Allies now had a mechanism that would allow them to seek punishment for such actions. After WWI, the Allied powers attempted to establish an international criminal court that would have the power to punish individuals found guilty of war crimes.

---

12 Howard Ball, *Prosecuting War Crimes and Genocide: The Twentieth-Century Experience* (Lawrence, KS: University Press of Kansas, 1999), 14 and 17.

13 These war crimes are defined in Articles 23-28 of the 1907 Hague Annex and in Ball, *Prosecuting War Crimes,* 15-16.

14 This is an amended version of a list compiled by Ball, *Prosecuting War Crimes,* 18-19. The most egregious of these crimes is the "forgotten genocide" of an estimated one million Turkish Armenians. This action by the Turkish government is the first genocide of the twentieth century, but not the last to go unpunished.

The Treaty of Versailles, signed June 28 1919, provided the legal right for the Allies to establish an international criminal court.[15] This court, if established, would serve the purpose of trying individuals' accused of committing war crimes. The jurisdiction of this court would extend not only to the common soldier, but also to military and governmental leaders. Section 227 specifically addressed the actions of Kaiser Wilhelm II, accusing him of "a supreme offence against international morality and the sanctity of treaties." As a result, the court would have the power to prosecute even the former German Emperor.

According to Howard Ball, more than one thousand two hundred individuals were identified as alleged war criminals and yet, no international court tried these individuals. The reason is that no international criminal court was ever established. Germany's Supreme Court tried and convicted a select number of cases however, most scholars believe that the sentences were insufficient for the crimes committed and most of those convicted received pardons within a few years. Due to the fact that the allied powers never established an international tribunal, there never was a "just" conclusion to World War I.

This point in history is important for many reasons. One, it sets the precedent for the establishment of a war crimes tribunal. Despite the fact that the international community did not establish a criminal tribunal, it is still crucial to future international law because the legal precedent for an international tribunal was in place. Second, the Treaty of Versailles also provided the legal precedent for the prosecution of military and governmental leaders, along with average soldiers and citizens. Because of this Treaty, it becomes apparent that many states believe that all individuals, regardless of rank or societal position, must be held accountable for their wartime actions. Finally, the United States established its' opposition to the formation of an international criminal court, foreshadowing its future belligerence to a permanent international criminal judicial system.

If one were to search for a primary reason why the international tribunal for World War I war crimes was not established, the lack of American support would have to top the list. The main American objection to the establishment of the tribunal concerned state sovereignty. The US viewed the proposed international criminal court as a violation of state sovereignty and therefore an illegal action on the part of the Allied Powers. Secretary of State Lansing also asserted that the tribunal lacked any legal precedent.[16] Without US support, the other Allied states lacked the political will to institute the tribunal and the opportunity for international justice slipped away.

---

[15] Articles 227-229 of the Treaty of Versailles, allowed for the establishment of an international court that would prosecute "persons accused of having committed acts in violation of the laws and customs of war."

[16] James F. Willis, *Prologue to Nuremberg: The Politics and Diplomacy of Punishing War Criminals of the First World War* (Westport, Conn: Greenwood Press, 1982), 68, has a discussion of Lansing's comments and the US position on the military tribunal.

The next step towards an international criminal court came in 1937 with the approval of the Convention for the Prevention and Punishment of Terrorism. In 1934, the assassinations of the King of Yugoslavia, King Alexander I, and the French Foreign Minister, in what many in the international community deemed acts of terrorism, spurred movement towards an ICC. With the memory of Archduke Franz Ferdinand's assassination all to clear, the Council of the League of Nations, at the request of the French government, established a committee to examine the means for dealing with terrorism. The result was the 1937 Convention on the Prevention and Punishment of Terrorism, along with a Convention for the Creation of an International Criminal Court. The purpose of the international criminal court was to act as a forum within which the prosecution of individuals guilty of terrorist acts could occur. At the Special Conference on the Repression of Terrorism, thirty-six nation-states approved these two conventions, but the ratification process did not prove so fruitful.[17] Once again, there was a lack of political will to establish such an institution. Only India ratified the Convention and thus another chance to establish an international criminal court failed.[18]

As a result of all these failed attempts to establish an ICC, one could conclude that the reality of establishing such an institution had simply not caught up with the rhetoric. Despite several proposals, the international community lacked the political will necessary for institutionalization. As a result, the idea of an international criminal court would have to remain just that, an idea. It would take another World War and a new round of atrocities before the community of states would establish another international criminal tribunal.

World War II and the Cold War

With the onset of World War II and the horrific atrocities committed by both the Nazi regime and the Japanese military between 1937 and 1945, there appeared an undeniable need for some sort of international institution of justice. What emerged out of the horrors of World War II were the first large-scale ad hoc international criminal tribunals, whose purpose was to try individuals for war crimes, crimes against peace, and crimes against humanity.[19] This event was certainly a major step towards international criminal justice and the formation of a permanent international criminal court.

---

[17] James F. Willis, *Prologue to Nuremberg,* 171-172.

[18] Blakesley, "Obstacles to War Crimes Tribunal," 285-286.

[19] M. Cherif Bassiouni, *The Statute of the International Criminal Court: A Documentary History* (Ardsley, NY: Transnational Publishers, 1998), 7. Earlier in this text, I described the trial of Peter von Hagenbach as the first international tribunal. But the magnitude of the Nuremberg and Tokyo trials provide them with the distinction of being the first large scale ad hoc international criminal tribunals.

World War II Military Tribunals

Nazi Germany was the site of one of the most horrific crimes ever committed. Describing the Jewish population as an infectious population that denies society of all beauty, nobility, and quality, Adolph Hitler instituted what is now known as the "Final Solution."[20] The result was the extermination of over six million Jews, homosexuals, gypsies, communists, and others.[21] The international community could not ignore the sheer magnitude of this genocide. Clearly the need for decisive punishment of those individuals responsible was necessary. The Allies, although split on the type of punishment to implement, finally decided on judicial proceedings in the form of an International Military Tribunal.[22]

The London Charter of August 8, 1945, established an International Military Tribunal at Nuremberg (IMT). The goal of the IMT was to prosecute those individuals' accused of war crimes, crimes against peace, and crimes against humanity.[23] As a result, Nuremberg became the primary historical precedent in the fight for an international criminal court. The establishment of the Nuremberg Court showed the international community that such immoral acts could and should be punished. Along with this, it added teeth to the earlier Hague Conventions and their codification of war crimes. This was truly the first major step forward in the struggle for international criminal justice.[24] But Nuremberg was not alone in its quest for international justice. On the other side of the globe the establishment of another tribunal was occurring. This court would try those individuals responsible for what one scholar calls, "The Forgotten Holocaust."[25]

---

[20] Hitler's description of the Jewish race is most clearly evident in *Mein Kampf (My Battle).* It is from this description that Hitler initiates his genocidal "solution" to the Jewish "problem."

[21] Ball, *Prosecuting War Crimes,* 38-44.

[22] At the time of Nazi surrender there were two choices for implementing justice: 1) judicial proceedings; or 2) executive action. The British favored executive action, which would result in the swift execution of Nazi leaders without any trial proceedings. The approval of such action would have truly been victor's justice. But despite the British calls for executive action, the establishment of the IMT at Nuremberg became the form of justice for German soldiers as the British reluctantly agreed to the Bernays Plan in May 1945. (Ball, *Prosecuting War Crimes,* 44-49.)

[23] For a definition of these crimes, see Greppi, "Evolution of Individual Criminal Responsibility."

[24] It should be noted that this court was a military court and therefore, the Allies established it to try those individuals accused of criminal activity only if they were part of the losing side. This was not a court to try all crimes committed during the Second World War; it was a court to try crimes committed by the Germans, as was the IMTFE a court to try crimes committed by the Japanese.

[25] Iris Chang, *The Rape of Nanking: The Forgotten Holocaust of World War II* (New York: Basic Books, 1997).

The war in the Pacific was replete with its own set of war crimes, crimes against peace, and crimes against humanity. Scholars of this time period often speculate that between 1937 and 1945, the Japanese military killed anywhere from six million to nineteen million Chinese.[26] This was not due to incidents of war, but instead was the systematic killing of a population of humans that the Japanese viewed as subhuman. One incident that highlights this sentiment is the Rape of Nanking. It was at Nanking, over a six to eight week period, that the Japanese military systematically murdered over three hundred and fifty thousand Chinese. Only the ten-week genocidal period in Rwanda, 1994, rivals the efficiency of this genocide.

It is because of such incidents as Nanking that at the conclusion of the war in the Pacific, the Allies, along with the United Nations War Crimes Commission, recommended the establishment of a military tribunal in the Far East. In September 1945, the Allied powers completed the final details concerning the establishment of an International Military Tribunal for the Far East (IMTFE) and in January of 1946, they announced the charter for the IMTFE to the world.[27]

These two International Military Tribunals are the first extensive forms of an international criminal court. As Bassiouni points out:

> The International Military Tribunal at Nuremberg, the International Military Tribunal in the Far East, and subsequent prosecutions by the Allies were significant precedents in the efforts to establish an effective system of international criminal justice. These historical precedents have developed new legal norms and standards of responsibility which have advanced the international rule of law...[28]

One can view these post-World War II tribunals as the foundation upon which the Rome Statute was built. However, that does not mean that these IMTs were without their shortcomings. In particular, many scholars have accused these tribunals of imposing "victors' justice" on their defeated enemies, Germany and Japan. Instead of instituting a criminal tribunal, which would lead to open investigations of all atrocities committed during World War II, the Allies established a court that only prosecuted the losers. These tribunals never prosecuted an Allied soldier or military commander. This is not due to the fact that the Allied forces did not commit possible war crimes, crimes against peace, and crimes against humanity. One could perceive incidents such as the bombing of Dresden and the use of atomic weapons as crimes against humanity. However, the construct of the IMTs, did not allow Allied personnel to be held responsible for

---

26 Chang, *Rape of Nanking,* 216-217.

27 Ball, *Prosecuting War Crimes,* 62-86, summarizes the history of war crimes committed in the Far East and the establishment of the IMTFE.

28 Bassiouni, *Statute of the ICC,* 9.

their actions. Simply stated, the IMTs were military courts of justice.[29] In other words, they were not internationally established courts of objective justice. Their sole purpose was to prosecute criminals from the losing nations, not the Allied forces. It was due to this biased jurisdiction that many scholars have deemed these proceedings a form of victors' justice and not objective justice.[30] If a truly objective form of international justice was to be established, future ad hoc tribunals would need to rectify this shortcoming.[31]

Despite this flaw, the establishment of the post-World War II criminal tribunals was still a major step forward in the quest for international justice. These institutions were the first to truly uphold the idea of an international moral authority and it is from this foundation that one can see the emergence of a permanent international criminal court. As Christian Tomuschat states:

> The Nuremberg and Tokyo trials represented a great leap forward after the horrors of World War II; namely, that no one should be left totally abandoned to the vagaries of his or her government and that, at least in situations where basic rights are infringed systematically and on a vast scale by power wielders, the international community will not stand idly by, restrained by the traditional rule of nonintervention from taking remedial action.[32]

Post-World War II Human Rights Movement

Accompanying the IMTs, and as a result of the atrocities committed during World War II, the international community initiated another monumental step forward in their quest for international justice. On December 9, 1948, the United Nations General Assembly approved the Genocide Convention and opened the treaty for signature. This treaty established an intersubjectively accepted definition of genocide and made the act of committing genocide illegal, whether committed in a time of war or peace.[33] The Genocide Convention also called for the enforcement

---

29 John Alan Appleman, *Military Tribunals and International Crimes* (Westport, CT: Greenwood Press, Publishers, 1971), 10-11, has a detailed discussion concerning the powers of military tribunals.

30 One example of how these military courts acted differently then many domestic courts is the fact that no appeals were allowed. Once the court rendered its decision the accused had no further recourse. Ball, *Prosecuting War Crimes,* 53-61.

31 Cedric Thornberry, "Saving the War Crimes Tribunal," *Foreign Policy* 104 (1996), 72-86, lays out the argument for victors' justice and also explains how the tribunals of the 1990s differ dramatically from both Nuremberg and Tokyo.

32 Christian Tomuschat, "International Criminal Prosecution: The Precedent of Nuremberg Confirmed," in *Prosecution of International Crimes: A Critical Study of the International Tribunal for the Former Yugoslavia,* ed. Roger S. Clark and Madeline Sann (Somerset, NJ: Transaction Publishers, 1996), 18.

33 Jack Donnelly, *International Human Rights* (Boulder, CO: Westview Press, 1998), 5; and Ball, *Prosecuting War Crimes,* 87-90.

of this treaty by an international penal tribunal.[34] This Article essentially laid the legal precedent for some form of an international criminal court.

Along with the Genocide Convention, the UN General Assembly also unanimously adopted the Universal Declaration of Human Rights.[35] The importance of this document was that it was the first comprehensive statement concerning the protection of human rights. It included such things as the protection of one's life, protection from torture and inhuman punishment, and the right to reside in an international environment that is conducive to the rights established in this document. What all of this post-World War II action demonstrates (both the codification and institutionalization) is that in the late 1940s, it appears as if the international environment was ripe for the establishment of an international criminal court.

With such an inviting environment in place, in 1947 the international community took its first definitive step towards the establishment of a permanent international criminal court, not just an ad hoc tribunal or a human right's treaty. It was in this year that the United Nations General Assembly instructed the Committee on the Codification of International Law to "prepare a draft code of offences against the peace and security of mankind."[36] At approximately the same time, the United Nations assigned a special rapporteur the task of formulating a draft code statute for an international criminal court. The rapporteur submitted his first report concerning the statute to the International Law Commission (ILC), formerly the Committee on the Codification of International Law, in March of 1950.[37] The report called for the formation of an international criminal court constructed on a definitive and comprehensive criminal code, thus bringing the two projects into one framework. From this moment forward, the draft code and the statute for an ICC were part of one larger endeavor.

At this point it appears as if momentum was building in favor of an international criminal court. In 1950, the UN General Assembly decides to establish a special committee whose sole purpose was to draft a statute for the establishment of an international criminal court. The statute was completed in 1951 and the first substantive attempt to institute an international criminal court was presented to the United Nations members.

The purpose of this court, according to the statute, would be to "try persons accused of crimes under international law, as may be presented in conventions or

---

34 The Convention on the Prevention and Punishment of the Crime of Genocide, Article 6.

35 It is important to note that the Universal Declaration of Human Rights was a declaration, not a treaty. The significance of this distinction is that a Declaration has no binding authority.

36 GA Resolution 174, UN, GAOR, 2nd Session, UN Doc. A/519 (1947).

37 The International Law Commission assumed the role of the Committee for the Codification of International Law in 1948.

special agreements among States parties to the present statute."[38] Unfortunately, the international community did not react to the draft statute with much enthusiasm. Among the Great Powers, only France supported the idea of a permanent international criminal court and even they did not press other states for its establishment. Thus, one could conclude that even among its supporters, the political will for an ICC was once again lacking.[39]

The ILC returned to the drafting process in an attempt to revise the 1951 statute so that it would be more attractive to the international community. In 1953, the committee developed a revised statute that attempted to cater to the concerns of the world's major powers. Some of the more profound changes in the statute included: a softening of the court's jurisdiction, voluntary participation by nation-states, and a provision that allowed states to withdraw from the court's jurisdiction with one year's notice.[40]

The UN General Assembly then tabled action on the revised ICC text until the ILC completed work on the Draft Code of Offences.[41] The problem was that the ILC did not complete the Draft Code of Offences for another twenty years. This was due to the ILC's inability to define "aggression", as it related to crimes of aggression. Thus, the international community never got the opportunity to debate or vote on the revised ICC statute of 1953.

Despite the flurry of human rights activities in the immediate post-World War II period, the failure to establish an international criminal court signaled the inception of a period in which the international community turned its back on international justice. Citing things like state sovereignty, the Cold War, and a lack of political will on the part of other nations, this period in time marked a distinct movement away from any attempt to codify and implement international humanitarian law. It seemed as if the formation of a permanent ICC had missed it best opportunity.

Cold War Era

The real tragedy of failing to form an international criminal court during the early post-World War II era is the failure to have an institution in place that may have

38 Article 1 of the Draft Statute for an International Criminal Court, 1951, reprinted in Bassiouni, *Statute of the ICC,* 741-748.

39 Bassiouni, *Statute of the ICC,* 13, and Ball, *Prosecuting War Crimes,* 194, discusses this lack of enthusiasm.

40 *Report of the Committee on International Criminal Jurisdiction,* UN GAOR 7th Session, supplement No. 12, at 21, UN Doc. A/26645 (1945). The ILC understood the need to have the support of the major powers if an effective international criminal court were to become a reality. That is why the court's statute contained so many substantive changes between 1951 and 1953.

41 The UN General Assembly concluded that the initiation of a debate on the ICC would not occur until the definition of "aggression" was agreed upon.

deterred, or at least been able to prosecute, the acts of genocide and crimes against humanity that persisted throughout the Cold War. Idi Amin's rule in Uganda,[42] the killing of some one hundred and fifty thousand civilians and the disappearance of another fifty thousand in Guatemala between 1966 and 1986, Pinochet's brutally repressive rule in Chile,[43] the massive slaughter of the Tutsi population in Rwanda between 1959 and 1973,[44] the repression of the East Timorese between 1975 and 1979,[45] among many others. Without a permanent international criminal court in place, there was no international forum in which to prosecute those responsible for such heinous crimes.

One of the more pronounced events in which an international criminal court could have acted as a possible deterrent, was the genocide in Cambodia. Even if it could not deter the perpetrators of the genocide, an international criminal court may have brought some sense of international justice to an otherwise unjust occurrence. Between 1975 and 1979, Pol Pot's Khmer Rouge slaughtered close to two million people in a calculated and systematic rule of terror.[46] This genocidal plan included the execution of all ethnic minorities living within Cambodia and the massacre of those deemed "undesirable" by Pol Pot.[47] A rapid and reasonable global reaction to this mass slaughter was nonexistent. If it were not for Vietnam's invasion of Cambodia in 1979 and the subsequent deposing of Pol Pot's regime, no one knows how long this madness would have continued. Since that time the international community has failed to take any substantive action to bring Pol Pot to justice. With his death on April 15, 1998, it became clear that no form of international justice would be brought to bear on Pol Pot himself.[48]

---

[42] Hans Peter Schmitz, "Transnational Activism and Political Change in Kenya and Uganda," in *The Power of Human Rights: International Norms and Domestic Change,* ed. Thomas Risse, Stephen C. Ropp and Kathryn Sikkink (Cambridge: Cambridge University Press, 1999), 39-77, and David Martin, *General Amin* (London: Faber and Faber, 1974).

[43] Stephen C. Ropp and Kathryn Sikkink, "International Norms and Domestic Politics in Chile and Guatemala," in *Power of Human Rights,* ed. Risse, Ropp and Sikkink, 172-204.

[44] Gerard Prunier, *The Rwanda Crisis: History of Genocide* (New York: Columbia University Press, 1995) and Alain Destexhe, "The Third Genocide," *Foreign Policy* 97 (1994-95), 3-17.

[45] Anja Jetschke, "Linking the Unlinkable? International Norms and Nationalism in Indonesia and the Phillipines," in *Power of Human Rights,* ed. Risse, Ropp and Sikkink, 134-171.

[46] Ball, *Prosecuting War Crimes,* 94-120, has an extensive discussion of the genocide in Cambodia.

[47] The minority groups included: Chinese, Vietnamese, Muslims, Chans, Laos and Thais. The group of "undesirables" was more ambiguous, but it was generally composed of those individuals that Pol Pot saw as a threat. This would include the intellectuals and the economic elite.

[48] Justice may be served on other Khmer Rouge leaders. On March 17, 2003, the United Nations and the Cambodian government established a draft agreement on the establishment

Even if the international community had established an international criminal court in 1951, this would not have guaranteed the prevention of such atrocities. However, the lack of an international forum for criminal justice also assured the Pol Pot's of the world that no international court would uphold the human rights' norms established between 1945 and 1949. An international criminal court may have had the ability to act as a deterrent or at least impose some semblance of justice concerning these unjust acts. Without an international criminal court, the international community lacked the necessary tools to uphold the human rights' norms established in the immediate post-World War II period. It is not until 1989 that a renewed sense of need for an international criminal court emerges.

Post Cold War Era

In 1989, Trinidad and Tobago resurrected the proposal for the establishment of an international criminal court. Due to an increased concern about drug trafficking, the United Nations' General Assembly called a special session to discuss the issue. What emerged from that session was a suggestion by Trinidad and Tobago that the United Nations establish an international criminal court to deal with this problem. As a result, the General Assembly called upon the International Law Commission to prepare a report concerning the formation of an international criminal court that would have jurisdiction over the prosecution of individuals' accused of drug trafficking. The following year the ILC submitted its report on the ICC, but that report called for the ICC to do more than just prosecute international drug trafficking.[49] The General Assembly began to warm to the idea of a permanent international criminal court and asked the ILC to continue its work on this subject. The ILC submitted a preliminary report on this matter in 1992, and then produced a more comprehensive report in 1993.[50]

At this point in time, the progression towards Rome was clearly gaining momentum. In 1994, after submitting a revised version of the 1993 text to the United Nations, the General Assembly agreed to create an ad hoc committee on the formation of an international criminal court. The primary goal of this ad hoc committee was to:

---

of an international criminal tribunal. The primary purpose of this tribunal is to prosecute former Khmer Rouge leaders.

[49] Report of the International Law Commission on the work of its forty-second session, UN Doc. A/45/10 (1990).

[50] See the Report of the International Law Commission on the work of its forty-fourth session, UN Doc. A/47/10 (1992) and the revised Report of the Working Group on the Draft Statute for an International Criminal Court, ILC, forty-fifth session, UN Doc. A/CN.4/L.490 (1993).

> Review the major substantive and administrative issues arising out of the draft statute prepared by the International Law Commission and, in light of that review, to consider arrangements for the convening of an international conference of plenipotentiaries.[51]

The international environment of the 1990s, as in the immediate post-World War II period, appeared ripe for the establishment of an international criminal court. This is attributable to several factors. One of the major impediments to the establishment of an international criminal court in the early 1950s was the onset of the Cold War. In 1989, however, the collapse of the Soviet bloc began and as a result, the end of the Cold War followed. With the onset of the post-Cold War period, the international environment appears altered and changed—both materially and ideationally. For instance, the international community now enters a period of time that many scholars see as unstable and unpredictable.[52] The international community also began to see an increase in UN peacekeeping operations,[53] a rise in internal or domestic wars,[54] and some scholars would claim, a decline in state sovereignty.[55]

It is now clear that this period in history was a profound moment of change and one of the resulting characteristics was a change in the global order's defining

---

[51] This was decreed on December 9, 1994 in General Assembly Resolution 49/53, Establishment of an International Criminal Court.

[52] Rosenau, *Domestic-Foreign Frontier,* 99-117, discusses this instability and captures it best with the term "fragmegration." Both integration and fragmentation marked the post-Cold War period. Fragmentation that leads to instability and insecurity in the international system and integration that tends to bring the actors of the world into a more interdependent relationship.

[53] The 1990s have seen a dramatic rise in the number of UN peacekeeping missions. During the Cold War, the UN deployed thirteen peacekeeping operations. In 1993 alone, the UN had seventeen Security Operations in effect and twelve of these were deployed in the post-Cold War era. Thomas G. Weiss, David P. Forsythe and Roger A. Coate, *The United Nations and Changing World Politics,* 2nd edition (Boulder, CO: Westview Press, 1997), 54 and 66. I would be remiss if I did not note that these numbers, although peaking in the immediate post-Cold War era, have declined after 1995.

[54] Internal wars have been much more a part of the international landscape in the 1990s. There have been internal wars in such diverse places as the former Yugoslavia, Rwanda, Indonesia, Sri Lanka, and Russia. It appears as if this type of conflict may become the norm in the post-Cold War era.

[55] Susan Strange, *The Retreat of the State: The Diffusion of Power in the World Economy* (Cambridge: Cambridge University Press, 1996), clearly takes aim at the idea of diminishing state sovereignty. In this text, Professor Strange cites such transnational actors as international organizations, organized crime, international accounting firms, and telecom networks as agents that are undermining the power of state sovereignty. Eric K. Leonard, "Seeking Sovereignty: Gaining Understanding Through Critical Analysis," *New Political Science* 23 (2001), also discusses the transforming nature of sovereignty and the decline of state sovereignty.

concept—state sovereignty. Claims of non-intervention were no longer unquestionable, borders appeared to be extremely permeable, and the authority of international organizations and non-state polities was on the rise.[56] This all adds up to an environment that is ripe for not only the establishment of an international criminal court, but also the formation of a number of strong intergovernmental organizations.[57]

Along with the onset of the post-Cold War era, the processes of globalization also appeared to be assisting in the formation of the ICC. The result is an international environment that is less state-centric and more interdependent. Such an environment is quite conducive to the formation of IGOs, due in part to the integrative aspects of globalization, but also the fragmentation that occurred because of this process.

In terms of the formation of an international criminal court, the importance of integration is that international news and current events are now globally broadcast within an instant. This greatly increases global awareness and human knowledge concerning human rights issues and violations of humanitarian law. Awareness of these abuses is clearly a precondition to action. The process of globalization, in particular its integrative aspect, has provided the international community with the political will to establish an institution that will protect human rights.[58]

The fragmentation process also promotes an environment that contributes to the formation of an international criminal court, in so far as globalization promotes fragmentation of nation-states and the re-emergence of multiple identities and loyalties, independence movements, ethnic conflict, and chaos.[59] Two ethnic conflicts that capture the chaotic nature of the post-Cold War era are those in the former Yugoslavia and in Rwanda. Both exemplify the fragmentation process and underscore the need for a permanent international criminal court.

Justice in the Former Yugoslavia

The post-Cold War conflict in the Balkans began in June 1991 with independence movements by Slovenia and Croatia. It was at this time that both republics

---

[56] Yale H. Ferguson, "Postinternationalism and the Future of IR Theory," in Heidi H. Hobbs (ed.), *Pondering Postinternationalism: A Paradigm for the Twenty-First Century?* (Albany, NY: State University of New York Press, 2000), 197-216, points out the rise in non-state polities and the need to view world politics outside of a state-centric paradigm.

[57] One example of this would be the World Trade Organization (WTO). Formed in 1995, this organization is clearly solidifying it place in the current international order and assuming a powerful role in world politics.

[58] Robert McCorquodale and Richard Fairbrother, "Globalization and Human Rights," *Human Rights Quarterly* 21 (1999): 758-763, discuss at length the integration process and its effects on human rights.

[59] Ferguson and Mansbach, "History's Revenge," discuss the rise of polities and the increase in independence movements since the end of the cold war.

declared their independence from Yugoslavia in an attempt to establish an independent sovereign state. The independence movement then spread to Bosnia-Herzegovina, Montenegro, and Kosovo. These wars have raged throughout the 1990s, with the death toll exceeding three hundred thousand and the number of displaced individuals reaching almost five million.[60] Unlike the situation in Cambodia, in the former Yugoslavia the international community decided to act, albeit in a delayed fashion.[61] In 1995, the western nations and the UN eventually took steps to end the conflict by assembling the warring parties around the negotiating table and implementing the Dayton Peace Agreement. This also brought about the formation of IFOR and the deployment of military personnel to oversee the implementation of the agreement.[62]

On May 25, 1993, the UN Security Council also passed resolution 827. The purpose of this resolution was the establishment of the International Criminal Tribunal for the Former Yugoslavia (ICTY). This ad hoc criminal tribunal was the first of its kind since the Nuremberg and Tokyo tribunals. The United Nations established the ICTY to prosecute individuals who were "responsible for serious violations of international humanitarian law committed on the territory of the former Yugoslavia since 1991."[63] Such offenses would include: grave breaches of the 1949 Geneva Conventions, violations of the laws or customs of war, genocide, and crimes against humanity.[64]

The formation of the ICTY was a momentous step towards the establishment of a permanent international criminal court. Despite the fact that the jurisdiction of the ICTY is limited both spatially and temporally, most scholars view it as the first real step towards international justice in the post-Cold War era. This court holds individuals responsible for their actions regardless of ethnicity or religious affiliation. Unlike the Nuremberg and Tokyo tribunals, it is difficult to accuse the ICTY of implementing victors' justice because it does not discriminate amongst the accused.[65] The ICTY is also predicated on established international law. The

---

[60] Ball, *Prosecuting War Criminals,* 125, discuss the death toll inflicted in the former Yugoslavia. The UN High Commission for Refugees places the number of displaced individuals at three million nine hundred thousand in 1995 and almost one million displaced during the war in Kosovo. All told, the number of displaced individuals in the former Yugoslavia is at least four million nine hundred thousand.

[61] Although the international community did react, it was a delayed reaction. It was not until the winter of 1995 that the United Nations, led by the United States and NATO, intervened decisively. Donnelly, *International Human Rights*, 139-143.

[62] With its deployment in 1995, IFOR was constructed of ninety thousand military personnel whose primary goal was to uphold the Dayton Peace Agreement.

[63] UN Doc. S/Res/827 (1993).

[64] Articles 2-5 of the Statute of the ICTY.

[65] Payam Akhavan, "Justice in the Hague, Peace in the Former Yugoslavia? A Commentary on the United Nations War Crimes Tribunal," *Human Rights Quarterly* 20 (1998): 781-782, discusses the fact that currently the ICTY has indicted and/or tried Croats,

statute cites the Nuremberg Principles, the Genocide Convention, and the 1949 Geneva Conventions as its legal precedent. Therefore, one can see this ad hoc tribunal as the rectification of previous shortcomings in international justice and a step forward in the quest to obtain an institutionalized form of international humanitarian law.

Clearly, the ICTY has not yet tried or even detained all of the responsible parties.[66] The tribunal has not even captured all of those that were most influential in initiating the "ethnic cleansing." Many scholars see this as a weakness of the tribunal and an example of the ineffectiveness of international law. Nevertheless, as Payam Akhavan points out:

> Whatever setbacks there may be in the short run, it is clear that punishment and deterrence are long-term propositions. The international community should not be under the illusion that justice for the former Yugoslavia is possible without time and determination. Deterrence and peace building are part of a long-term investment and a broader commitment on the part of the international community to the eradication of the prevailing culture of impunity.[67]

Scholars who are so quick to dismiss the ability of the ICTY to bring about justice in the former Yugoslavia are, according to Akhavan, impatient. This ad hoc tribunal is simply another step in "the progressive establishment of an international criminal jurisdiction."[68] The international community and the scholars who analyze it should not disregard its significance too quickly. The establishment of the ICTY may well be one of the most crucial steps on the path to a permanent ICC.

Judging Genocide in Rwanda

Along with the establishment of the ICTY, on November 8, 1994 the UN Security Council adopted Resolution 955, which established the International Criminal Tribunal for Rwanda (ICTR). The tragedy of Rwanda is clearly one of the worst in modern history. Between April 6, 1994 and early July 1994, the Hutu population massacred between five hundred thousand and eight hundred thousand minority

---

Serbs, and Muslims, thus showing the neutral character of the court. The tribunal also investigated charges of war crimes committed by NATO during their bombing campaign over Kosovo and Serbia. Although these charges were dismissed, this investigation of NATO actions also shows the neutral character of this court.

66 Yves Beigbeder, *Judging War Criminals: The Politics of International Justice* (London: MacMillan Press, Ltd., 1999), 160-163, is quick to point out that the main problem with the ICTY is its lack arrests, although with the arrest and subsequent trial of Slobodan Milosevic this criticism may be losing validity.

67 Akhavan, "Justice in The Hague," 813.

68 Akhavan, "Justice in The Hague," 815.

ethnic Tutsis.[69] As Gerard Prunier points out, "the daily killing [in Rwanda] was at least five times that of the Nazi death camps."[70]

In tragically familiar fashion, the United States and the international community failed to respond immediately to the genocide in Rwanda. In fact, the United Nations, the US, and most other capable institutions and nation-states failed to act while the genocide was still occurring; this despite numerous warnings from UN peacekeepers that the situation in Rwanda was one of genocidal madness.[71] Eventually action was taken by the international community, but not before the lives of eight hundred thousand to one million people were lost in one hundred days.

The sole purpose of the ICTR is to:

> Prosecute persons responsible for genocide and other serious violations of international humanitarian law committed in the territory of Rwanda and Rwandan citizens responsible for genocide and other such violations committed in the territory of neighboring states between January 1st 1994 and December 31, 1994.[72]

Some scholars have accused the ICTR, as with its predecessor the ICTY, of failing to fulfill its mandate. However, the ICTR has currently convicted twenty individuals and has fifty-seven detained in Arusha, Tanzania.[73] Thus, it is hard to argue that the tribunal is not fulfilling its mandate. Granted, this process may be slow and at times faulty, but it clearly shows an attempt to implement an ideal of international justice to an unjust situation. As one scholar stated:

> Ethnic cleansing" in the former Yugoslavia and genocide in Rwanda have assumed a similar role in the post-Cold War era as the twin pillars of moral outrage upon which the beginnings of an international criminal jurisdiction can be discerned. Therefore, although the Yugoslav tribunal [and the ICTR] might be regarded as yet another expression of the reactive nature of the international human rights system, it is a

69 The number of dead differs depending on the source that one cites. However, most scholars accept the fact that no less than eight hundred thousand people died in just one hundred days. Ball, *Prosecuting War Crimes,* 155-185; Fergal Keane, *Season of Blood: A Rwanda Journey* (London: Penguin Books, 1995); and Gerard Prunier, *The Rwanda Crisis: History of Genocide* (New York: Columbia University Press, 1995), provide a history of the genocide in Rwanda and explain the ethnic basis of this massacre.

70 Prunier, *Rwanda Crisis*, 261.

71 Ball, *Prosecuting War Crimes,* 163-164 and the Organization of African Unity's report, "The Preventable Genocide," document the repeated warnings by UN officials and peacekeepers as does the writing of the UN Force Commander Lt. General Romeo Dallaire, *Shake Hands With the Devil: The Failure of Humanity in Rwanda* (New York: Carol & Graf Publishers, 2003).

72 United Nations Security Council Resolution 955.

73 Statistics taken from website: <http://www.ictr.org> on May 1, 2005.

> significant step forward in comparison with other situations where genocide was committed with complete impunity.[74]

These two tribunals represent a growing consensus or international norm concerning the necessity of the institutionalization of humanitarian law. The next step in the quest for global justice is the formation of a permanent international criminal court that supplants the need for ad hoc tribunals.

Building Towards Rome

In 1989, the discussion of forming a permanent international criminal court returned to the international consciousness. As stated earlier, the idea of an ICC was resurrected in reference to the prosecution of international drug traffickers. The onset of the end of the Cold War appeared to produce an environment that was conducive to the idea of establishing an ICC and the International Law Commission seized on the opportunity. In 1993, the ILC produced a comprehensive text on the formation of the ICC.[75] Then in 1994, the ILC submitted a modified version of this text to the General Assembly. As a result, the road to Rome began to both take formal shape and gain increased momentum.[76]

The 1994 Report of the International Law Commission became the foundation for the 1998 Rome Statute. In this draft statute, there is a discussion of the Court's jurisdiction, investigation process, prosecution, trial proceedings, composition of the Court, cooperation with nation-states, and enforcement. In order to adequately analyze the proposed statute, the General Assembly approved the establishment of an ad hoc committee for the purpose of reviewing the ILC document.[77] After meeting for two sessions during the spring and summer of 1995, the ad hoc committee recommended that a UN preparatory committee (PrepCom) be established. In December 1995, the UN General Assembly officially formed the PrepCom for the purpose of drafting a final statute for the formation of an international criminal court.[78] The General Assembly instructed the PrepCom:

> To discuss further the major substantive and administrative issues arising out of the draft statute prepared by the International Law Commission … with a view to proposing a

---

74 Payam Akhavan, "The Yugoslavia Tribunal at a Crossroads: The Dayton Peace Agreement and Beyond," *Human Rights Quarterly* 18 (1996): 269.

75 Revised Report of the Working Group on the Draft Statute for an International Criminal Court, ILC, 45th Session, May 3-July 23, 1993, A/CN.4/L.490 (1993).

76 The 1994 modified text, Report of the International Law Commission on its 46th Session, Draft Statute for an International Criminal Court, May 2-July 22, 1994, A/49/10 (1994), was the first substantive step towards the Rome Statute taken in the 1990s.

77 UN Doc. A/Res/49/53.

78 UN Doc. A/Res/50/46.

widely acceptable consolidated text of a convention for an international criminal court as a next step towards consideration by a conference of plenipotentiaries.[79]

The PrepCom sessions were open to all members of the UN General Assembly. The first session convened on March 25, 1996, and lasted until April 12, 1996. This session dealt primarily with the most fundamental issues of the draft statute and the proposed Court. The PrepCom began by tackling the following issues: how the ICC would interact with national domestic courts, trigger mechanisms of the Court, jurisdiction, and state cooperation with the Court.[80] The draft definition of the three "core crimes" also emerged from this inaugural PrepCom session.[81]

The PrepCom met again in August 1996 and began a discussion and debate on the procedural issues of the Court, the rights of the accused, and the relationship that the ICC would have with the UN and more importantly, the Security Council. Despite the abundance of progress on many of these issues, the delegates who attended the PrepCom meetings acknowledged that a tremendous amount of work remained. In the PrepCom's report to the General Assembly, the delegates stated that:

> The Preparatory Committee wishes to emphasize the usefulness of its discussions and the cooperative spirit in which the debates took place. In light of the progress made and with an awareness of the commitment of the international community to the establishment of an international criminal court, the Preparatory Committee recommends that the General Assembly reaffirm the mandate of the Preparatory Committee ... [due to the fact that] the Preparatory Committee, on the basis of its scheme of work, considers that it is realistic to regard the holding of a diplomatic conference of plenipotentiaries in 1998 as feasible.[82]

The UN General Assembly did reaffirm the mandate of the Preparatory Committee and as a result, the PrepCom convened four more times prior to June 1998. The goal of these PrepCom meetings was to draft a statute for the ICC that they would submit to a conference of plenipotentiaries. The purpose of the conference would be to gather delegates from as many states as possible in an attempt to draft a final statute that result in the establishment of a permanent international criminal court. The culmination of over fifty years of work seemed to be at hand and it now

---

[79] UN Doc. A/Res/50/46 at paragraph 2.

[80] Fanny Bendetti and John L. Washburn, "Drafting the International Criminal Court Treaty: Two Years to Rome and an Afterword on the Rome Diplomatic Conference," *Global Governance* 5 (1999), detail the PrepCom agenda and its subsequent discussions.

[81] The three "core crimes" are genocide, crimes against humanity and war crimes. The definitions for these crimes were all based on established international law and will be discussed at greater length in the next chapter.

[82] UN Doc. A/51/627 paragraph 368 and 369.

seemed plausible that a vote on the institutionalization of humanitarian law might finally occur.

With the renewed mandate in hand, the PrepCom proceeded with four more sessions in an attempt to hammer out a final draft text.[83] They began by focusing on the Court's jurisdiction and the definition of the "core crimes." In the first session they returned to the trigger mechanisms for Court action and the concept of complementarity (or the relationship between the ICC and domestic courts). Future meetings centered on the procedural issues of the Court and finally, at the last pre-Rome PrepCom meeting,[84] the participants drafted a final statute and prepared it for presentation in Rome.[85]

Rome and Beyond

On June 15, 1998, the United Nations Diplomatic Conference of Plenipotentiaries on the Establishment of an International Criminal Court officially began. Over the next thirty-three days, delegates from one hundred and eighty-five nation-states would come together to discuss and debate the one hundred and sixteen article, one hundred and seventy-three page PrepCom draft statute. The goal of this Conference was the approval of a final draft statute on an International Criminal Court, but that process would not be an easy one. It became obvious from the outset that certain issues would be more contentious then others. These issues included: the principle of complementarity, jurisdiction, trigger mechanisms, and the Court's relationship with the UN Security Council.

Actors Involved

Prior to the Rome Conference some states had already defined their positions on the ICC and its draft statute. One group of states, entitled the "Like-Minded States", favored the establishment of a strong and independent court.[86] This group

[83] The official PrepCom sessions were not the only meetings concerning the establishment of the Rome Statute. Along with the PrepCom sessions, there were several informal sessions that met to discuss the draft articles. These sessions proved extremely useful to the process of drafting the statute and are generally considered to be a crucial component to the rapid formalization process of the draft statute.

[84] I use the term "pre-Rome PrepCom meetings" because since the Rome conference, PrepCom has continued to meet in order to clarify some key issues and strengthen the existing treaty.

[85] The acceptance of Italy's invitation to host the Conference of Plenipotentiaries on the Establishment of the International Criminal Court was formalized in General Assembly Resolution A/51/160 of December 15, 1997, thus establishing Rome as the host city.

[86] The "Like-Minded states" emerged during the PrepCom sessions and the informal meetings prior to the Rome Conference. This group of states was an eclectic group of states

was probably the most outspoken collection of states concerning the need for an international criminal court and as a result, they emerged as leaders during the Rome Conference.

Opposing the Like-Minded Group was the United States, along with a loosely bound group of permanent Security Council members and non-democratic states (the P-5).[87] The United States' opposition to the court centered on the concept of national sovereignty. The US delegates were concerned that if the Like-Minded States established an ICC with an independent prosecutor who had the power to initiate investigations on their own, then the Court could bring US soldiers to trial outside of the US court system. It was this fear of an ICC prosecutor "running wild" and impinging on the national sovereignty of not only the US, but all sovereign states, that fueled US opposition.

According to US delegates, an ICC must first respect the concept of national sovereignty and second, it must not be vulnerable to usage as a political tool. In other words, the US wanted to make sure that any permanent ICC would remain under the control of the Security Council and, as a result, the United States.[88] Thus, the United States did not technically oppose the establishment of a permanent ICC, just an ICC that the US does not have veto power over. As David Scheffer, US Ambassador at-large for War Crimes Issues and US delegate representative to the Rome Conference, stated:

> The United States has had and will continue to have a compelling interest in the establishment of a permanent international criminal court… Since 1995, the question for the Clinton administration has never been whether there should be an international criminal court, but rather what kind of court would be in order to operate efficiently, effectively and appropriately.[89]

As the Conference progressed, it became quite obvious that the US and the Like-Minded Group were going to clash over numerous issues contained in the draft

---

whose international presence ranged from Germany at the high end, to Samoa at the low end. The Like-Minded Group was ultimately composed of more than sixty states. I will discuss the specific goals of the Like-Minded Group at length in chapter five.

[87] The main opponents to the final draft Statute were the United States, Israel, China, Iran, Iraq, Libya and the Sudan. All of these states voted against the final draft of the Rome Statute.

[88] David J. Scheffer, "US Policy and the Proposed Permanent International Criminal Court," *US Department of State Dispatch* 8 (1997): 20-22, repeatedly refers to the primacy that the Security Council must play in jurisdiction of the court—only with Security Council approval should the ICC be able to take action. William Schabas, "United States Hostility to the International Criminal Court: It's All About the Security Council," *EJIL* 15 (2004): 701-720, also supports the notion that the US will only approve a Security Council controlled ICC.

[89] David J. Scheffer, "The United States and the International Criminal Court," *The American Journal of International Law* 93 (1999): 2.

statute. In the end, the US refused to approve the Rome Statute because, according to American representatives, it failed to adequately address their concerns. Despite US opposition, the participants overwhelmingly approved the Rome Statute, due in no small part to the growing number of non-aligned states that joined the Like-Minded Group. Much of the credit for this successful vote has to go to the non-governmental organizations that were in attendance.

The Non-Governmental Organization (NGO) coalition for an International Criminal Court (CICC) was a major actor in the formation of the Rome Statute. At the time of the Conference, the coalition had over eight hundred non-governmental organizations working for their position and this generally assisted the Like-Minded states and their cause. The NGO coalition was strongly in favor of an independent court with universal jurisdiction.[90] NGOs such as Amnesty International, Human Rights Watch, Lawyers Committee for Human Rights, and the International League for Human Rights, provided vital information and analysis to the delegates through informal meetings and aggressive campaigning tactics. In short, these NGOs provided the delegates with an expert's analysis of the subject matter and as a result, became a crucial component to the final draft statute.[91]

Negotiations

At the outset of the Conference there was a distinct plan on how things should progress, what issues the delegates would discuss, and which committees should discuss them. The brain trust of the PrepCom formulated this plan of attack at an informal meeting in Courmayeur, Italy, May 4-8, 1998.[92]

The Courmayeur Plan, as it came to be known, established a pragmatic plan for success in Rome. At this meeting it was first decided that the Plenary would only convene during the first week of the conference. Second, June 17th was agreed upon as the first date in which the Committee of the Whole and the Drafting Committee would meet.[93] Finally, it was established that discussion of Parts I and

90 Bassiouni, *Statute of the ICC,* 25, has an extensive list of the participation NGOs.

91 The NGO coalition was especially helpful to the smaller states. The NGO coalition was able to give them information concerning occurrences in meetings they could not attend and information that may not have been available to their delegates. Their impact on these nation-states was tremendous.

92 The PrepCom's Bureau, the elected conference chair, the elected committee of the whole chair, the elected drafting committee chair, the coordinators of the PrepCom working groups and the Secretariat attended this informal meeting. Bassiouni, *Statute of the ICC,* 26-29, discusses the specific details of the Courmayeur meeting.

93 The Committee of the Whole and the Drafting Committee were to be the main organs of the Rome Conference. The Committee of the Whole would receive texts from the working groups, debate the issues within these texts, and then decide whether to refer the text to the Drafting Committee. If it were accepted by the Committee of the Whole, they would refer it

III of the Draft Statute should come first, due to their likely acceptance by the convening diplomats. The Courmayeur group believed that such a ploy would give the Conference some momentum and establish a foundation for success.

With the commencement of the Rome Conference it rapidly became apparent that the Courmayeur Plan would not work. The main problem was that a large portion of the delegates attending the Rome Conference had not participated in the PrepCom meetings. As a result, the Committee of the Whole and its working group found themselves in the position of constantly having to rehash the same issues that were already debated in the PrepCom meetings.[94] It was obvious that the Conference leadership must formulate and initiate a new tactical plan otherwise the entire Rome Conference would grind to a halt and end in failure.

In order to avoid such a situation, several "informal working groups" were created. Many of these groups were then broken down into even smaller "informal-informal working groups."[95] According to participants at the Conference, a tremendous amount of the work on the final draft occurred in these smaller informal groups. A typical day for a delegate at the Rome Conference would consist of official working group meetings, supplemented by "informals" in which, as one observer put it, "the real negotiations took place."[96]

The use of "informals" as supplemental to the formal meetings appeared to be working. Progress was occurring on many of the contentious issues and a final draft was beginning to take shape. On the last day of the Conference, Chairman Philippe Kirsch decided that the Bureau's text would be presented to the Committee of the Whole for possible adoption. The Committee of the Whole met on Friday July 17, 1998 to discuss adoption of the final draft Statute. At this time, India and the United States attempted to introduce final amendments to the draft. Norway's delegate introduced a "no action" motion, which was basically a motion to table the amendments, in order to avoid a total collapse of the Conference. The result was an affirmative vote of one hundred and fourteen votes in favor, sixteen against, and twenty abstentions on the "no action" motion concerning India's amendment. On the American proposal the vote was one hundred and thirteen in favor, seventeen against, and twenty-five abstentions for the "no motion" action.[97] Cherif Bassiouni described the scene as follows:

> After the second vote, which was final [on the US proposal], the delegates burst into a spontaneous standing ovation which turned into rhythmic applause that lasted close to

---

to the Drafting Committee whose job it was to formalize the language and place the text into the final draft, which, subsequently, would need re-approval by the Committee of the Whole. Kirsch and Holmes, "Rome Conference," note 4 and 5 discuss this process in detail.

94 Bassiouni, *Statute of the ICC,* 29.

95 Bassiouni, *Statute of the ICC,* 29.

96 Donald W. Jackson, "Creating a World Court Is Like Making Sausage—Except It Takes Longer," *The Texas Observer,* June 30, 1998: 4.

97 Bendetti and Washburn, "Drafting the ICC," 26, and Bassiouni, *Statute of the ICC,* 31.

> 10 minutes, while some delegates embraced one another, others had tears in their eyes. It was one of the most extraordinary emotional scenes ever to take place at a diplomatic conference. The prevailing feeling was that the long historic journey that started after World War I had finally reached its destination. It was truly a historic moment of great significance for all who had worked so hard to bring about the momentous results.[98]

The final plenary session convened at around nine o'clock that evening. After the American delegation called for one more unrecorded vote on the Statute, the official tally was taken and the Rome Conference delegates overwhelmingly approved the final Statute. As stated earlier, the final vote was one hundred and twenty in favor, seven against, and twenty-one abstentions. The Rome Conference had achieved its ultimate goal and the Rome Statute of the International Criminal Court was finally opened for signatures. The long journey towards the establishment of an International Criminal Court had reached a critical moment, and one can mark the events of June 15-July 17, 1998 as a momentous occasion not only for humanitarian law, but for international law and international cooperation in general.[99]

Conclusion

With the approval of the Rome Statute of the International Criminal Court, the possibility of establishing a permanent ICC was finally realized. The international community had overwhelmingly approved the Statute and despite American opposition, they had concluded that the formation of an ICC was best for the global community. This fact is empirically evident by the rapid ratification process, the current functioning institution, along with the number of signatories (137) and ratifying states (98).

The Rome Conference signified the onset of a more cooperative environment within the realm of humanitarian law. When one considers the history behind the establishment of a permanent International Criminal Court, the results achieved at Rome can only be considered a great achievement. The Rome Conference initiated the institutionalization of humanitarian law and an overwhelming majority of states

98 Bassiouni, *Statute of the ICC,* 31-32.

99 Numerous accounts of the Rome Conference exist and I reference many of them. But for the purpose of this text I relied mainly on the description given by M. Cherif Bassiouni, *Statute of the ICC*. Bassiouni was present not only for the Rome Conference, but also for the PrepCom meetings. Bassiouni was the Chairman of the Drafting Committee for the Rome Statute and thus, played an integral role in the Rome Conference. He is also a professor at DePaul University and has written extensively on the establishment of an international criminal court. Bassiouni recorded much of the events that occurred in this process, both prior to and during Rome, making his account of the Conference extremely accurate and detailed.

agreed to pass the Statute, sign the Statute, and eventually ratify the Statute. Today, the ICC is a fully functioning international organization that is undertaking investigations in several different situations.

However, the Rome Statute is also significant outside of this particular issue-area. The conference at Rome was a model for how to pursue international cooperation and negotiations. The negotiating process was open and diplomatic, and the ability of a hegemon to dictate the rules and procedures of the Conference did not seem to apply. The Conference also allowed for non-state actors to play a significant role. The CICC was a major participant in the conference and one could argue that without the actions of the CICC, the international community would never have approved the Rome Statute.

The passing of the Rome Statute and the approval of a permanent International Criminal Court signify a major achievement for the global community. This Statute not only shows that cooperation and enforcement may be possible within the area of humanitarian law, but also that the international environment in general appears more amiable towards cross-border cooperation. The question that now remains is whether this Conference, and its successful outcome, signals the onset of a new global governance structure?

Chapter 3

The Rome Statute

> In the prospect of an international criminal court lies the promise of universal justice. That is the simple and soaring hope of this vision. We are close to its realization. We will do our part to see it through to the end. We ask you…to do yours in our struggle to ensure that no ruler, no State, no junta and no army anywhere can abuse human rights with impunity.
>
> Kofi Annan, United Nations Secretary-General

Introduction

With the conclusion of the Rome Conference on July 17, 1998, the final Statute of the International Criminal Court was completed. An overwhelming number of delegates approved the Statute and this despite the multiple concessions made by a large number of the participants. The final Statute was certainly not a perfect document and it was not approved by unanimous agreement however, the final Statute was a major accomplishment for the international community. It shows the world's resolve to prevent violations of humanitarian law and uphold an ideal of international justice. As Philippe Kirsch, Chairman of the Committee of the Whole, and John T. Holmes, Canadian delegate to the Rome Conference, stated:

> The statute is not a perfect instrument; no internationally negotiated instrument can be. It includes uneasy technical solutions, awkward formulations, and difficult compromises that fully satisfied no one. But it is a balanced instrument, furnished with enough strength to ensure the effective functioning of the court and sufficient safeguards to foster broad support among states… The establishment of an international criminal court is a historic achievement, the culmination of many decades of hope and hard work. It is our responsibility to keep in mind the raison d'etre of the court, which is the protection of victims, and to ensure its success.[1]

The goal of this chapter is to engage some of the specifics of the Statute in order to understand how the ICC proposes to protect the world's victims and ensure the impartial functioning of the Court for future generations. Due to the massive size of the document, I will only analyze what many scholars consider the most important (or at least most contentious) aspects of the Rome Statute: jurisdiction,

---

1 Kirsch and Holmes, *Rome Conference*, 11-12.

trigger mechanisms, complementarity, the ICC's relationship with the United Nations, enforcement, and obstacles to ratification.[2]

Aside from these issues, the majority of the Statute deals with the rights of the accused, the composition and administration of the Court, and the financing of the Court. These issues, although crucial to the functioning of the ICC, were not as hotly debated at the Rome Conference. Thus, by understanding the more contentious issues, I believe that it becomes easier for us to first, gain a better understanding of the Court's purpose, and second, use this understanding to analyze its formation in a more detailed manner. However, before going into the specifics of the Court, we must first understand why the formation of the International Criminal Court is so important to world politics; and to accomplish this we must first discuss some of the benefits the Court will provide the global community.

The Benefits of the Court

The preamble of the Rome Statute establishes the purpose of the International Criminal Court. In general, the Court will seek "to guarantee lasting respect for and the enforcement of international justice."[3] Prior to the Rome Statute, the only forms of international criminal justice, concerning individuals and not states, were ad hoc tribunals, and although these tribunals served their purpose well, scholars often accused these tribunals of both "selective justice" and a lack of rapid response.[4]

---

2 The Rome Statute of the International Criminal Court is constructed of twelve parts and one hundred and twenty-eight articles. The rationale for analyzing the aforementioned issues is due to the contentious nature of these issues and the centrality of these issues to the functioning of the ICC. I am not alone in singling out these particular issues. When analyzing the Rome Statute, the following authors also chose to center on some or all of these issues: Nanda, "Establishment of Permanent ICC"; Berg, "Permanent International Criminal Court," Yves Beigbeder, *Judging War Criminals: The Politics of International Justice* (London: MacMillan Press, Ltd., 1999), Helen Duffy, "Toward Eradicating Impunity: The Establishment of an International Criminal Court," *Social Justice* 26 (1999): 115, Alejandro Teitelbaum, "Statute of the International Criminal Court: A Critique," *Social Justice* 26 (1999): 107-114, and Bertram Brown, "The Statute of the ICC: Past, Present, and Future," in *The United States and the International Criminal Court: National Security and International Law,* ed. Sarah B. Sewell and Carl Kaysen (Lanham, MD: Rowman & Littlefield Publishers, Inc., 2000), 61-84. These issues not only make-up a large portion of the Rome Statute, they have been the major issues discussed by both governments, during the ratification process, and within scholarly analysis.

3 Rome Statute of the International Criminal Court, Preamble paragraph 11.

4 As Mark W. Janis, "The International Court," in *International Courts for the Twenty-First Century,* ed. Mark W. Janis (Dordecht, The Netherlands: Martinus Nijhoff Publishers, 1992), 13-43, points out, the other major International Courts, the International Court of

Preventing Selective Justice

"Selective justice" is an accusation levied against not only the post-World War II tribunals (selective justice within the tribunal), but against the entire practice of establishing ad hoc international tribunals (selective justice in terms of establishment). In terms of selective justice within an ad hoc tribunal, critics of these tribunals commonly referred to this type of action as "victors' justice." Critics accuse both the Nuremberg and Tokyo Military Tribunals of imposing victors' justice.[5] This charge stems from the fact that the vanquished had no choice but to accept the type of justice imposed on them, while the victors would go unpunished for any actions or atrocities that were committed on their part during the Second World War. Scholars also assert that the proceedings at these two International Military Tribunals were simply "show trials." The defendants in these cases are often cited as not having any judicial procedural protection or adequate time to prepare a defense. Thus, the courts at Nuremberg and Tokyo are often seen as an act of injustice in their own right.[6]

More importantly, the ad hoc tribunal system is seen as implementing "selective justice" in terms of the incidents over which the international community establishes a tribunal. Historically, the international community has established several ad hoc tribunals including: Nuremberg, Tokyo, the former Yugoslavia, Rwanda, East Timor, Cambodia, Sierra Leone, and Iraq. This begs the question, why only these situations? Why not establish an international ad hoc tribunal for crimes committed in Chile? Why not one for crimes committed in Uganda? Why not one for crimes committed against Turkish Armenians? Unfortunately there is no answer. For one reason or another, the great powers of this world saw these four cases as more important then the others.[7] It was a

---

Justice (ICJ), its predecessor the Permanent Court of International Justice and the Permanent Court of Arbitration, have all dealt with states, not individuals. The most recognizable of these institutions, the ICJ, has been in place since 1946 but is generally considered a weak institution. One of the reasons for this perceived weakness is the fact that the ICJ only hears cases between state governments, not individuals. Couple this with the fact that the ICJ's jurisdiction is not compulsory and the weakness of the institution becomes self-evident. David P. Forsythe, "Politics and the International Tribunal for the Former Yugoslavia," in Roger S. Clark and Madeline Sann (eds.), *The Prosecution of International Crimes: A Critical Study of the International Tribunal for the Former Yugoslavia* (Somerset: NJ: Transaction Publishers, 1997), 185-207 has a more detailed discussion of the ICJ and its strengths and weaknesses.

5 Thornberry, "Saving the War Crimes Tribunal," 72-73 and Bassiouni, *Statute of the ICC,* 8.

6 Thornberry, "Saving the War Crimes Tribunal," 72-73.

7 The signing of the London agreement on August 8, 1945 established the Nuremberg tribunal. Russia, the United States Great Britain, and France established this agreement. The Tokyo tribunal was initiated by the recommendation of the United Nations War Crimes

subjective judgement by a group of statesmen working without an objectively defined criterion for establishing a criminal tribunal. Such action only solidifies the criticism that a system of international justice predicated on an ad hoc tribunal system allows for "selective justice."

Permanency

Another innate problem of the ad hoc tribunal system is that it often fails to act in a timely manner. This is simply due to the fact that the tribunals are ad hoc, and therefore establishment of a tribunal takes time. With the establishment of a permanent ICC the tools of justice are already in place. There is no need for broad agreement among the international community to take action and there is no delay in the pursuit of justice because of infrastructure problems. Past tribunals needed the approval of the Security Council or the approval of a set of key nation-states before their establishment. The Rome Statute already has the approval of the international community. A permanent ICC also has the necessary infrastructure in place, thus allowing for rapid reaction to acts of genocide, crimes against humanity, crimes of aggression, and war crimes. Put simply, a permanent ICC already has the tools of justice assembled and approved.[8]

Individual Accountability

The establishment of the ICC also allows individuals to be brought to justice, not just governments. One of the many criticisms leveled at the International Court of Justice is that it does not hold individuals accountable, only governments. However, as the judgements at Nuremberg stated, "crimes against international law are committed by men, not abstract entities, and only by punishing individuals who commit such crimes can the provisions of international law be enforced." The ICC now contains the legal right to try individuals for their actions and punish them accordingly.[9] Therefore, the establishment of a permanent International Criminal

---

Commission. The International Tribunal for the Former Yugoslavia was established officially established with the passing of Security Council Resolution 827 and Rwanda's tribunal resulted from Security Council Resolution 955. The point is that all of these ad hoc tribunals came about from the actions of great powers and as a result, they are "selective" in their imposition of justice.

8 Berg, "Permanent International Criminal Court," discusses the advantages of a permanent International Criminal Court as opposed to the ad hoc tribunals that the international community has used in the past. She cites such advantages as established international approval of the ICC mandate, a permanent group of assembled experts within the field, and having adequate funds to pursue international justice.

9 Rome Statute of the International Criminal Court, Article 25.

Court is a great assistance in establishing a system of international justice at the global level.[10]

Overcoming the Nation-State System

The establishment of an International Criminal Court also rectifies the failure of the nation-state system to protect human rights. Traditionally, the protection of individual human rights was considered a domestic issue. The principle of state sovereignty gave nation-states supreme authority over their citizenry. As a result, the international community did not view intervention by an outside authority for violations of "universal" human rights as an option.[11] The upholding of the principle of state sovereignty would not be a problem if states adequately addressed violations of human rights. However, as history has shown us, this is simply not the case. As one author described the sovereign state system, "Westphalia is another of the West's failures."[12]

The ratification of the Rome Statute is a clear step towards rectifying the failures of the nation-state system (at least in terms of humanitarian law). The ICC serves as the international institutionalization of humanitarian law and has the jurisdiction to act when states fail to uphold their obligation to protect human rights. Nation-states no longer shoulder the protection of citizens from war crimes, genocide, crimes against humanity, and crimes of aggression by themselves. Instead, the international community now has a mechanism for action and a legal process for the rectification of state failure.

Deterrence

Finally, a permanent International Criminal Court *could* also act as a deterrent to future humanitarian law violators. With the first indictment, arrest, conviction, and enforcement of the sentence, the Court will send a message to all those who might consider violating international humanitarian law.[13] That message is that the international community is finally saying "never again" and backing this statement

---

[10] Bruce Broomhall, *International Justice and the International Criminal Court* (Oxford: Oxford University Press, 2003) provides a good description of the transformative nature of international justice.

[11] The defining characteristic of a system predicated on the concept state sovereignty is the principle of non-intervention. Thus, any conception of human rights within this type of system is tied directly to the state and its authority. Krasner, "Sovereignty, Regimes and Human Rights," discusses this very principle.

[12] Ken Booth, "Human Wrongs and International Relations," *International Affairs* 71 (1995): 123.

[13] It is important to note that without enforcement, the ICC will not have the ability to deter—conviction is not enough.

with the institutionalization of humanitarian law.[14] The ICC acts as the mechanism for upholding these norms, thus forcing individuals to consider the consequences of violating these norms.[15] This is not to say that the ICC *will* deter criminal actions. Clearly the existence of functioning courts and enforcement capabilities does not always equate into deterrence. Nevertheless, with the presence of a permanent ICC, there is a chance that some criminal actions will not occur because of the impending consequences. Therefore, although the ICC will not deter all criminals, the Court does have the ability to prevent some criminal actions.

Given the fact that the international community has granted the ICC the mandate of enforcing established humanitarian law, it is clear that the permanent International Criminal Court will have to serve numerous purposes. From rectifier of past shortcomings in humanitarian law, to a deterrent of future violations, it is clear that the ICC now shoulders a tremendous amount of expectations. But what types of mechanisms does the Rome Statute contain that will assist in achieving these purposes? In general, what is the legal construct of the ICC?

Particulars of the Rome Statute

The final Rome Statute is constructed of one hundred and twenty-eight articles that are divided into thirteen parts. These thirteen parts vary in the issues they cover. They range from the establishment of the Court, to the appeal process and enforcement, to financing and entry into force.[16] The Statute is based on three underlying principles. The first is the principle of complementarity between the Court and state parties. The second is that the Court must only deal with the most

---

14 This statement "never again" refers to the reaction of the international community after the atrocities of the Holocaust. The problem is that such atrocities did occur again, several times. The permanent ICC would serve as a message that this time the global community is serious. The institutionalization of humanitarian law through the establishment of the ICC would show the world that perpetrators of this law would now be held accountable.

15 Cassel, "Why We Need the ICC," discusses the deterrent factor at greater length showing that the ratification of the ICC is a statement of "zero tolerance" for crimes against humanity. Lawyers Committee for Human Rights, *Establishing an International Criminal Court: Major Unresolved Issues in the Draft Statute* (New York, NY: International Criminal Court Briefing Series, 1996), 3-5, also gives a brief synopsis of why an international criminal court is needed. Their list includes many of the issues discussed in this work, but also several other issues.

16 The thirteen parts of the Rome Statute are as follows: *Establishment of the Court; Jurisdiction, Admissibility and Applicable Law; General Principles of Criminal Law; Composition and Administration of the Court; Investigation and Prosecution; The Trial; Penalties; Appeal and Revision; International Cooperation and Judicial Assistance; Enforcement; Assembly of State Parties; Financing; Final Clauses.*

serious crimes of humanitarian law. Third, the Statute must also remain within the realm of established international law.[17]

In order to adequately understand the importance of this institution, it is necessary to discuss some of the more important issues embodied in the Rome Statute. In particular, this narrative must discuss the Court's jurisdiction, trigger mechanisms, the concept of complementarity, the role of the prosecutor and the Security Council, and finally enforcement. Let us begin with a discussion of jurisdiction and what constitutes the "core crimes."

Jurisdiction

Part 2 of the Rome Statute discusses the jurisdiction of the Court. As stated in Article 5, the International Criminal Court has jurisdiction over the following four crimes: crime of genocide, crimes against humanity, war crimes, and the crime of aggression. The Court has jurisdiction over these crimes from the time the Statute enters into force therefore, the ICC is temporally bound to the point of its ratification.[18] No crimes committed prior to July 1, 2002, are within the Court's jurisdiction.

Scholars often refer to the crimes themselves as the "core crimes" of international humanitarian law.[19] The definitions of the crime of genocide, crimes against humanity, and war crimes are all predicated on established international law. The crime of aggression is more problematic, but I will return to this later.

The crime of genocide is defined in Article 6 of the Rome Statute. The wording of this definition is taken directly from the 1948 Genocide Convention and reads as follows:

> For the purpose of this Statute, "genocide" means any of the following:
> [A]cts committed with intent to destroy, in whole or in part, a national, ethnical, racial, or religious group, as such:
> (a) Killing members of the group;
> (b) Causing serious bodily or mental harm to members of the group;
> (c) Deliberately inflicting on the group conditions of life calculated to bring about its physical destruction in whole or in part;

---

[17] These three principles permeate the majority of the Rome Statute text and are defined by Mahnoush H. Arsanjani, "The Rome Statute of the International Criminal Court," *The American Journal of International Law* 93, (1999): 24-25.

[18] Rome Statute of the ICC, Article 10.1.

[19] Such scholars as Berg, "Permanent International Criminal Court," Lawyers Committee for Human Rights, *The Rome Treaty for an International Criminal Court: A Brief Summary of the Main Issues* (New York, NY: International Criminal Court Briefing Series, 1998), and Marie-Claude Roberge, "The New International Criminal Court: A Preliminary Assessment," *International Review of the Red Cross* 93 (1998): 671-691, use the term "core crimes."

(d) Imposing measures intended to prevent births within the group;
(e) Forcibly transferring children of the group to another group.[20]

The delegates attending the Rome Conference unanimously accepted this definition and rapidly incorporated it into the Statute. Under this article, not only does the Court have the right to impose punishment for acts of genocide, but also conspiracy to commit genocide, public incitement to commit genocide, attempted genocide, and complicity in genocide.

Article 7 discusses the nature of crimes against humanity. The definition of these crimes proved more difficult to negotiate. The definition that exists in the final Statute is a broad definition that goes beyond previous definitions. Both the Nuremberg Charter and the ad hoc tribunals of the 1990s contained definitions of such crimes, but the Preparatory Committee determined that the definitions found in these documents were insufficient.[21] The definition employed in the final Rome Statute includes acts of: murder, extermination, enslavement, deportation or forcible transfer of a population, imprisonment or severe deprivation of physical liberty, torture, rape, sexual slavery, enforced prostitution, forced pregnancy, enforced sterilization, other forms of extreme sexual violence, persecution against any identifiable group or collectivity, enforced disappearance of persons, apartheid, or other inhumane acts of a similar character.

The Court considers all of these actions crimes against humanity as long as they are "committed as part of a widespread or systematic attack directed against any civilian population."[22] It is also important to note that the Rome Statute does not require that such acts be committed within the context of an armed conflict. Therefore, according to the Rome Statute's definition, crimes against humanity can also be committed in times of civil strife or even peace.[23]

Article 8 of the Rome Statute discusses war crimes. As with the previous two crimes, the Statute's final definition of war crimes is also predicated on established international law. In particular, the lengthy definition of what constitutes a war crime is based on grave breaches of the 1949 Geneva Conventions (including Protocol I, Protocol II and violations of article 3 common to the four Geneva

---

[20] The only change from the Genocide Convention definition to the Rome Statute definition is the replacement of the word "Convention" for the word "Statute".

[21] Originally the PrepCom looked at the ICTY definition of crimes against humanity as defined in Article 5 of the Statute of the Yugoslav Tribunal and the ICTR definition found in Article 3 of the Rwanda Tribunal. Both proved inadequate and therefore there was a need to broaden the definition to encompass a greater number of actions. Arsanjani, "Rome Statute of the ICC," 30-32, and Darryl Robinson, "Defining 'Crimes Against Humanity' at the Rome Conference," *The American Journal of International Law* 93 (1999): 43-57.

[22] Rome Statute of the ICC, Article 7.1.

[23] Robinson, "Defining Crimes Against Humanity," 46.

Conventions) and the Hague Convention of 1907.[24] The resulting definition is extremely inclusive and encompassing. It includes: willful killing, torture or inhuman treatment, extensive destruction and appropriation of property, unlawful deportation, taking of hostages, intentionally targeting civilian populations, use of poison weapons or gases, rape, sexual slavery, starvation, among numerous other violations of international law.[25]

A major point of discussion at the Rome Conference was whether the definition of war crimes should apply to internal conflicts. The Court was established to have jurisdiction over war crimes when they are "committed as part of a plan or policy or as part of a large-scale commission of such crimes."[26] In paragraph 2 (b), the Statute establishes that this crime applies in situations of international armed conflict, but not "situations of internal disturbances and tensions, such as riots, isolated and sporadic acts of violence or other acts of a similar nature."[27] Such acts are already included in the Rome Statute's definition of crimes against humanity, thus providing the Court with the ability to prosecute these actions.

The last crime within the Court's jurisdiction is the crime of aggression.[28] This particular crime has proved a sticking point for the establishment of an international criminal court since the early post World War II era. In 1954, the United Nations' General Assembly prevented the formation of an ICC because the ILC could not define "aggression."[29] The UN Special Committee finally defined the concept in 1974, but this issue has remained a contentious one. The 1974 definition was rather expansive, but the primary content of the definition was as follows: "Aggression is the use of armed force by a State against the sovereignty, territorial integrity or political independence of another State, or in any other manner inconsistent with the Charter of the United Nations, as set out in this definition."[30]

This definition went on to include the following acts as evidence of aggression: invasion or attack by an armed force of a State, bombardment by an armed force of a State, blockade of ports or coasts by an armed force of a State, the use of mercenaries by a State to carry out acts of armed force and any other act that the

---

24 There are also sections of the war crimes article that overlap with the Convention on the Rights of the Child (1989) and the Convention for the Protection of Cultural Property (1954).

25 For the entire definition of War Crimes see the Rome Statute of the ICC, Article 8.

26 Rome Statute of the ICC, Article 8.1.

27 Rome Statute of the ICC, Article 8.2 (d) and (f).

28 Rome Statute of the ICC, Article 5.1 (d).

29 Bassiouni, *Statute of the ICC,* 14.

30 Report of the Special Committee, Supp. No. 19, A/9619 of the Twenty-Ninth Session, 1974, Article 1. Reprinted in Benjamin B. Ferencz, *Defining International Aggression: The Search for World Peace* (Dobbs Ferry, New York: Oceana Publications, Inc., 1975), 562.

Security Council determines is an act of aggression under the provisions of the Charter.[31]

With the renewed discussion of an ICC in the 1990s, the debate concerning a definition of crimes of aggression once again took center stage. With none of the post-Cold War ad hoc tribunals' prosecuting this crime, the Preparatory Committee did not have any recent precedent to call upon that dealt with individual acts of aggression.[32] Despite the definitional problem, it was clear that the Preparatory Committee was determined to see that this issue was discussed at Rome.[33] In fact, the crime of aggression was included in the draft statute for the Rome Conference and it included three definitions that would be presented as options to the attending delegates.[34] As the Conference progressed it became clear that there was support for the inclusion of this crime in the final Statute, but once again, there was a lack of consensus on how to define this crime.[35] The result is as follows:

> The Court shall exercise jurisdiction over the crime of aggression once a provision is adopted in accordance with articles 121 and 123 defining the crime and setting out the conditions under which the Court shall exercise jurisdiction with respect to this crime. Such a provision shall be consistent with the relevant provisions of the Charter of the United Nations.[36]

The crime of aggression is included in the list of crimes within the jurisdiction of the Court, but its definition is yet to be determined. Even upon defining this crime, the definition must then pass through the procedures of an amendment to the Statute, as defined in Articles 121 and 123. The Post-Rome Preparatory Committees have taken up this issue, but at the point of writing this text no consensus has been reached.

It should now be apparent that the jurisdiction of the ICC is quite broad. It includes genocide, crimes against humanity, war crimes and eventually crimes of aggression. It is important to note that the Court substantiated none of these crimes or their definitions. Instead, they are all based on legal precedent and established international law. This is important because it shows that the Court is not trying to

---

31 Report of the Special Committee, Supp. No. 19, A/9619 of the Twenty-Ninth Session, 1974, Article 1. Reprinted in Ferencz, *Defining International Aggression,* 562-563.

32 Even the definition found in General Assembly Resolution 3314 of December 1974, is not precedent. This is because the 1974 definition limits its scope to crimes committed by states. As a result, the 1974 definition of aggression is not legally binding due to the fact that it deals with states, not individuals.

33 Arsanjani, "Rome Statute of the ICC," 29-30.

34 Report of the Preparatory Committee on the Establishment of an International Criminal Court: Draft Statute and Draft Final Act, Article 5. Reprinted in Bassiouni, *Statute of the ICC,* 120-122.

35 Arsanjani, "Rome Statute of the ICC," 30.

36 Rome Statute of the International Criminal Court, Article 5.2.

initiate a new form of international law, it is simply trying to uphold and institutionalize existing legal precedent.

Trigger Mechanisms

The exercise of jurisdiction, or trigger mechanisms, was a very contentious issue at the Rome Conference. At the heart of the debate was whether state parties, the Security Council, and/or the independent prosecutor could refer a matter for investigation to the Court. A large contingent of states, along with the NGO coalition (CICC), wanted the ICC to have *universal* and *inherent* jurisdiction over the four core crimes.[37] Universal in the sense that no state would fall outside of the Court's purview; inherent in that the prosecutor would have the inherent power to pursue a criminal investigation without having to consult another authority.

The United States strongly opposed the idea of an international criminal court with both universal and inherent jurisdiction. For the United States delegates, the idea of an independent prosecutor who possessed the power to trigger an investigation into any state's domestic realm without having to seek authority from another source was ludicrous. The US saw this as a clear violation of the principle of state sovereignty and the foundation for a politicized Court whose actions would not be undertaken to uphold the norms of international justice, but the self-interests of its member states. US ambassador to the UN, Bill Richardson, explained US concerns in the following manner:

> There is also a need for checks and balances with respect to the decisions of a single Prosecutor, who in theory also could be influenced by personal and political considerations. If the Prosecutor has sole discretion to initiate investigations and file complaints—as some delegations have sought under the rubric of "inherent jurisdiction"—the results could be more idiosyncratic, possibly even more political, than the decisions of the Security Council.[38]

US objections to the implementation of universal and inherent jurisdiction led to the need for negotiations at the Conference. The US proposed that the UN Security Council control the Court's trigger mechanisms.[39] This scenario would be similar to the practice of the war crimes tribunals in the former Yugoslavia and Rwanda. The prosecutor would have wide discretion within the situation once the

---

37 Kirsch and Holmes, "Rome Conference," 8-9.

38 This excerpt is taken from a speech given by Bill Richardson to the General Assembly on October 31, 1996. Reprinted in Ball, *Prosecuting War Crimes,* 203.

39 Scheffer, "US Policy," 2, clearly defines the Clinton administration's policy on the ICC and it is clear that the Bush administration concurs with this position. See Georg Nolte, "The United States and the International Criminal Court," in *Unilateralism and U.S. Foreign Policy: International Perspectives,* ed. David M. Malone and Yuen Foong Khong, (Boulder, CO: Lynne Rienner Publishers, 2003), for an analysis of the Bush administration's policy towards the ICC.

Security Council approved the Court's jurisdiction over that situation. The US position clashed with a German proposal, which called for universal jurisdiction and an independent prosecutor. The result was a compromise between these two positions.

The final draft of the Rome Statute established both preconditions for the exercise of jurisdiction and the trigger mechanisms for an investigation. The Court has jurisdiction over a situation if one of the following conditions is met:

> (a) A situation in which one or more of such crimes [a stated in Article 5 of the Rome Statute] appears to have been committed is referred to the Prosecutor in accordance with Article 14;[40]
>
> (b) A situation in which one or more of such crimes appears to have been committed is referred to the Prosecutor by the Security Council acting under Chapter VII of the United Nations;[41] or
>
> (c) The Prosecutor has initiated an investigation in respect of such a crime in accordance with Article 15.[42]

In other words, the Court may initiate an investigation if a state party, the Security Council, or the prosecutor refers a situation to the Court. If any of these actors determines that any of the crimes defined in Article 5 have been committed, they may refer the case to the prosecutor for further investigation. The case is then in the hands of the prosecutor and he/she must decide whether there is sufficient evidence to proceed.

Although this appears to be an approval of universal jurisdiction, it is not. Certain preconditions must be met prior to the Court exercising its jurisdiction. These preconditions establish the territorial jurisdiction of the Court and limit the application of its power. In short, Article 13 does not give the Court universal jurisdiction because a state party cannot refer any situation to the prosecutor and the prosecutor cannot investigate any situation. Spatial considerations determine where and when the Court may exercise its power.

---

40 Article 14 discusses the process by which a state party may refer a case to the prosecutor. This referral must specify the circumstances surrounding the crime and include proper documentation that proves that such a crime has occurred.

41 Chapter VII of the United Nations Charter involves the action that the Security Council can take in situations where there is a threat to peace, a breach of peace or an act of aggression.

42 Rome Statute of the ICC, Article 13. Article 15 of the Rome Statute describes the process that must be undertaken if the Prosecutor is to initiate an investigation without referral by either a State Party or the Security Council. This article states that the prosecutor may initiate an investigation *proprio motu*, but that in order to proceed with the investigation and seek an indictment, the prosecutor must submit a request to the Pre-Trial Chamber and receive their authorization. As mentioned earlier in this text, the Court is also temporally bound in that it does not have retroactive jurisdiction.

According to Article 12, the Court has jurisdiction within the territory of a state which is party to the Statute. Therefore, if a one or more of the crimes defined in Article 5 are committed on a state's territory that is party to the Statute, then the ICC has jurisdiction.[43] The ICC also has jurisdiction if the crime was committed on board a vessel or aircraft that is registered by a state that is party to the Statute.[44] The ICC's jurisdiction also extends to a situation in which the perpetrator of the crime is a national of a state that is party to the Statute.[45] Finally, the ICC also has jurisdiction over a non-party state if that state voluntarily accepts the Courts jurisdiction or the United Nations Security Council refers the situation.[46]

In combining both the preconditions and the trigger mechanisms, what results is the following: either a state that is party to the Statute, the Security Council, or the prosecutor can trigger an investigation as long as the crime occurred on a party state's territory, or a vessel or aircraft that is registered to that state, or the perpetrator is a national of a party state. The only other instances in which the ICC could act in a non-party situation are if a non-party state consented or if the Security Council referred it to the Court. If the Security Council refers a situation to the Court, then universal jurisdiction does apply.[47]

To better understand the issue of jurisdiction, the following hypothetical situation is instructive. If Hosni Mubarak commits a crime against humanity (after July 1, 2002) when would the Court be able to act? If Egypt is not party to the Statute and the crime occurs within Egyptian territory, then the Court has no jurisdiction over the crime unless Egypt invites the ICC to investigate or the UN Security Council refers the situation. Since Egypt is not party to the Statute, so neither the territory on which the crime was committed or the nationality of the perpetrator are party to the Statute. But if Mubarak commited his crimes in Turkey, and Turkey is a party to the Statute, then the ICC could act.

A more simplistic understanding applies to crimes committed in a member state's territory. Suppose General Mladic, a Bosnian Serb, were to commit an ICC defined crime in Serbia, and Bosnia had ratified the Statute, then the Court could prosecute Mladic. General Mladic's national state is, hypothetically, party to the Statute. In general, it all keys on the spatial point of the crime or the nationality of the perpetrator. If neither the State nor the perpetrator's state is party to the Statute, then the Court has no jurisdiction, unless the state voluntarily consents to an ICC investigation or if the Security Council refers the situation to the Court. The referral of a situation by the Security Council is the one and only instance in

---

43 Rome Statute of the ICC, Article 12.1.

44 Rome Statute of the ICC, Article 12.2 (a).

45 Rome Statue of the ICC, Article 12.2 (b).

46 Rome Statute of the ICC, Article 12.3.

47 Arsanjani, "Rome Statute of the ICC," 26, discusses Article 13 (b) and the provision concerning the Security Council's ability to initiate an investigation in any territory, regardless of the State's relationship to the Court. A recent example of this power is the UN Security Council's recent approval of ICC jurisdiction in the non-party state of Sudan.

which universal jurisdiction applies. Aside from this type of referral, the ICC is constrained by issues of territory, nationality and temporal considerations.

Complementarity

The Court must also incorporate the principle of complementarity when considering whether they have legal jurisdiction. The principle of complementarity concerns the relationship that the International Criminal Court has with the national authorities and domestic courts of state parties. A major concern for many nation-states is that the formation of the ICC perpetuates a situation in which the infringement of state sovereignty is inevitable.[48] PrepCom believed that complementarity would allow for the institutionalization of humanitarian law, while still preserving the principle of state sovereignty and allaying the concerns of many states.

According to Article 17.1 of the Rome Statute, the principle of complementarity states that:

> [T]he Court shall determine that a case is inadmissible where:
> (a) The case is being investigated or prosecuted by a State which has jurisdiction over it, unless the State is unwilling or unable to genuinely carry out the investigation or prosecution;
> (b) The case has been investigated by a State which has jurisdiction over it and the State has decided not to prosecute the person concerned, unless the decision resulted from the unwillingness of the State genuinely to prosecute;

In short, the relationship of the ICC with national judicial systems is a complementary one. If, and only if, the domestic judicial system cannot properly investigate or prosecute the alleged crime does the ICC have jurisdiction. The inability to investigate or prosecute would most likely be the result of a lack of national infrastructure or a collapse of the state's domestic judicial system. Unwillingness to investigate or prosecute is not as easy to define.

The Rome Statute holds that if a state is unwilling to investigate a crime, then the ICC has the right to prosecute the accused.[49] The Court shall determine unwillingness by whether one or more of the following situations exists: (1) the national judicial proceedings were undertaken for the purpose of shielding the

[48] Berg, "Permanent International Criminal Court," Louise Arbour and Morten Bergsmo, "Despite Shortcomings, a Court Deserving Support," *UN Chronicle* 35 (1998): 12-13; Kenneth W. Abbott, "International Relations Theory, International Law, and the Regime Governing Atrocities in Internal Conflicts," *The American Journal of International Law* 98 (1999): 361-379; and Arsanjani, "Rome Statute of the ICC," all discuss the issue of complementarity and the fear by many states that without this principle their state sovereignty would no longer be secure.

[49] Rome Statute of the ICC, Article 17.2.

accused from criminal responsibility; (2) the court proceedings have been unjustifiably delayed, showing the state's lack of intent to impose justice; (3) if the judicial proceedings are being undertaken, they are not being undertaken in an impartial and neutral manner. As a result, the Statute of the International Criminal Court asserts that international justice is not being served; therefore, the Court has a right to intervene and prosecute.

These are the three situations in which the ICC can impose its jurisdiction on a nation-state and take over the investigation and trial. The reason for the establishment of this type of system is that the Court is meant to function for the interests of the victims and the international community as whole, not individual states.[50] But at the same time, the Court is established to "be complementary to national criminal jurisdictions."[51] As a result, it became crucial to the effectiveness of the ICC that the delegates establish specific guidelines concerning situations in which "unwillingness" by states to prosecute was occurring.

In the aforementioned situations, Article 17.2 (a-c), the Court can claim primacy in a criminal case and override a state's jurisdiction on that case. Many states, including the US, see this as a clear violation of national sovereignty and the concept of non-intervention. But if the ICC is to establish a sense of universal justice, then the provision for the Court's primacy over incapable or unwilling domestic legal systems is crucial. Without the inclusion of complementarity and the Court's jurisdictional primacy in certain situations, the ability of states to protect their own citizens from criminal responsibility is greatly increased and the ability to ascertain international justice is greatly decreased.[52]

The ICC and the United Nations

Advocates of the ICC have yet to determine the exact relationship of the Court with the United Nations. Article 2 stipulates that the Assembly of States Parties

---

[50] Kofi Annan stressed this goal of the ICC in his opening speech at the Rome Conference. In this speech Annan stated that "the overriding interest [of the court] must be that of the victims, and of the international community as a whole…It must be an instrument of justice, not expediency. It must protect the weak against the strong." The entire speech can be found on the UN website <www.un.org/icc/>

[51] Rome Statute of the ICC, Preamble paragraph 10.

[52] One could argue that the concept of complementarity, although necessary to an effective ICC, still needs elaboration. The concept is often seen as ambiguous and underdeveloped. Therefore, scholars such as Madeline Morris, "Complementarity and Conflict: States, Victims and the ICC." In *The United States and the International Criminal Court: National Security and International Law, ed.* Sarah B. Sewall and Carl Kaysen, (Lanham, MD: Rowman & Littlefield Publishers, Inc., 2000), 195-212, have called for a more carefully developed policy concerning the ICC's use of complementarity. With this further development, Morris sees the "very real risk that the ICC will create injustice rather than justice," 208.

must approve a future agreement regarding the relationship between these two entities. Although the Court's relationship to the UN is important, it is the Court's relationship with the Security Council that is truly contentious.

I discussed the contentious nature of the Security Council's role in the ICC earlier in this chapter, but the importance of this issue warrants some reiteration. The Rome Statute does establish a role for the Security Council. The Security Council can refer a situation to the prosecutor for investigation.[53] Thus, the Security Council is one of the trigger mechanisms of the ICC, but it is also the most powerful of trigger mechanisms. This is due to the fact that not only can the Security Council initiate an investigation, but they can also initiate an investigation regardless of the state's relationship to the Court (as the Sudan case demonstrates).

Acting under Article VII of the UN Charter, the Security Council can refer a situation to the prosecutor regardless of whether the territory on which the alleged crime occurred is a party to the ICC, or whether the accused is a national of a state party. In other words, the Security Council is the only trigger mechanism that has the ability to grant the Court universal jurisdiction.

Accompanying this powerful provision is the fact that the Security Council can ascertain a deferral of any ICC investigation for a period of twelve months. According to the Rome Statute:

> No investigation or prosecution may be commenced or proceeded with under this Statute for a period of 12 months after the Security Council, in a resolution adopted under Chapter VII of the Charter of the United Nations, has requested the Court to that effect; that request may be renewed by the Council under the same conditions.[54]

Although many states, such as the US, feel that the Rome Statute does not grant enough power to the Security Council, it should now be clear that the Rome Statute has granted a reasonable amount of power to this entity. In fact, many states see Article 16 as a mechanism by which the Security Council could subject the Court to its political influence. The end result, according to these states, is that the ICC has the potential to simply become a political tool of the Security Council instead of a means for achieving international justice.[55] Nevertheless, whether one desires greater Security Council control or less, no one can deny that the final Statute of the ICC grants the Security Council a crucial role in the workings of the Court.[56]

---

53 Rome Statute of the ICC, Article 13 (b).

54 Rome Statute of the ICC, Article 16.

55 Ved P. Nanda, "The Establishment of a Permanent International Criminal Court: Challenges Ahead," *Human Rights Quarterly* 20 (1998): 422-423, discusses the issue of Security Council power and both opposition and advocation of their power.

56 One should also note that technically, according to Article VII of the UN Charter, the Security Council has the ability to initiate any action it desires, as long as it has the consent of all of its members.

Their actions will certainly have a bearing on the future of the ICC and the cases that it pursues.

Enforcement

The final issue to discuss is the enforcement mechanisms for the ICC. As with most intergovernmental organizations, enforcement of the Rome Statute relies on the state parties. Scholars often see this reliance as the achilles heal of international law. John Fried describes this as the "jailer theory" of international law.[57] This theory depicts the foundation of international law as a sizable body of accepted norms that lacks any reliable enforcement capabilities. Without the ability to enforce these norms, international law remains a weak form of international justice.

The main problem concerning enforcement is that international law tends towards a system of self-help.[58] The institutionalization of international law usually comes in the form of an intergovernmental organization (IGO). An IGO is an association of states that are bound together in their quest to advance a common goal.[59] An IGO is predicated on the power of state members and despite their transsovereign mandates, IGOs still rely on sovereign states to enforce the underlying treaty that formed the IGO.[60] This is no different for the International Criminal Court, which clearly fits the definition of an IGO.

In order to enforce the Court's judgements, the ICC must rely on the state parties to cooperate. Without their cooperation, the ICC is unable to fulfill its mandate. Arrests, transfer of prisoners, and enforcement of Court sentences all rely on the cooperation of member states.[61] If member states refuse to uphold the norms contained within this Statute, then the ICC will simply become a dead letter treaty. The only recourse that the ICC has to a state's failure to comply is referral of the matter to the Assembly of State Parties or the United Nations' Security

---

[57] John H. E. Fried, "International Law—Neither Orphan Nor Harlot, Neither Jailer Nor Never-Never Land," in *International Law: Classic and Contemporary Readings,* ed. Charlotte Ku and Paul F. Diehl (Boulder, CO: Lynne Rienner Publishers, 1998), 27.

[58] Perceived may be a better word, because although many scholars and policymakers view the system of international law as a self-help system, the provisions established in the UN Charter, chapter VI and VII can circumscribe it.

[59] Robert L. Bledsoe and Boleslaw A. Boczak, *The International Law Dictionary* (Santa Barbara, CA: ABC:CLIO, 1987), 75-76.

[60] Ursula C. Tafe, Intergovernmental Organizations," in *Beyond Sovereignty: Issues for a Global Agenda,* ed. Maryann K. Cusimano (Boston: Bedford/St. Martin's Press, 2000), 231-234, discusses the reliance that IGOs have on nation-states despite the changing international environment and the rise in transsovereign problems.

[61] The specifics of these issues are all contained within the Rome Statute. The arresting of accused criminals is contained in Article 89. The conditions for transfer are also found in Article 89, along with Article 93.7. The enforcement of sentencing is found in Article 103.

Council,[62] and even then the enforcement mechanism relies on the action of nation-states. This issue of enforcement is crucial to an analytical understanding of the ICC, and in subsequent chapters this narrative will continue this issue. At this point it is important to note that the enforcement mechanism of the ICC, as with most IGOs, does appear to rely solely on member states. The question that must be addressed is whether this reliance will prevent the formation of a strong and effective International Criminal Court?

Obstacles to Effectiveness

There are two major obstacles to the establishment of an effective Court: 1) lack of US support; 2) the challenge that the Court poses to the concept of state sovereignty and non-intervention.[63] The lack of US support has been an underlying theme throughout this chapter. As was previously discussed, US opposition to the Rome Statute rests primarily on the fear that the ICC will unfairly prosecute US service members or citizens. In the eyes of the United States, the ICC is an institution with the capability to initiate prosecution against American service members or citizens simply because of political motivations. For instance, if a member state did not agree with US foreign policy or its subsequent actions, the US believes they could initiate an investigation of American activities not in the name of international justice, but in the name of political gain.[64]

The result of this apprehension is that the US refused to approve the Rome Statute at the conclusion of the Conference and despite President Clinton's signing of the Statute, the Bush administration has "unsigned" the Statute, threatened to withhold funds to those states that do not provide American immunity from the Court, and even passed legislation that allows for the invasion of the Netherlands to free any American held by the ICC.[65] The question that arises from this

---

62 Rome Statute of the ICC, Article 87.7.

63 These are certainly not the only obstacles. One could cite such things as a lack of enforcement, failure to adhere more strictly to established international law, the conflict the Court's structure poses between individual liberty and a continental model of justice, among others. Numerous authors have discussed these obstacles. A short list of some discussions of these obstacles follows. Jelena Pejic, "The Tribunal and the ICC: Do Precedents Matter?" *Albany Law Review* 60 (1997): 841-860; Arbour and Bergsmo, "Despite Shortcomings"; Blakesley, "Obstacles to War Crimes Tribunal"; Ball, *Prosecuting War Crimes*; and the Association of the American Law Schools Panel on the International Criminal Court, *American Criminal Law Review* 36 (1999): 223.

64 Thomas Omestad, "The Brief for a World Court," *US News and World Report,* 6 October 1997; and Scheffer, "US Policy," and "United States and the ICC," summarize the US position on the ICC.

65 President Clinton himself warned against ratifying the treaty when he signed it. Upon signing the Statute, Clinton urged his successor not to send the treaty to Congress for ratification. Clinton said, "I will not, and do not recommend that my successor, submit the

situation is whether the ICC can be an effective tool of global justice without US support?

In addition to US opposition, some scholars and policy-makers perceive the ICC as a mechanism intended to undermine state sovereignty—not simply US sovereignty, but all nation-states' sovereignty. Arguably, state sovereignty has been a guiding principle in world politics since approximately 1648.[66] As a result, nation-states, as a collectivity, have defended their right to sovereignty and all that accompanies this concept. With the approval of the Rome Statute, some states feel that the Court's mandate violates their sovereign powers. The Court's ability to pursue individuals within a state's territorial boundaries and assert legal jurisdiction over internal crimes is often cited as a violation of state sovereignty. In short, the ICC does have the ability to override the primary purpose of state sovereignty, non-intervention.[67]

Will the ICC be able to overcome the aforementioned obstacles? That remains to be seen. Even if these obstacles are overcome, there may be other obstacles that will prevent the effective implementation of the Statute. Clearly, there are still a plethora of problems awaiting advocates of a permanent International Criminal Court. However, none of this should undermine the tremendous progress that has been made in upholding principles of international justice. As this narrative will depict, the ICC is part of an evolutionary process of norms and its historical significance should not be underestimated.

Conclusion

This chapter has introduced readers to the Rome Statute of the International Criminal Court. As readers can now see, this treaty is extremely detailed and complex. It contains one hundred and twenty-eight Articles that cover topics as widely divergent as jurisdiction, to rights' of the accused, to financing the Court.

---

treaty to the Senate for advice and consent until our jurisdictional fundamental concerns are satisfied." Betsy Pisik, "Clinton Calls for Global Court; Conservatives Fear Jeopardizing GIs," *The Washington Times,* January 1, 2001, A1. As stated above, President Bush took this advice to heart and subsequently "unsigned" the Statute in spring of 2001.

66 Many international relations scholars feel that 1648 and the Peace of Westphalia signifies the moment in which the concept of state sovereignty became the dominating ontology for understanding world politics. Even if one wants to squabble with the moment of 1648, it is clear that state sovereignty has been a dominant constitutive principle since the inception of international relations as a field in the early twentieth century.

67 The final Rome Statute took the issue of state sovereignty into consideration and backed off the ideas of inherent and universal jurisdiction in order to placate fears of a loss of state sovereignty. But as Blakesley, "Obstacles to War Crimes Tribunal," 282-283, points out, despite complementarity the fear still exists and this fear has caused some states to either not sign the Statute or even if they did sign it, vow not to ratify it.

Frankly, the ICC Statute is too grand in stature to be accurately described in one chapter. Therefore, this chapter was established to serve as an introduction to the Statute and some of its more important components.

What this chapter did accomplish is an elementary analysis of some of the more important issues of the ICC including: jurisdiction, trigger mechanisms, complementarity, the role of the UN Security Council, and possible obstacles to ratification. The next six chapters will map alternative ways to understand the formation of the ICC, as opposed to simply describing the institution. By employing three different analytical perspectives, readers should ascertain a clearer understanding of the implications and consequences of the formation of the ICC on world politics.

Chapter 4

Mainstream Cooperation Theory

> Cooperation is elusive enough, and its sources are sufficiently multifaceted and intertwined, that it constitutes a difficult subject to study. It is particularly hard, perhaps impossible, to investigate with scientific rigor. No sensible person would choose it as a topic of investigation on the grounds that its puzzles could readily be "solved." I study it, despite the lack of rich multi-case data suitable for the testing of hypotheses and despite the relative paucity of relevant theory, because of its normative significance.
>
> Robert Keohane[1]

Introduction

The formation of the International Criminal Court is clearly the result of international cooperation. From the inception of the Preparatory Committee, through Rome, and now to the current initiation of ICC work, there are numerous examples of international cooperation among nation-states. One of the goals of this text is to try and understand this cooperative formation process by engaging several different analytical perspectives. The question that I must first address is which analytical perspectives to engage?

The field of international relations is so ripe with analytical and theoretical perspectives that one is often left baffled by which perspective is most relevant to the project at hand. However, in this case I believe that the choice is quite clear. If we are going to analyze the formation of an international institution like the ICC, then we must first engage the mainstream theory on regime formation and cooperation—neoliberal institutionalism.

In general, international relations scholars would consider neoliberal institutionalism to be the mainstream theory concerning cooperation and international organizations.[2] International relations scholars have employed this theory to not only analyze existing cooperation, but also to advocate cooperation among states. It was not until the 1980s that the contemporary theory of neoliberal institutionalism finally began to take shape. Through the work of scholars like

---

1 Keohane, *After Hegemony,* 10.

2 Hasenclever, Mayer and Rittberger, *Theories of International Regimes,* 23, state that neoliberalism "has come to represent the mainstream approach to analyzing international regimes, and the other two schools...regularly make reference to its arguments in order to give their own positions a clear profile."

Robert Keohane, Robert Axelrod, Arthur Stein, and others, this theory of international relations has become a primary counter-theory to Kenneth Waltz's neo-realism.[3] With the end of the Cold War and the subsequent understanding that cooperation amongst international actors is possible, it appears as if neoliberal institutionalism is finding a new core of followers. The formation of institutions like the ICC appears to provide neoliberal scholars with a new set of relevant cases. As a result of these factors, it appears that neoliberalism is in some ways experiencing a renaissance in the post-Cold War era.

Neoliberal institutionalism main goal is to understand cooperation amongst international actors, despite the existence of an anarchical system.[4] In order to achieve this goal, neoliberalism analyzes the international system through the use of six guiding principles:

1. The global system is anarchical in its structure.
2. States are the primary actors in international relations, although international non-state institutions do play a significant role.
3. States are rational-unitary actors, but they also share complementary interests with other states.
4. In so far as these complementary interests exist, cooperation among states is possible and this cooperation often occurs under the auspices of international organizations in order to diminish cheating, create iterativeness, and reduce costs of transactions.
5. Hegemony is not a necessary factor for the maintenance of cooperation and the regimes that are formed from this cooperation.
6. In pursuing their interests, states seek absolute, not relative gains. Therefore, states will evaluate intentions as much as capabilities.[5]

---

3 Kenneth Waltz, *Theory of International Politics* (New York: McGraw-Hill, 1979), in many ways re-invents the realist tradition and propels it back to its position as the dominant paradigm in international relations theory. Neoliberalism attacks much of what Waltz is arguing, but as will become apparent, neoliberals also accept many of the basic realist principles. Some of these principles include: acceptance that the international system is anarchical and that states are the primary actors of global politics, but not the only actors. This makes the theory more palatable to realists who are attempting to understand the rise in cooperation that occurs during the late 1970s and 1980s. Keohane, *After Hegemony,* and Baldwin, *Neorealism, Neoliberalism*, provide us with a list of neoliberalism's primary principles. Ole Waever, "The Rise and Fall of the Inter-paradigm Debate," in *International Theory: Positivism and Beyond,* ed. Steve Smith, Ken Booth and Marysia Zalewski (Cambridge: Cambridge University Press, 1997), 163-164, discusses the convergence of these two perspectives, which he calls the neo-neo synthesis.

4 Keohane, *After Hegemony,* 6, and Axelrod and Keohane, "Achieving Cooperation," clearly establish the goal of neoliberal institutionalists as understanding cooperation despite the presence of an anarchical system.

5 This list has been compiled from numerous core works of neoliberal institutionalist theory. These works include: Keohane, *After Hegemony*; Axelrod and Keohane, "Achieving Cooperation;" and Keohane, Institutional Theory, Realist Challenge."

Cooperation, as Keohane warns his readers, is difficult to investigate scientifically.[6] This is due to the fact that cooperation among nation-states is an elusive concept that scholars often understand through a variety of central variables.[7] This makes a positivistic analysis of cooperation and the study of the ICC nearly impossible. Nevertheless, the fact that cooperation does occur within world politics makes a study of institution formation important, and if one is to engage this subject, one should first engage it through the lens of the mainstream perspective. Therefore, this chapter's primary focus will be on the history and evolution of neoliberal institutionalism and the resulting theory.

In the next chapter, I will employ neoliberal institutionalism to understand the formation of the Rome Statute and the ICC. As a result of its basic principles, this analysis will primarily center on the actions of nations-states, although it will not ignore the role of non-state actors. This analysis will also assess the role of absolute versus relative gains in the states decision to sign and/or ratify the Rome Statute. Ultimately, this form of analysis will demonstrate that the emergence of cooperation did occur despite the anarchical construct of the international system. But let us begin our assessment of cooperation theory with a short history of this perspective and its current evolutionary form.

Theoretical History

It is necessary to begin this historical analysis with the first debate in international relations theory and a brief discussion of utopian or idealist thought. I will then move on to discuss the functionalist perspective and the complex interdependence movement. Ultimately, this analysis will reach the current state of liberal theory—neoliberal institutionalism and its relationship to the neorealist school of thought.

Inter-war Idealism

Utopianism or Idealism was part of the "first debate" in international relations theory.[8] This theory was a direct result of World War I and its primary goal was to

---

6 Keohane, *After Hegemony,* 10.

7 As Hasenclever, Mayer and Rittberger, *Theories of International Regimes,* 6, show us, at a minimum international cooperation can result from any of the following variables: power, interest, or knowledge.

8 Some scholars have also referred to utopianism or idealism as liberalism or pluralism. It is important to note that no matter the term associated with this line of thinking, the underlying philosophical tenets are the same. During the inter-war period, idealist scholars were engaged in a theoretical debate with proponents of realist thinking. This is usually referred to as the first debate in international relations theory. For a more detailed discussion of this debate, see Steve Smith, "Self-Images of a Discipline: A Genealogy of

prevent such a horrific event from occurring again.[9] Numerous scholars have attempted to calculate how to prevent war and the tensions that lead to war. In general, the idealist camp believes that: 1) war is an irrational act; 2) that it is usually the result of leadership and not mass public opinion; 3) that misunderstandings between leaders are the primary cause of war; and 4) that the implementation of mediating structures (international organizations) can assist in rectifying these misunderstandings.[10]

Idealists generally believe that progress can occur and that the war-ravaged system of the early twentieth century can be altered into a more peaceful and stable system. As one scholar stated: "The distinctive characteristic of these writers [idealists] was their belief in progress: the belief, in particular, that the system of international relations that had given rise to the First World War was capable of being transformed into a fundamentally more peaceful and just world order."[11]

In order to achieve such an idealistic goal, these scholars advocated both the growth of international organizations and the election of a more enlightened leadership. If the international community is to prevent war, then international actors must take action both at the international and domestic level. In attempting to prevent war, the first step is to establish a cooperative system in which discussion and mediation amongst nation-states take place within established organizational structures. These organizational structures serve as institutions within which state's conflicting views can be resolved peacefully. This line of thinking perceives the major cause of war as a lack of international organization. As Leonard Woolf explained, if we are to avoid war then:

> There must be international law and a regular method of making it; there must be organs of international government and organs for interpreting the law and settling disputes; there must be the machinery and procedure for common international actions and from making changes to meet changed conditions; there must be international control of

---

International Relations Theory," in *International Relations Theory Today,* ed. Ken Booth, Steve Smith (University Park, PA: The Pennsylvania University Press, 1995), 1-37.

9 The primary objective of preventing war is best exemplified in the work of Alfred Zimmern, "Organize the Peace World," *Political Quarterly* 5 (1934): 156. In this article, Zimmern states, "the overriding objective of policy in the present generation…is the prevention of war."

10 This list is developed from the writings of numerous idealist scholars. This list includes: Norman Angell, *The Great Illusion: A Study of the Relations of Military Power to National Advantage* (London: William Heinemann, 1912); James Shotwell, "Alternatives for War," *Foreign Affairs* 6 (1928): 459-467; Zimmern, "Organize the Peace World"; Leonard Woolf, "DeProfundis," *Political Quarterly* 10 (1939): 463-476; and Alfred Zimmern, *The League of Nations and the Rule of Law: 1918-1935* (London: MacMillan, 1945). Hollis and Smith, *Explaining and Understanding International Relations,* 17-20 also succinctly summarizes the foundational components of idealism.

11 Hedley Bull, 2nd ed., *The Anarchical Society: A Study in World Politics* (New York: Columbia University Press, 1995), 34.

national power and provision for common action in the face of a resort to war or the threat of war by any nation.[12]

In short, the formation of international organizations could very well serve as the mechanism that prevents war. A major part of their role is the fact that these international organs of law and dispute settlement mechanisms assist in the prevention of misunderstandings between state leaders.[13] In other words, these institutions will provide state leaders with a forum in which they could air their differences and possibly achieve a peaceful resolution. This is important because according to inter-war idealism, one of the primary causes of war is misunderstanding amongst leadership.

Along with the formation of these international organizations, idealist scholars also assert the need for better domestic leadership. Idealism perceives individuals as rational entities, but war as an irrational act. As a result, an educated and enlightened individual will never pursue war as a national policy. Therefore, one of the primary ways to prevent war is to instill "proper" leadership. With an enlightened leadership at the helm, the futility of war becomes self-evident and the initiation of war as a method of achieving ones' foreign policy is viewed as irrational.[14]

With the inception of idealism as a theory of international relations, the foundations for neoliberal institutionalism were established. Idealism noted the anarchical nature of the international system, the need for and the ability to achieve cooperation among states, and the positive role for international organizations. All of these attributes found their way into neoliberal thought, while others, like the importance of leadership, were abandoned along the way. However, the evolutionary history of liberal thought has many more twists and turns, so let me now turn the readers' attention to the functionalist movement of the subsequent decades.

Functionalism

The second stage in this evolutionary process is the genesis of functionalist thought in the 1940s and 1950s. The primary author of functionalist thought is David Mitrany.[15] Mitrany perceives the post-World War II world as one of growing

---

12 Woolf, "DeProfundis," 474-475.

13 Shotwell, "Alternatives for War" and Woolf, "DeProfundis," clearly advocate the use of international organizations as a mediating mechanisms.

14 Zimmern, "Organize the Peace World," advances the premise of needing an educated leadership in order to prevent war.

15 David A. Mitrany, *A Working Peace System: An Argument for the Functional Development of International Organization* (London: Royal Institute of International Affairs, 1943), is cited as the seminal work on functionalist theory. Paul Taylor, "Functionalism: The Approach of David Mitrany," in *Framework for International*

complexity. According to Mitrany, the number of technical issues that exists in the world is far too many for states, acting as autonomous entities, to resolve. Mitrany believes that this growth in technical issues necessitates a cooperative environment in which "experts" work collaboratively to solve these issues. This collaborative approach assists in serving human needs, not just state needs. In this sense, one can view functionalism as an attempt to overcome the cultural, ideological and nationalistic differences that exist between nation-states.[16]

This is clear when we recognize that Mitrany emphasizes that the solutions to the global community's problems lay not only in collaborative efforts, but more specifically, in collaborative efforts by technocratic experts, not politicians. The emphasis on experts instead of politicians gives functionalism its cross-national underpinnings. According to Mitrany, the international community should no longer look to the state and the formal politicians for solutions to the world's problems. Instead, we need to look to the functional experts within these issue-areas, no matter their national or ideological background.

As stated above, Mitrany believes that the problems of this world are becoming increasingly complex and technical in nature. A majority of these technical issues are, as he defined them, apolitical. These problems involve economic, social, and scientific issues that affect a multiplicity of states. Due to the functional need for a solution to these problems, Mitrany asserts that cooperation between states and their respective technical experts must occur, regardless of ideological or nationalistic differences. Thus, the functionalists believe that these interests are exogenously given and that the primary obstacle to obtaining these interests is the state and its political infrastructure.[17] Mitrany acknowledges that cultural, ideological, and nationalistic differences exist between the world's states. Such differences hinder any opportunity at solving the global community's problems cooperatively. The only way to overcome this obstacle is the formation of new institutions that transcends national institutional structures.[18]

When considering whether to cooperate or not, it is important to note that Mitrany perceives the international system as fundamentally relying on something other then a zero-sum game. Functionalism sees the system as either a variable-

---

Cooperation, ed. A.J.R. Groom and Paul Taylor (London: Pintner Publishers, 1990), 125-138, has a nice summary of Mitrany's theory.

16 Lucien M. Ashworth, *Creating International Studies: Angell, Mitrany and the Liberal Tradition* (Brookfield, VT: Ashgate Publishing Company, 1999), 95-99, explains this particular component of functionalism at length.

17 Jennifer Sterling-Folker, "Competing Paradigms or Birds of a Feather? Constructivism and Neoliberal Institutionalism Compared," *International Studies Quarterly* 44 (2000): 100-101, describes this in greater detail.

18 Mitrany, *Working Peace System,* 29.

sum or positive-sum game.[19] The importance of such an assertion for functionalists is that it now becomes possible to implement a system that benefits the entire global community. However, if such a cooperative system is to exist, the international community must build on the collaborative interests that are served by both experts and functionalist organizations. This is because functionalism does not believe that states are oriented towards a more cooperative environment. Therefore, it will be the role of the technical experts and the functional organizations that they create to overcome the atomized orientation of the state. In other words, functional organizations will show the system's primary actor, nation-states, that cooperation is a beneficial action for all.

Mitrany believes that as greater amounts of successful cooperation take hold the ability to trust other actors (including states) in future collaborative projects will intensify. This process, termed *ramification,* will lead to cooperation in numerous issue areas and gradually build a web of integration that will alleviate the need for conflict or war.[20] The establishment of functional organizations will provide for a more stable and cooperative international system thus, the relative benefits of cooperation lead to a new form of multilateralism among global actors, in particular nation-states, and eventually to the formation of more and more regimes and international organizations.[21] For functionalism, this is the road to a peaceful world system.

Neofunctionalism

In the late 1950s and 1960s, Ernst Haas began building on Mitrany's work. The result was an analytical perspective that international relations scholars now call neofunctionalism. Neofunctionalism bases much of its logic on functionalism, but refuses to acknowledge the difference between political and non-political issues. The technical tasks that Mitrany and functionalism examine are, according to Haas and his neofunctionalist theory, political. The reason for this rationale is that without the acceptance of the issue by the political elite, neofunctionalism believes

---

[19] Paul R. Viotti and Mark V. Kauppi, 3rd ed. *International Relations Theory: Realism, Pluralism, Globalism and Beyond* (Needham Heights, MA: Allyn and Bacon, 1999), 212-213, summarize this line of reasoning.

[20] Functionalist theory was spurred on by the successful creation of the European Coal and Steel Community in 1952 and the European Economic Community in 1956. Both of these entities provide empirical confirmation of the positive benefits of integration and simply add credence to Mitrany's functionalist theories.

[21] The most important benefit that functionalism grants to participating states is the sharing of costs. With the establishment of functionalism, the cost of rectifying transnational problems is no longer a unilateral burden. As a result, if actors share the costs, they can also share the benefits. Thus, functionalists see the international system as predicated on a positive-sum game.

that no substantive cooperation will occur.[22] To Haas, integration is a process in which *political actors* form a new understanding of preference in order to achieve their interests.[23] Therefore, if the political elites simply ignore Mitrany's experts, then no cooperation will occur and the integration process simply stalls. According to Haas, Mitrany's experts need the approval of the political elites.

For Mitrany and the functionalist tradition, cooperation begins with experts due to the fact that states cannot overcome the cultural, ideological, and nationalistic differences that exist between them. Haas accepts this fact but goes beyond its simplistic solution. Instead of accepting that cooperation between states will eventually occur because of ramification, Haas argues that in order for cooperation to occur, it must begin and end with politicians and statesmen. Relying on the cooperative efforts of functional experts may not be enough to initiate cooperation among the real actors in the international system, states. If integration is to occur, the political elites must perceive this integration to be beneficial to their self-interest. If they do not then no cooperation at the state level will occur.[24]

In an attempt to show how cross-border cooperation can occur, Haas and neofunctionalist theory place a large emphasis on regional integration.[25] Haas believes that political elites who share a regional setting are more likely to pursue integration than with those outside of their regional setting. Thus, Western European leaders are more likely to undertake collaborative, cross-border efforts to rectify problems amongst themselves then with leaders from outside Western Europe.[26] Haas argues that shared interests among states, which neofunctionalism also take as exogenously given, appear to be more prevalent within regional boundaries then outside of them. If political elites within a particular region can agree on institutional preference formation to achieve their interests, then the ramification process can continue.

---

[22] James E. Dougherty and Robert L. Pfaltzgraff, Jr. 4th ed., *Contending Theories of International Relations: A Comprehensive Survey* (New York: Addison-Wesley Educational Publishers, 1997), 423.

[23] Ernst B. Haas, *The Uniting of Europe: Political, Social and Economic Forces, 1950-1957* (London: Stevens, 1958), 16.

[24] Ernst B. Haas, *Beyond the Nation-State: Functionalism and International Organization* (Stanford, CA: Stanford University Press, 1964), 94-98.

[25] Ernst B. Haas, "Turbulent Fields and the Theory of Regional Integration," *International Organization* 30 (1975): 173-212, describes the theory of regional integration at length.

[26] Leonard Woolf, *The War for Peace* (New York: Garland Publishing, 1972), is the foundation for this idea of regionalism. In this work, Woolf argued that regionalism would exist, but that its roots would be cultural and historical affinities. Thus, the only strong regional constellation Woolf acknowledged was Western Europe. Despite this emphasis on regional federations, Woolf does see some sort of world government as necessary, but the formation of regional federations may prove useful in obtaining this ultimate goal.

Haas calls this ramification process *spillover,* but its meaning is the same.[27] Spillover refers to the process by which one collaborative effort leads to greater collaboration due to the benefits that actors derive from cooperation. As in functionalism, Haas believes that the process of cooperation will snowball as more successful efforts to achieve interests occur. The major difference between these two theoretical positions is the importance that Haas places on political elites and the need to involve them in the integration process. Without their acceptance, Mitrany's functional experts can simply be ignored. In other words, Haas does not accept Mitrany's notion that "integration" is somehow de-politicized. Neofunctionalism is predicated on the ability of political elites to understand that their self-interest is best served through cooperation with other political elites.

Complex Interdependence

The final theoretical predecessor to neoliberal institutionalism, complex interdependence, is part of the 1970s challenge to realist thought. The main authors of this theory are Robert Keohane and Joseph Nye, who in their classic 1977 text lay out the foundation for this novel theory.[28] Building on the previous liberal/functional theories, Keohane and Nye describe three main characteristics of complex interdependence: 1) multiple channels; 2) an absence of hierarchy among issues; and 3) due to the presence of complex interdependence, the primacy of military force is no longer a given.[29]

If we begin with the first proposition, complex interdependence asserts that multiple channels of contact have the effect of connecting the world's different societies. According to this perspective, a web of interaction builds among the community of international actors, thus creating an atmosphere of interdependence. This interdependence occurs through interstate, transgovernmental, and transnational relations, which bind the global community's governmental and nongovernmental entities together.[30] Thus, the connections between global actors need not be inter-governmental. The multiplicity of channels that exist will ostensibly perpetuate greater cooperation among international actors and initiate a process in which these actors can now functionally cope with the impending transnational problems. Keohane and Nye cite major international airports as a

---

[27] E. Haas, *Beyond the Nation-State,* 48.

[28] This theory has its roots in Robert Keohane and Joseph Nye Jr., ed., *Transnational Relations and World Politics,* (Princeton, NJ: Princeton University Press, 1971), but the bulk of this discussion is derived from Robert Keohane and Joseph Nye Jr., *Power and Interdependence: World Politics in Transition,* (Boston: Little Brown, 1977).

[29] Keohane and Nye, *Power and Interdependence,* 24-29.

[30] Keohane and Nye, *Power and Interdependence,* 25, define the type of channels that exist as follows: "*Interstate* relations are the normal channels assumed by realists. *Transgovernmental* applies when we relax the realist assumption that states act coherently as units; *transnational* applies when we relax the assumption that states are the only units."

way to "confirm the existence of multiple channels of contact among advanced industrial countries."[31]

What is important about this proposition is that Keohane and Nye assert that the number of ways in which societies interact has greatly expanded. It is no longer simply state elites meeting within the bounds of foreign offices. According to this theory, the multiple channels that tie societies together now consists of formal and informal interaction amongst both government elites and non-government elites (such as multinational corporations, international banks, etc.).[32]

Complex interdependence also asserts that the number of issues affecting the world's international actors has become much larger and more diverse. Due to this expansion of international issues, Keohane and Nye argue that the primary determinant of foreign policy is not always going to be military security issues. Other issues, such as economic, social, and domestic issues all play a role in foreign policy formulation and as a result, there is no hierarchy of issues. This proposition is radically different then the mainstream thinking of that time which stipulates that military and security issues always assume primacy over other issues.[33] Complex interdependence alters that perception and argues that military and security issues do not and should not dominate the foreign policy agenda of the world's nation-states. The result is a web of multiple, overlapping issues that all demand attention. Due to the fact that there are such a plethora of issues facing international actors, Keohane and Nye believe that the necessity of international organizations, for functional reasons, is compelling. According to their theory, only through the establishment and use of international organizations will the global community find viable management or solutions to these issues.

Finally, reverting back to the original goal of inter-war idealism, complex interdependence theorizes that with an increase in state interdependence, the likelihood of war will diminish—at least among highly industrialized states.[34] This does not mean that the use of military force is obsolete. What Keohane and Nye propose is that by tying two governments together in an interdependent relationship, the use of force between these two states is no longer the primary policy option. This is due to the cost, relatively calculated by the states, and uncertainty of war.[35] However, the inception of more and more international organizations will also alleviate the prospect of war by increasing interdependence.

---

[31] Keohane and Nye, *Power and Interdependence,* 25.

[32] Keohane and Nye, *Power and Interdependence,* 24-26.

[33] This line of thinking is prevalent in the mainstream theory of the 1970s, realist theory. For proponents of this theoretical approach, security and military issues were of the utmost importance and never took a backseat to anything.

[34] Recall that the primary goal of the inter-war period idealists was the prevention of war. Keohane and Nye, *Power and Interdependence,* reassert this goal and theorize about how the international community can achieve this goal.

[35] Keohane and Nye, *Power and Interdependence,* 27-29.

Thus, the result of this increased interdependence is, at least to some extent, the achievement of the inter-war idealist's goal—mitigating conflict.

Power also plays a role in interdependence theory and in order to understand this role, Keohane and Nye introduce two measurements of power within interdependent relationships: sensitivity and vulnerability.[36] Sensitivity refers to the degree of "responsiveness within a policy framework."[37] In other words, sensitivity refers to an actors' perceived effect of policy change within an interdependent relationship. If one country is sensitive to an alteration in the interdependent relationship, then that country is clearly at a power disadvantage.

However, sensitivity is not the only dimension of power within an interdependent relationship; one must also account for vulnerability. Vulnerability "rests on the relative availability and costliness of the alternatives that various actors face."[38] In other words, if the original relationship breaks down, the costs incurred by actors in implementing alternative policies would be a measure of vulnerability. Keohane and Nye use the following example: "Two countries, each importing 35 percent of their petroleum needs, may seem equally sensitive to price rises; but if one could shift to domestic sources at moderate costs, and the other had no such alternative, the second state would be more vulnerable than the first."[39]

Thus, in analyzing global relations within the complex interdependence paradigm, one must account for the dyadic power dimensions of sensitivity and vulnerability. According to complex interdependence theorists, by grounding one's analysis of power within this dyadic model, international relations scholars should be better able to predict bargaining advantages and, to some extent, outcomes.

Complex interdependence is the penultimate liberal precursor to neoliberal institutionalism. Through the historical evolution of this theoretical perspective, scholars have altered certain attributes of liberalism, while others have simply been discarded. However, the core of the liberal tradition remains—international relations is not simply about power and coercion, it is often about cooperation; cooperation for the purpose of achieving common interests and alleviating the cost of unilateral action. Neoliberal institutionalism maintains this core, but also strays from many of the principles of their theoretical predecessors. One can view neoliberal institutionalism as an attempt to rectify not only the problems of functionalist thinking, but also neo-realist thought. As Keohane stated in 1993:

> [I]t is crucial to remember that it [neoliberal institutionalism] borrows as much from realism as from liberalism: it cannot be encapsulated as simply a "liberal" theory

---

36 Keohane and Nye, *Power and Interdependence,* 11-19.

37 Keohane and Nye, *Power and Interdependence,* 12.

38 Keohane and Nye, *Power and Interdependence,* 13.

39 Keohane and Nye, *Power and Interdependence,* 13.

opposed at all points to realism. Indeed, it is almost as misleading to refer to it as liberal as to give it the tag of neorealism."[40]

Neoliberal Institutionalism

As stated earlier in this chapter, neoliberal institutionalism is predicated on six basic principles:[41]

1. States are the primary units of analysis;
2. states are rational-unitary actors;
3. these states exist within an anarchical system;
4. complementary interests exist among states, therefore cooperation is possible;
5. relative gains are conditional;
6. hegemony is not a necessary factor for cooperation.

This preliminary list of neoliberal attributes clearly shows the debt Keohane owes not only to previous liberal thinkers, but also to neorealism.[42] Neoliberalism does deal with the act of cooperation among actors and the interest-based rationale for this type of action; but it also deals with concepts like anarchy, self-interest, and nation-states. These latter concepts are directly attributable to realist/neorealist thinking and its fundamental principles.[43] Nevertheless, one should not assume that neoliberalism is simply a derivative of Waltz and neorealism. There are fundamental differences between these two schools of thought.

The primary difference between these two schools of thought being that realist thought is a power-based theory, while neoliberalism is interest-based.[44] In other words, understanding regime formation from a realist perspective would attribute the process to coercion and hegemonic power. Neoliberal institutionalism, which believes that institution building, although difficult, is not as difficult as realists

---

[40] Keohane, "Institutional Theory, Realist Challenge," 272.

[41] International relations scholars refer to neoliberal institutionalism by several different titles. These include: neoliberal, institutionalism, contractualism, functionalism, and pluralism. For the purpose of this text, I will refer to this theory as either "neoliberal institutionalism," "institutionalism," or "neoliberalism."

[42] James K. Oliver, "The Balance of Power Heritage of Interdependence and Traditionalism," *International Studies Quarterly* 26 (1982), 384, makes the argument that Keohane and Nye's theory of complex interdependence was much closer to classical realism. The convergence of NLI with realism only proves Oliver's point.

[43] Keohane, "Institutional Theory, Realist Challenge," 271, admits this himself. He states that institutionalist thought is neorealist in the fact that it "assumes states are the principle actors in world politics and that they behave on the basis of their conceptions of their own self-interests."

[44] Hasenclever, Mayer, and Rittberger, *Theories of International Regimes,* 26-27, explain the differences between power-based and interest-based theories at length.

assert, contends that regimes will form primarily because of mutual interests among states. Hegemonic power can be helpful in the formation process, but it is not the dominant causal factor. As a result, if the hegemon's power declines, the cooperative arrangement or regime that the international community created will persist. This is due to the fact that the international community, or at least those participating in the regime, have invested a large amount in the formation process of the regime and do not want to lose their investment. Therefore, when analyzing the formation of the Rome Statute from an institutionalist perspective, the primary reason for its formation must be complementary interests. A hegemon may help the process, but the presence of such an entity is not needed either for formation or maintenance. Before this text proceeds to an analysis of the ICC from a neoliberal institutionalist perspective, it is important to first explore the major attributes of neoliberalism in order to adequately understand this analytical perspective.

State-Centered

Breaking from most of his liberal predecessors, Keohane asserts a much more state-centered theory than any of the previous liberal thinkers (including himself and Joseph Nye). The inter-war idealist, functionalists, and complex interdependence literature all emphasized alternate international actors. Many of Keohane's liberal ancestors viewed the state as the primary obstacle to cooperation and peace and yet, neoliberal thinking emphasizes the primacy of the state.[45] Obviously international institutions are important to the neoliberal rationale, but Keohane would remind us that the construct of these institutions is states and these states are pursuing their self-interest.

Keohane does note that if we were to relax this premise, cooperation could still occur. In other words, if states were not the major entities in the world, Keohane still believes that cooperation would occur between transnational entities and regimes would still form.[46] Scholars often construe this addendum to Keohane's theory as an invitation for neoliberals to analyze non-state actors. However, at no

---

45 This applies to almost the entire liberal tradition. Inter-war idealists saw the state as one of the primary causes of war, functionalists saw the need to use technical elites to initiate cooperation, and complex interdependence took into account numerous other actors besides the state. Only neo-functionalism approximates the primacy of the state found in neoliberal institutionalist writings. However, viewing the state as an obstacle to cooperation does not preclude its status as the primary unit of analysis. In fact, one could argue that Keohane believes that such an understanding of the state necessitates this linkage.

46 Keohane, *After Hegemony,* 111 note 1, states that: "This chapter does not discuss the implications of relaxing the assumption that the major entities in world politics are governments, but there is no apparent reason to believe that such a shift in premises would make the creation or maintenance of international regimes less likely. Transnational organizations can cooperate in pursuit of shared interests and must take international institutions into account..."

time within his writings does Keohane relinquish the premise that states are the primary actors in world politics. He acknowledges the importance of transnational actors, but never considers them the central unit of analysis. Therefore, rather than perceiving this statement as an invitation for neoliberal scholars to study non-state actors, scholars should view it as a reassertion that, at this point in time, states are still the major unit of analysis for international relations and neoliberalism.[47] His assertion that relaxing the state-centric paradigm does not hinder cooperation is simply a hypothetical situation that allows the reader to see that cooperation, under anarchy, is not contingent on states being the key actors. To reiterate though, this does not mean that Keohane views transnational actors as the primary units of analysis. As he reasserts in 1995, "institutionalist theory assumes that states are the principle actors in world politics."[48]

Rational-Unitary Actors

The second principle of neoliberal institutionalism is that states are rational-unitary actors that seek to fulfill their self-interests. Neoliberalism expects states to behave as rational egoists. Their motivation for action is the pursuit of their own self-interest. This assumption is indistinguishable from the core premises of realist theory, except that the outcome of this rational egoism is not a Hobbesian state of nature in which everyone is at war with everyone.[49] Instead, this premise leads institutionalists to believe that cooperation and institution building is the rational behavior of nation-states seeking to fulfill their self-interest.[50]

An addendum to this premise is that when states pursue their self-interest, this does not preclude a mutuality of interests. In many instances, states do share common interests. This is a key component of neoliberal institutionalism because without a mutuality of interests, cooperation is virtually impossible.[51] However, it

---

[47] This footnote was written in Keohane, *After Hegemony*, 111, but even in his later work, such as "Institutional Theory, Realist Challenge," Keohane continues to work within a state-centric paradigm. It appears, therefore, that Keohane still feels that states are the primary actors in world politics.

[48] Keohane, "Institutional Theory, Realist Challenge," 271.

[49] Thomas Hobbes, *Leviathan* (1651; reprint, London: Penguin Books, 1985), 186.

[50] Keohane, "Institutional Theory, Realist Challenge," 273-274. The formation of this type of analysis is derived from the functionalist school of thought and the work of David Mitrany, *Working Peace System.* It was the functionalists that first placed a large emphasis on the rationality of states and the need to view cooperation as part of a rational thought process by these actors. One could assert that this outcome is also akin to Hobbesian philosophy, because self-interested actors in the state of nature also cooperated to create the social contract. However, realists tend to conveniently overlook this aspect of Hobbesian thought.

[51] Keohane, *After Hegemony,* 6, and Robert Keohane, "Neoliberal Institutionalism: A Perspective on World Politics," in *International Institutions and State Power: Essays in*

is equally important to note that a mutuality of interests between states does not automatically result in cooperative arrangements. Harmony is different then cooperation. Therefore, according to neoliberal institutionalism, despite the mutuality of interests, there are times when cooperation fails.[52] I will return to this point when discussing why cooperation, within an anarchical system, is possible.

Anarchy

The next premise of neoliberal institutionalism is that states exist in an anarchical system. Keohane and Axelrod define anarchy as "a lack of common government in world politics, not… a denial that an international society…exists."[53] Neoliberal institutionalists perceive this state of anarchy to be constant, but this does not mean that structured interaction does not exist. Advocates of this theory believe that anarchy, or a lack of government, is an accepted attribute of world politics. Unlike realist thought, however, neoliberals do not believe that such a characteristic severely hampers or prevents cooperation from occurring. Common interests do exist between states and as a result, cooperation occurs. Nevertheless, this cooperation exists within an anarchical system, and neoliberal institutionalism acknowledges the fact that the structure of the system has a large impact on states' actions. As a result, neoliberalism asserts a strong, yet not exclusionary, systemic approach to international relations.[54] The anarchical system impacts state actions, but unlike the (neo)realist logic that theorizes that this type of system leads to a war of all against all, neoliberals see cooperation occurring within the anarchical system. A return to the previous discussion of complementary interests explains why.

Common Interests

Taking a cue from their functionalist ancestors, neoliberals assert that common interests do exist among states. They cite these complementary interests as necessary conditions for cooperation, but not sufficient in and of themselves for cooperation. So how and why does cooperation occur within an anarchical system?

International Relations, ed. Robert Keohane (Boulder, CO: Westview Press, 1989), 2, discuss the fact that common interests do exist among states. Scholars such as Keohane often cite the use of game theory, especially Prisoner's Dilemma, as verification that mutual interests do exist.

52 Keohane, *After Hegemony,* 6; and Hasenclever, Mayer and Rittberger, *Theories of International Regimes,* 30.

53 Axelrod and Keohane, "Achieving Cooperation," 226.

54 Keohane, *After Hegemony,* 25-26, discusses the importance of starting with a systemic level analysis. However, Keohane concludes this section by stating that a systemic analysis is not comprehensive. Keohane still sees the need for an analysis of domestic politics, albeit in a secondary role.

Keohane and other institutionalists take a mutuality of interests among states as a given, but this still does not result in automatic cooperation among these actors. The primary reason is that cooperation is not synonymous with harmony. If states resided in a system of absolute common interest (harmony), then cooperation would not be necessary. The existence of a harmony of interests among states would simply allow these states to pursue their self-interest with the knowledge that all other actors in the system hold complementary interests. As Keohane states, "Harmony refers to a situation in which actors' policies…automatically facilitate the attainment of others' goals."[55] The result is an apolitical system in which regimes and intergovernmental organizations are unnecessary because cooperation is unnecessary.[56]

Nevertheless, the international system is not a harmonious one. Instead, it is fraught with conflict, and the inception of cooperation is simply a reaction to that conflict.[57] In other words, if the system were void of any discord, then cooperation becomes unnecessary. But due to the fact that the system is not a harmonious one, cooperation becomes a mechanism by which states achieve their common goals regardless of the anarchy that exists around them. According to Keohane: "intergovernmental cooperation takes place when the policies actually followed by one government are regarded by its partners as facilitating realization of their own objectives, as the result of a process of policy coordination."[58]

This distinction between harmony and cooperation helps us to define cooperation, but it does not tell us why states cooperate. Keohane shows us that harmony is not a central part of the world system and that cooperation is a possible solution to the discord that exists. If states choose to cooperate, one could view this action as an attempt to initiate an environment in which states can fulfill their mutual interests. But what are the reasons why states cooperate?

In order to address this question it is necessary to combine all that we now understand about neoliberal institutionalism and apply it to the anarchic world. According to neoliberal institutionalists, cooperation occurs because states act primarily as rational egoists who share mutual interests. The most efficient way to achieve utility maximization is through the formation of a regime or international institution.[59] Regimes act as facilitators of cooperation by providing states with information, reducing uncertainty among states, reducing transaction costs and establishing expectations concerning actors' behavior.[60] In other words, regimes make cooperation a more palatable and efficient option. By lowering costs and

---

55 Keohane, *After Hegemony,* 51-52.

56 Keohane, *After Hegemony,* 51-55, and Axelrod and Keohane, "Achieving Cooperation," 226, contain an in depth discussion of harmony versus cooperation.

57 Keohane, *After Hegemony,* 54.

58 Keohane, *After Hegemony,* 51-52.

59 It is clear from Keohane's discussion of regimes, *After Hegemony,* 57-63, that he views international institutions as regimes.

60 Keohane, *After Hegemony,* 85-97.

providing information, regimes act to facilitate cooperation by limiting uncertainty and showing states the mutual benefits of cooperation. Therefore, despite the self-interested egoism of states, cooperation is possible because the mutuality of interests is, or can become, common knowledge among states.

According to Keohane and neoliberal institutionalists, the actualization of these interests occurs through the formation of regimes. States form regimes as a method of gaining their exogenously given goals. In other words, states believe that the benefits derived from cooperation far outweigh those of unilateral action. Therefore, states acting in a rational manner naturally form regimes to increase their personal gains. One can view this formation process as part of a strategic game, undertaken by states, in which they wish to further their interests through cooperation. Through institution building, states are able to gain their exogenously given interests. It is important to emphasize that state's interests are *a priori* to regime formation; regimes do not define state's interest. Therefore, cooperation is simply a method by which a state obtains their previously defined, exogenously given interests.

It is now apparent that the premise of exogenously given interests is crucial to an understanding of neoliberal institutionalism. This premise is deeply rooted in the realist aspect of this theory and assumes that states maintain a set of *a priori* interests.[61] As a result, neoliberal institutionalism does not consider state's interests as dynamic however, institutional preference is. According to Keohane:

> I neither explore how economic conditions affect patterns of interests, nor do I investigate the effects of ideas and ideals on state behavior. The theory that I [Keohane] develop takes the existence of mutual interests as given and examines the conditions under which they will lead to cooperation.[62]

As the global environment changes, so too will the institutional preference for achieving states' *a priori* interests. Thus, it is at the point where these exogenously given interests overlap with other actors' interests thus making cooperation a possibility.[63] One concern that I have with this type of analysis is that it does not question how states construct their common interests. The result is that neoliberal institutionalism's explanatory power of global politics appears incomplete.

---

[61] Sterling-Folker, "Competing Paradigms," 100-104, traces the theoretical foundations of exogenously given interests.

[62] Keohane, *After Hegemony,* 6. Keohane also expands on this premise in his later work, Keohane, "Institutionalist Theory, Realist Challenge," 274-278.

[63] It is important to remember that the prevalence of common interests does not automatically equate into cooperation. Discord can result despite the presence of common interests among states. Keohane is describing a cooperative process, not the presence of harmony. According to neoliberal institutionalists, if harmony existed there would be no need for cooperation. Keohane, *After Hegemony,* 12-13.

Relative versus Absolute Gains

This brings us to the next premise of neoliberal institutionalism—states are not solely concerned with relative gains. If states were only concerned with relative gains this would seriously limit the prospects for cooperation. This is not to say, as many neorealists assert, that relative gains are a non-factor for neoliberalists.[64] Keohane acknowledges the importance of relative gains to nation-states, but views these gains as highly conditional.[65] Relative gains are only important when a state's intent upon receiving those gains is to use them against another state. Therefore, it is important to evaluate not only the capabilities of a state, but also its intentions. If a state accrues asymmetrical gains from a cooperative relationship, but their intent is not to dominate another state, then the relative gains are insignificant. In such a situation it is the absolute gains that matter most. In essence, whether or not a state achieves greater relative gains through cooperation is not foremost in the participants' mind; it is the absolute gains accrued by each actor that matters most.[66] If the intention of a state to dominate other states were abundantly clear, then neoliberals would concede a consideration of relative gains must now be a fundamental part of the final equation. If relative gains are part of the decision-making process, then neoliberals must admit that the prospect for cooperation between states is minimal.

Keohane goes on to show that in cooperative situations involving multiple actors, the concept of relative gains becomes even more insignificant.[67] In such a situation, the question becomes which relationship will prevent cooperation? If state A gains relative to state B, but not to state C or D, then will state A cooperate? The conclusion of a neoliberal perspective is that scholars cannot adequately address this situation unless they know the *intentions* of each state, not just their capabilities. If state C or D does not intend to use their relative gains against state A because they are allies, then state A will cooperate because of their ability to accrue absolute gains. In such a situation, neoliberal institutionalists

---

[64] Joseph M. Grieco, "Anarchy and the Limits of Cooperation: A Realist Critique of the Newest Liberal Internationalism," *International Organization* 42 (1988): 485-507, asserts that the primary concern of the nation-state is relative gains. Since Grieco claims that neoliberal theorists only emphasize absolute gains and, therefore find the theory fundamentally flawed.

[65] Keohane, "Institutional Theory, Realist Challenge," 274-278.

[66] Keohane does not rely on his own analysis to justify this point. In "Institutional Theory, Realist Challenge," Keohane cites the work of Robert Powell, "Absolute and Relative Gains in International Relations Theory," *American Political Science Review* 85 (1991): 1303-1320, and Duncan Snidal, "Relative Gains and the Pattern of International Cooperation," *American Political Science Review* 85 (1991): 701-726, to uphold his argument concerning the conditionality of relative gains.

[67] This will be important to my analysis of the Rome Statute because of the multiple states involved in that negotiation.

would not consider relative gains a detrimental factor to cooperation.[68] However, if state C does intend to use their gains against state A, then state A will not cooperate despite the possibility of relative gains. The point Keohane is trying to make is that relative gains are conditional and therefore, they will not always act as an obstacle to cooperation. If relative gains are not part of the equation, that is, if a state is gaining absolutely, then cooperation under anarchy is not only possible, but also probable.

Hegemony

The final premise of neoliberal institutionalism concerns the concept hegemony. Neorealist and power-based theories assert that hegemony is a necessary component for regime formation and cooperation.[69] Neoliberal institutionalism counters this argument by stating that regime formation and maintenance can occur without a nation-state acting as a hegemon. Throughout his 1984 text, Keohane constantly refers to post-hegemonic cooperation. At one point in the text Keohane states that:

> Without ignoring the difficulties that beset attempts to coordinate policy in the absence of hegemony, this book contends that non-hegemonic cooperation is possible, and that it can be facilitated by international regimes…Cooperation is possible after hegemony not only because shared interests can lead to the creation of regimes, but also because the conditions for maintaining existing international regimes are less demanding than those required for creating them.[70]

Clearly neoliberal thought does not necessitate the existence of a hegemon for cooperation to occur; cooperation, for the institutionalists, occurs as the result of shared interests among states and the ascertaining of absolute gains through regime formation. Although hegemony may assist in the formation process, hegemonic coercion does not play a primary role for neoliberalism. As a result, power-based theories of cooperation are viewed as a misconception of the current global system.[71]

---

68 Keohane, "Institutional Theory, Realist Challenge" 276, uses a similar example to show the highly conditional nature of relative gains.

69 Hasenclever, Mayer and Rittberger, *Theories of International Regimes,* 83-135, provide us with a detailed discussion of the power-based theory of regime formation.

70 Keohane, *After Hegemony,* 50.

71 One can view the dialogue between Keohane and Grieco during the late 1980s and 1990s as a power-based versus interest-based debate. In this debate Keohane shows the reason why hegemonic conceptions of cooperation are misguided. Central to this analysis is the conditionality of relative gains.

Conclusion

This chapter has provided my readers with a basic understanding of the general arguments used by neoliberal institutionalists. By borrowing ideas not only from the liberal—functionalist perspective, but also from the neorealists, neoliberal institutionalism has formed a state-centered paradigm that discusses the existence of cooperation within an anarchical system. This theory views the basis of cooperation as a mutuality of exogenously given interests that often results in the formation of international regimes; regimes that serve as mechanisms through which states pursue and achieve their self-interest. It is possible to view the International Criminal Court as such a mechanism. As a result, the next chapter analyzes the formation of the Rome Statute and the resulting International Criminal Court from a neoliberal perspective. The goal of this endeavor is to begin the understanding process of what some scholars see as a highly improbable institution.[72] However, the ICC is now a functioning institution that was begot from cooperative endeavors. It is these cooperative endeavors that IR scholars must now try and understand.

---

72 Realist/neorealist thinkers who advance a power-based theory of cooperation would accept the improbability of this regime. Joseph M. Grieco, "Anarchy and the Limits of Cooperation," and "Understanding the Problem of International Cooperation: The Limits of Neoliberal Institutionalism and the Future of Realist Theory," in *Neorealism and Neoliberalism: The Contemporary Debate,* ed. David A. Baldwin (New York: Columbia University Press, 1993), 301-338; and Krasner, "Sovereignty, Regimes and Human Rights," are the most prominent of these scholars.

Chapter 5

The Primacy of the State

> Through your collective efforts you have created a Statute that will establish the international criminal court that has long been recognized as the missing link in the international legal system. You have deliberated with great care and patience and have negotiated through very difficult passages. That you had to overcome great obstacles was not a surprise. The questions that you successfully resolved have posed a challenge to the United Nations for more than 50 years – a challenge that you now have met.
>
> Hans Corell[1]

Understanding the ICC

During the Rome Conference it became evident that a large number of state and non-state actors approved of the formation of an International Criminal Court. The overwhelming support for the Rome Statute for an International Criminal Court exemplifies the neoliberal idea that cooperation among states is possible despite the anarchical nature of the world system. This support was solidified on April 11, 2002, when the requisite number of ratifications occurred, thus bringing the Rome Statute into force on July 1, 2002. In order to better understand the formation of this unique institution, neoliberal institutionalism has to address three primary questions: 1) why have so many states approved the Statute; 2) why has the United States so vehemently opposed the Statute; 3) what has the impact of American opposition been on the formation process? A critical part of addressing these questions entails a discussion of why the mainstream theory of international relations (realism/neorealism) is not applicable to this case. I will attempt to achieve this goal by briefly examining the ICC in light of the hegemonic factors important to this cooperative endeavor.

Hegemony and/or Cooperation?

Neoliberal institutionalism is predicated on the idea that cooperation occurs because of shared interest, not coercive power. The formation of the Rome Statute clearly adheres to this principle of neoliberalism. Therefore, in my attempt to

---

1 This quote is part of a statement made at the conclusion of the Rome Conference of the International Criminal Court, July 17, 1998. Hans Corell was the Secretary General Representative at the Rome Conference.

address the question of why such a large number of states approved the Rome Statute, it is necessary to begin with this core premise.

The overwhelming support received during the Rome Conference, by not only the organizations that make up the CICC but also state actors, is not attributable to a form of hegemonic leadership. Contrary to the principles of cooperation under hegemony (as embodied in the realist writings of Robert Gilpin), the formation of the ICC lacked the support of the world's only superpower.[2] In fact, the sole global superpower, the United States, not only voted against the Statute at the conclusion of the Rome Conference, but they continue to undermine the work of the ICC today. As a result of this lack of hegemonic leadership, the first question that I must address is why is the United States so vehemently opposed to the ICC?

United States Opposition to the ICC

David Scheffer, former American Ambassador at Large for War Crimes Issues and Head of the United States' delegation to the Rome Conference, has authoritatively summarized the US position on the Rome Statute.[3] In a statement delivered to the US Senate Foreign Relations Committee, Scheffer cites seven objections to the Rome Statute.

First, the United States objects to any form of jurisdiction over non-party states. According to Scheffer, "Official actions of a non-party state should not be subject to the court's jurisdiction if that country does not join the treaty, except by means of Security Council action under the UN Charter."[4] The Rome Statute does allow jurisdiction over individuals of non-party states if the crime occurs on the soil of a party state.[5] In such a case, the ICC can prosecute the accused individual even if that individual is not a national of a party state. The United States government believes that this form of jurisdiction puts its service members at risk regardless of whether the US Senate ratifies the Rome Statute. In short, the United States government considers the inclusion of this article as both a limiting factor to American involvement in world affairs (because of the concern about ICC jurisdiction) and a violation of international treaty law.

2 Hasenclever, Rittberger and Mayer, *Theories of International Regimes,* 83-136, discusses power-based theories of regime formation. One interpretation of power-based theories states that regime formation can only occur if that regime is supported by a hegemon.

3 Scheffer's arguments are clearly laid out in numerous articles and speeches delivered by the Ambassador. These include "Development at the Rome Treaty Conference," *US Department of State Dispatch,* 9 (1998): 19-23; "US Policy and the Proposed Permanent International Criminal Court," and "The United States and the International Criminal Court." I believe it is fair to say that the current administration of George W. Bush concurs with all of Scheffer's points and has in fact taken a hard line approach against the ICC.

4 Scheffer, "Development at Rome," 2.

5 Rome Statute of the ICC, Article 12.2(a).

The "principle of unanimity" has always served as the foundation of international treaty law.[6] According to this principle, a treaty or regulation is considered binding on a state without that state's consent. Therefore, in regards to the Rome Statute, US representatives argue that unless the United States government formally consents to the regulations of the Court (through ratification), then its laws are not binding on American citizens. In general, the US government believes that any attempt to prosecute a citizen of a non-party state is a violation of established international law and the principle of unanimity. As a result, the formation of the ICC, as established in the Rome Statute, lacks any legal basis. Therefore, the US considers ratification of this Statute a violation of established international law.

There is a counter-argument to this portion of US opposition. Due to the fact that the Rome Statute is predicated on established international law, the idea that its jurisdiction violates the principle of unanimity is illogical. According to Roy S. Lee, established international law already recognizes universal jurisdiction over the core crimes. Previous conventions and treaties, such as the Hague Conferences, the Genocide Convention, and the Geneva Conventions, have already established the law.[7] As opposed to David Scheffer, Roy Lee and other legal scholars contend that universal jurisdiction is already a part of international law. Therefore, the United States' claim against the ICC prosecuting individuals of non-party states lacks validity. Both positions are grounded in international law, but one could argue that the international community's overwhelming vote in favor of the Rome Statute was a vote in favor of Lee's interpretation.

Second, the US desires an "opt-out" clause that allows states to "assess the effectiveness and impartiality of the court before considering whether to accept its jurisdiction."[8] At the request of the French government, the Statute did include a seven-year opt-out provision for war crimes; however the United States was angling for an opt-out clause on all core crimes. The majority of participating delegates did not think such a clause to be prudent, thus they denied the United States' request.[9]

The third objection concerns amendment procedures. Under the amendment procedures of the Rome Statute, state parties which do not agree to amendments of Articles 5, 6, 7, and 8 (these articles concern the definitions of the core crimes), do

---

6 Louis Henkin, "The Politics of Law-Making," in *International Law: Classic and Contemporary Readings,* ed. Charlotte Ku and Paul F. Diehl (Boulder, CO: Lynne Rienner Publishers, 1998), 20, describes the formation of international law and the primacy of this principle within the law-making process.

7 Roy S. Lee, "The Rome Conference and its Contributions to International Law," in *The International Criminal Court: The Making of the Rome Statute—Issues, Negotiations, Results,* ed. Roy S. Lee (The Hague: Kluwer Law International, 1999), 29.

8 Scheffer, "Development at Rome," 3.

9 Rome Statue of the ICC, Article 124.

not fall under the Court's jurisdiction concerning these amendments.[10] In other words, if a state party does not agree to an amendment of the aforementioned articles they do not apply to that state. The US fought for this provision and succeeded in its inclusion in the Rome Statute; however, the aspect of this provision that Scheffer objected to was the fact that the ICC's jurisdiction over newly formed or amended crimes automatically extends to non-party states.[11] This is because these states, due to their non-party status, do not have the opportunity to vote on amendments. Therefore, when an amendment passes, a non-party state has no choice in whether jurisdiction concerning that amendment applies to their nationals. If a national of their state commits the new crime on the territory of a party state that accepted this amendment, then that national is accountable to the ICC. Scheffer cites this as a violation of state sovereignty and an overreaching of ICC jurisdiction.

The fourth US objection concerns the creation of a *proprio motu*, or self-initiating prosecutor. The Rome Statute allows the prosecutor to initiate criminal investigations on his or her own.[12] This of course only applies when the ICC's preconditions for jurisdiction are met, but the US still believes that such expansive authority by the prosecutor "risk[s] diversion of its [the Court's] resources, as well as embroil the court in controversy, political decision-making and confusion."[13]

Fifth, the US opposes the inclusion of the crime of aggression. The basis of this argument lies in the fact that currently, no agreed upon, established definition of this crime exists and historically, attempts to define this crime have been quite contentious. Therefore, the US believes that a Security Council decision is the only legitimate method for initiating an investigation of this crime. Basically, this objection protests against the lack of Security Council power over the ICC, which the US views as a necessary condition of any just court.

The US also objected to the inclusion of crimes of terrorism and drug crimes within the Court's jurisdiction. On the final day of the Conference, the delegates decided to include these crimes by adopting them in an annexed resolution. The resolution's inclusion in the Statute is contingent upon the definition of these crimes by the Court. US opposition to the inclusion of such crimes is due to the fact that ICC jurisdiction over these crimes would "undermine essential national and transnational efforts, and actually hamper the effective fight against these crimes."[14] Thus, the US desires leaving these crimes within national jurisdiction.

The seventh and final objection concerns Article 120 of the Rome Statute. This Article simply states that, "No reservations may be made to this Statute." The US wanted the opportunity to voice its reservations concerning certain portions of the

---

10 Rome Statute of the ICC, Article 121.5.

11 Scheffer, "Development at Rome," 21.

12 Rome Statute of the ICC, Article 15.

13 Scheffer, "Development at Rome," 3.

14 Scheffer, "Development at Rome," 3-4.

Statute while still signing and ratifying the treaty. The inclusion of Article 120 served as another reason for American opposition.[15]

It should now be clear that the specifics of the Rome Statute do not mesh with the US conception of an international justice system. Along with the aforementioned objections there is also the question of constitutionality. This question centers on whether American ratification of the Rome Statute is even constitutional? Scheffer and other government officials have not specifically raised this question however, other ICC opponents have. One could speculate that the reason why Scheffer did not acknowledged this factor is that the ratification process actually is constitutionally acceptable. According to Ruth Wedgewood, "there is no forbidding constitutional obstacle to US participation in the treaty."[16] She cites five principles that allow the US to constitutionally ratify the Rome Statute. 1) The US participation in past tribunals has impacted American lives and property. Thus, the precedent has already been established. 2) The ICC embodies the US principles of due process and individual rights. 3) If the US government and not the ICC tried the crimes that come under the ICC's jurisdiction, they would occur in military courts. Since these military courts differ dramatically from US common law trials, the applicability of different standards of judgement is not a viable argument (ie: a lack of a jury trial). 4) The well-drafted rules and procedures of the ICC avoid many of the pitfalls found in the two ad hoc tribunals of the 1990s. 5) The Status of Forces Agreements (SOFAs) protects American military personnel from local arrest. According to SOFA, the US President is the final arbitrator over extradition matters; therefore, if he/she deems the case unfair, then he/she can refuse to extradite the accused individual to The Hague.[17]

It is clear that the Rome Statute lacks the support of the global hegemon and it is doubtful that the US will ever support the treaty in its current form. With the US firmly entrenched against the Rome Statute, an understanding of the ICC from a power-based perspective would conclude that cooperation was impossible and that the formation of the ICC is implausible. Neoliberal institutionalism provides us with a more accurate account of the events in Rome, because neoliberalism looks beyond hegemony. According to neoliberal institutionalism, cooperation did occur because among those one hundred and twenty states that voted in favor of the Rome Statute, the one hundred thirty-seven signatories, and ninety-nine ratifications, a shared or mutual interest existed.

---

[15] The Bush administration continues to work against the functioning of the ICC. This is evident by his administration's "unsigning" of the Statute, the passing of The Hague Invasion Act, and the attempt to tie foreign aid to Article 99 acceptance.

[16] Ruth Wedgewood, "The Constitution and the ICC," in *The United States and the International Criminal Court: National Security and International Law,* ed. Sarah B. Sewall and Carl Kaysen (Lanham, MD: Rowman & Littlefield Publishers, Inc., 2000), 121.

[17] Wedgewood, "The Constitution and the ICC," 120-127, contains a more detailed discussion of these principles and the question of ICC constitutionality.

Interest-based Cooperation

For neoliberals, a mutuality of interests is the only rationale for this type of collaboration. However, for many scholars, the applicability of interest-based theory never extends beyond the economic realm. Stephen Krasner, for one, views interest-based cooperation within the issue-area of human rights as impossible. According to Krasner, neoliberalism asserts that cooperation is undertaken to overcome market failure.[18] Since human rights' atrocities are not a product of market failure, then neoliberalism cannot adequately address this issue. Krasner states that any formation of a human rights regime must be a function of powerful states within the system enforcing a set of human rights' norms.[19] As shown in the previous section, and contrary to Krasner's assertions, the formation of the Rome Statute did not arise in such a manner. The imposition of international norms by a hegemonic state did not occur in Rome. Instead, the ICC resulted from a cooperative effort amongst numerous state delegates who believed that it was in their state-interest to approve such an institution. This despite the fact that market-failure was not an issue for the actors in Rome. It would appear that the cooperative effort of the participants in Rome discredits Krasner's assertions and shows that interest-based cooperation can occur within the issue-area of human rights.

According to the neoliberal paradigm, there are several crucial factors that lead to the formation of the ICC. First, neoliberals consider the participating states to be rational actors who seek to fulfill their own interests. Second, the mutual goal of the Rome Conference participants is the security of a known and enforceable system of international justice. Third, neoliberal theory believes that states' interests are static. That is, they are exogenously given and the primary goal of all states is to fulfill those interests.[20] If we employ this neoliberal line of thinking, then it is plausible to claim that a large number of nation-states desired the aforementioned goal, and the ensuing conflict amongst these actors was the result of institutional preference, not basic interests. In order to justify this claim, I must first undertake an analysis of state negotiation stances.

---

18 Krasner, "Sovereignty, Regimes and Human Rights," 139. Keohane would agree that market failure is a crucial and possibly primary initiator of international cooperation. But for Keohane, as opposed to Krasner, this does not nullify the chance that cooperation could occur because of reasons other than market failure.

19 Krasner, "Sovereignty, Regimes and Human Rights," 141.

20 Sterling-Folker, "Competing Paradigms," explains the premise of exogenously given interests in much greater detail. Drawing on the work of Keohane, Sterling-Folker shows that neoliberals believe that interests are given, but that institutional preference on how to achieve these interests is not. This is where cooperation is most important, because without it state's interests cannot be fulfilled.

Negotiating Positions

To uphold the principles of the neoliberal paradigm, it must be true that most participants at the Rome Conference desired an ICC. Even the US stated its desire for an international criminal court. Their (US) opposition to the Rome Statute stems from issues of jurisdiction, not from the formation a court itself.[21] Therefore, the primary bone of contention for the American delegation and other opponents of the ICC is institutional, not interest-based. The US desires the formation of an international criminal court, but not in the form constructed at Rome. The conflict between the US and the "Like-Minded" states is over how to construct the institution, not over the institution itself.[22]

Most of the participating states fall into one of three groupings: the Like-Minded Group, the Non-aligned states, and the permanent Security Council members (P-5).[23] All three groupings take a different tact on the negotiations, but in order to achieve success at the Rome Conference an overwhelming majority of these states needed to agree on an underlying interest that would eventually lead to an agreement concerning institutionalization. The approval of the Rome Statute occurred as a result of tremendous cooperation; cooperation that, according to the neoliberal perspective, occurred between states.

Like-Minded Group

The Like-Minded countries were the strongest advocates for an independent and powerful ICC. In general, this group of states shared one common interest: the rapid creation of a permanent international criminal court. These states realized that the opportunity to establish such an institution had already slipped away at least once (post World War II), and they believed that if the international community did not act fast, the current movement might also fall short.[24] In order to achieve their goal, the Like-Minded states played a crucial role not only during

21 Scheffer, "The US and the ICC," clearly states that the US is not opposed to the formation of an international criminal court, but the US is opposed to the Rome Statute. This is primarily due to the issue of jurisdiction and the lack of control the US has over the proposed ICC. The US delegation made it very clear that they would support an ICC, but only if the majority of jurisdictional power resides in the Security Council.

22 Recall that the Like-Minded states are a group of ICC supporters who vehemently oppose many of the changes that the US proposed at Rome. The interesting aspect of these competing perspectives is that a large number of Like-Minded states are traditional American allies. See chapter two for more details on this group of states.

23 The reason for only analyzing nation-state stances at this point is because of the analytical position being employed. Neoliberal institutionalism analyzes world politics within a state-centered paradigm. Therefore, according to this theory, any discussion of the tactics or perspectives of non-state actors is secondary to the actions of states.

24 Bendetti and Washburn, "Drafting the ICC," 20.

the Rome Conference, but also at the PrepCom meetings leading up to the Conference.

Over a three-year period, the Like-Minded Group fought to establish a strong and independent ICC by often leading the PrepCom meetings and always maintaining a high level of visibility. Their efforts did not go unnoticed. Other states began to see the importance of this issue and slowly began to gravitate to the Like-Minded Group. At the time of the ILC Draft Statute for an International Criminal Court, the Like-Minded Group consisted of only a dozen or so countries. However, as the process progressed and the other states became aware of the group's intentions, the number of adherents to their position began to swell. By the opening of the Rome Conference the group was composed of forty-two states. By the end of the Conference the group totaled more than sixty countries.[25] This dramatic increase in membership is empirical evidence that the Like-Minded Group's guiding principles resonated true with a large portion of the global community.

It was in December 1997 that the Like-Minded Group explicitly stated what their bloc of countries desired. At the December PrepCom meeting, the Like-Minded Group centered their future goals on the following six guiding principles.[26] First, they desired an ICC that would be independent of the United Nations Security Council. This would assist in the de-politicizing of this institution and prevent the major powers of the world from vetoing prosecutions that were not in their best interest.

Second, in a further attempt at de-politicization of the Court, the Like-Minded Group also advocated the idea of an independent prosecutor. This principle would grant the prosecutor the power to initiate, *proprio motu,* an investigation. Such a principle would provide the Court a greater degree of independence from both member states and the Security Council, thus granting the Court greater legal legitimacy.

Third, the Like-Minded Group advocated the extension of the inherent jurisdiction of the Court to cover all core crimes. This principle would achieve two major functions. First, it would improve upon the traditional two-track approach to jurisdictional issues that currently exists in international courts and tribunals. Historically, if a state is party to an international court or tribunal, this did not necessarily equate into inherent acceptance of the court's jurisdiction.[27] In the case

---

25 Bendetti and Washburn, "Drafting the ICC," 30, and William R. Pace, "The Relationship Between the International Criminal Court and Non-Governmental Organizations," in *Reflections on the International Criminal Court: Essays in Honour of Adriaan Bos,* ed. Herman A. M. von Hebel, Johan g. Lammers, Jolien Schukking (The Hague: T. M. C. Asser Press, 1999), 205, both document these numbers.

26 Bendetti and Washburn, "Drafting the ICC," 21, and Pace, "Relationship Between ICC and Non-governmental Organizations," 206, discuss this list of defining principles.

27 Lee, "Rome Conference Contributions," 28, cites Article 36 of the Statute of the International Court of Justice.

of the ICC, immediately upon ratification the Court ascertains automatic jurisdiction within the party state.[28] Second, it allows for greater prosecutorial independence of the Court. By not allowing any opt-in or opt-out clauses, the ability of the Court to pursue prosecutions is increased, regardless of state consent.[29]

Fourth, the Like-Minded Group calls for the full cooperation of states with the ICC. The necessity of such a proposal is obvious when considering the plethora of tasks that the Court has to undertake. The ICC is still an institution that is constructed of nation-states and it relies on the assistance of these states for the functioning and enforcement of the Court and its decisions. According to the Rome Statute, the ICC is entirely reliant on member states for the discharge of its functions.[30] Without the full cooperation of states, the Court will not be able to function in an effective and/or efficient manner. This applies to several different aspects of the Court, but I will briefly discuss three.

Within the approved Statute there are several activities that necessitate a cooperative relationship between Court and states. One such area is the investigation and prosecution of the core crimes. Article 93 dictates that state parties must assist the Court in identification of persons, taking of evidence, questioning of accused, service of documents, transfer of persons, execution of searches, protection of witnesses, and more. The Court's resources, as prescribed in the Rome Statute, are insufficient for undertaking a proper investigation on its own. Thus, the Like-Minded Group saw the need for state cooperation in this area and they were successful in codifying this relationship in the final Statute.

Another area in which state cooperation is crucial is the enforcement of Court decisions, including the detention of convicted individuals. Article 103 provides a clear example of the state parties' role in enforcement. This Article dictates that member states penitentiary systems will serve as the detention centers of convicted individuals. There is no ICC detention facility for long-term imprisonment. Thus, without full member state cooperation, effective enforcement of the Court's verdicts is not possible, thus rendering the Court impotent.

Along with the need for enforcement, the Court also relies heavily on member states for financing. The Rome Statute dictates that:

---

[28] Rome Statute of the ICC, Article 12.1.

[29] The idea of a consent regime was advocated by the US for all crimes except genocide. But as will be shown, the US position on this issue eventually failed. Mahnoush H. Arsanjani, "Reflections on the Jurisdiction and Trigger Mechanism of the International Criminal Court," in *Reflections on the International Criminal Court,* ed. Herman A. M. von Hebel, Johan G. Lammers and Jolien Schukking (The Hague: T. M. C. Asser Press, 1999), 59-61.

[30] The functioning of the Court is reliant on the member states, because without the cooperation of these states the Court could not acquire evidence, arrest the accused, enforce sentences, or finance the daily proceedings. As with most international organizations, the necessity of state cooperation is clear.

> The expenses of the Court and the Assembly of States Parties…shall be provided by the following sources:
> (a) Assessed contributions made by States Parties
> (b) Funds provided by the United Nations…[31]

This reliance on state funding makes the functioning of the Court dependent on state cooperation. The money is generally assessed from state parties; therefore their cooperation in paying this assessed contribution is critical to the survival of the Court. As all of the aforementioned areas indicate, without a high level of member state cooperation (in multiple areas of the final Rome Statute) the goal of constructing a reliable, credible, and effective ICC is implausible. Thus, the foresight of the Like-Minded Group appears to be crucial to the future capabilities of this institution.

The Like-Minded Group's fifth principle advocated the idea of the ICC as final decision-maker on all issues of admissibility. This objective is essential to the Like-Minded states because of their desire to establish an independent Court. As they perceive it, one way to insure the fair and independent functioning of the Court is to place the burden of admissibility solely with the elected judges. This alleviates the politicization of the Court by state members and assists in the pursuit of an objective decision-making process that is essential in the pursuit of justice.

The final principle espoused by the Like-Minded Group is a commitment to a successful diplomatic conference in Rome. This group of states realized that more than a half-century's worth of work was dependent on a five-week conference. They were not under the impression that this step in the formation process would be an easy one; therefore they wanted to explicitly state their commitment to a successful outcome at the Conference. The approval of the Rome Statute on July 17, 1998, is the result of the Like-Minded Group's dedication to this project. And although some of their principles were embodied in the Statute, while others were not, it is clear that this group of states was crucial to the negotiating process. However, the Like-Minded states were not the only state actors involved. Two other groups of states also played an important role.

Non-aligned Movement

The Non-aligned movement was composed of another group of states that were involved in the pre-Rome negotiations. This group consisted mainly of non-Western states that wished to initiate a counter-movement to the Western, Security Council powers. India served as the leadership of this group, with a group of Gulf States forming the secondary leadership role. In general, the Non-aligned movement was in favor of an ICC, but only if certain conditions were included. One, they felt it imperative that the Statute include nuclear weapons in the list of

---

31 Rome Statute of the ICC, Article 115.

prohibited weapons; two, the necessity to eliminate any control of the Court by the Security Council.[32]

Despite their well defined agenda, this group lacked staying power. One of the primary deficiencies of this group was the lack of total cohesiveness and weak leadership. These flaws eventually led the members of the Non-aligned movement to break away and gravitate to either a more regionally based grouping, or towards the Like-Minded states.[33] Thus, their impact on the negotiations was minimal, although in many ways they did bolster the Like-Minded Group's numbers, giving them an edge over the permanent Security Council states.

Security Council States?

The third group of states that evolved during the negotiating process was misnamed the P-5, after the permanent Security Council members. As this section will show, the P-5 quickly became the P-2—with only China and the United States voting against the final Statute.

As stated earlier, the United States opposed the formation of the ICC for the following reasons:

1) any form of jurisdiction over non-party states;
2) no "opt-out" clause concerning jurisdiction of core crimes;
3) amendment procedures that do not allow states to avoid jurisdiction;
4) an independent or *proprio motu* prosecutor;
5) the inclusion of the crime of aggression as a core crime;
6) the inclusion of crimes of terrorism and drug crimes;
7) a no reservation clause.[34]

With these objections as the cornerstone to their opposition, the United States and China, along with a select few rogue states, entered the negotiation process as the main opponents to the Like-Minded Group. During both the PrepCom meetings and the Rome Conference, the P-5 opposed both the Like-Minded Group's call for an independent court and the Non-aligned movements desire to include the use of

---

32 Bendetti and Washburn, "Drafting the ICC," 31.

33 Bendetti and Washburn, "Drafting the ICC," 31 and 33, explain the dissipation of the group. This fragmentation is also obvious when looking at the alignment of the states at the Rome Conference. Three general groupings were present: the Like-Minded states, the Security Council members and regional blocs from Africa, Asia, and the Americas. But despite gravitation to other groups, the final Declaration of the Thirteenth Ministerial Conference of the Non-Aligned Movement contained a statement of support for the ICC (articles 97-99). *The International Criminal Court Monitor,* June 2000, 6, reported on the Non-aligned movements support.

34 Scheffer, "Development at Rome," and "United States and the ICC," discuss these objections. I summarize them at length earlier in this chapter.

nuclear weapons.[35] The main objective of this group was to establish a Court that would have close ties to the Security Council, thus allowing these states to maintain their veto power over this institution. This perspective was obviously contradictory to the Like-Minded principles and as a result, the competing negotiating positions were established.

Cooperation Among States

The final outcome of the Rome Conference was overwhelming support of the Statute, despite the presence of two competing positions concerning the construction of the ICC. As a result of this conclusion, I must now address two questions: 1) how did the final Statute come about; 2) how, if at all, were these two opposing views reconciled?

Pursuing these questions from a neoliberal institutionalist perspective leads us to the negotiating process among states. The foundation of the Rome Statute lies with the Draft Statute for an International Criminal Court, published by the ILC in 1994. The pre-Rome negotiations were primarily undertaken through a set of PrepCom meetings in which delegates discussed and amended the draft Statute. This was by no means an easy task. Over a three year period the PrepCom participants struggled to form a final draft Statute that would serve as an acceptable foundation for a diplomatic conference. Over six PrepCom sessions and numerous informal sessions, delegates amended, altered, and transformed the 1994 Draft Statute until the working text contained one hundred and sixteen articles, with several options and hundreds of brackets.[36]

During this three-year process, the positioning of the participant states began to take shape. Although the Like-Minded Group formed around the time of the ILC Draft Statute, it was not until December 1997 that they stated their foundational principles. At this point the P-5 had also established their position on the Statute, but the defection of the United Kingdom to the Like-Minded Group severely hampered their negotiating position.[37] Despite this defection, it became obvious to both sides that without high-level cooperation, the formation of a permanent ICC would be impossible. Thus, during both the PrepCom meetings and the Rome Conference, it became obvious to both groups of states that they would have to make concessions.

One way to assess the concessions that these states made is to analyze the gains and losses of the American delegation.[38] As stated earlier, at the close of the Rome

---

35 Kirsch and Holmes, "Rome Conference," 4.

36 Arsanjani, "Rome Statute of the ICC," 22.

37 Scheffer, "US Policy", describes the pre-Rome conference position of the US.

38 This is due to the fact that observers of the conference often consider the US position on the Rome Statute synonymous with the P-5 position on the Statute.

Conference the US still felt that the Statute needed a tremendous amount of alteration. Nevertheless, this does not mean that the US and the rest of the opposition states did not make significant gains during this negotiation process. According to David Scheffer, the P-5 states achieved numerous objectives prior to Rome. Ironically, the successful implementation of some of the P-5's objectives may have resulted in the ultimate defection of the UK, France, and Russia from the P-5 group.[39]

First, the US felt that they had gained an improved form of complementarity. Under the principle of complementarity, the ICC must defer to a state's national courts. Only if the national court is unable or unwilling to prosecute the case does the ICC have jurisdiction.[40] This principle protects the national sovereignty of state parties and also upholds the premise of *ne bis in idem*. As a result, although the US did not achieve the exact form of complementarity they desired, Scheffer did admit that it was an improvement over the previous form.[41]

Second, the final Statute granted the UN Security Council the power to halt the Court's action in certain circumstances. According to Article 16 of the Rome Statute:

> No investigation or prosecution may be commenced or proceeded with under this Statute for a period of 12 months after the Security Council, in a resolution adopted under Chapter VII of the Charter of the United Nations, has requested the Court to that effect; that request may be renewed by the Council under the same conditions.

Thus, the role of Article 16 is to provide the Security Council with a mechanism through which they can stop or prevent an ICC investigation or prosecution. This component was crucial to the US because it provides them with greater authority over the initiation of investigations and the possible prosecution of individuals by the ICC.[42]

---

39 Scheffer, "Development at Rome," 19-20. It is important to note that although some scholars still refer to the post-Rome US contingency as the P-5, at this point in time the P-5 only includes two of the permanent members of the Security Council—the US and China.

40 Rome Statute of the ICC, Article 17.1-2 and Article 20. John T. Holmes, "The Principle of Complementarity," in *The International Criminal Court: The Making of the Rome Statute—Issues, Negotiations, Results,* ed. Roy S. Lee (The Hague: Kluwer Law International, 1999), 41-78, discusses the nuances of this principle at length. One important component of this principle is the fact that the decision concerning unwillingness is to be determined by a panel of three ICC judges. Thus, the ultimate power of prosecution lies with this group of individuals.

41 Scheffer continued to harbor fears that some states may use the ICC as a political tool against US soldiers. The ultimate goal of the US, both during the Clinton administration and now during the Bush administration, is to exclude American service members from the jurisdiction of the Court altogether.

42 Lionel Yee, "The International Criminal Court and the Security Council: Articles 13(b) and 16," in *The International Criminal Court: The Making of the Rome Statute—Issues,*

Third, the Rome Statute upholds the confidentiality of national security information. Article 72 of the Rome Statute declares that in instances where a state believes that the disclosure of information or documents will prejudice the national security of that state, they have the right to "intervene in order to obtain resolution of the issue." In short, the Article provides states with the ability to block the introduction of certain testimony or evidence into the Court proceedings if that state deems it a threat to their national security. This Article is another way in which the ICC upholds the norm of state sovereignty, an ideal that the United States holds in high regard.

Fourth, due process and the protection of the accused were included as major parts of the Rome Statute. The Rome Statute's Articles 55, 66 and 67 deals with the rights of the accused and clearly parallel American domestic judicial proceedings.[43] These Articles provide the accused with the right to be promptly informed of their alleged crimes, the right to remain silent, the presumption of innocence, to have adequate time and facilities to prepare for a defense, the right to counsel, the right to a timely trial, the right to the assistance of a competent interpreter, and others. Clearly the participants of the Rome Conference wanted to uphold the individual rights that the US holds so dear and this desire is embodied, much to Scheffer's delight, in the final Statute.

Fifth, rigorous qualifications were established for the appointment of judges. As per Article 36.3-8, nominated individuals shall be of a high moral character, exhibit competence in the proceedings of not only criminal law and procedure, but also international humanitarian law and the law of human rights. The election process entails a secret ballot vote by the Assembly of State parties and the result of that election is that no two judges shall be from the same state. The US saw the need for rigorous qualifications and election proceedings because this would provide the Court with the ability to fight against any form of politicization that might impinge on its ultimate goal of upholding international justice.

Finally, as stated in Article 115, assessed contributions by state parties constitute the majority of the Court's funding. If the Court receives any funding from the UN, the General Assembly must approve of it first. Delegates of the Rome Conference also determined that they, the state parties, shall be the final overseers of the Court's action. In other words, the Court is ultimately accountable to the state parties. This provides the member states with the final voice over all of the Court's actions.[44]

Negotiations, Results, ed. Roy S. Lee (The Hague: Kluwer Law International, 1999), 143-152.

[43] Leonard, "Discovering the New Face of Sovereignty," discusses the relationship between American domestic law and the ICC's proceedings.

[44] Scheffer, "Development at Rome," mentions fourteen objectives that the US achieved. I consider the seven mentioned in this text to be the most representative.

These concessions were tantamount to the interests of many of the P-5 members. One could speculate that the objectives achieved by the US and the P-5 were enough to sway several key members of the original P-5 group into approving the Rome Statute. In the end, the Rome Statute received the support of several of the permanent Security Council members. The United Kingdom pledged its loyalty to the Like-Minded Group seven months prior to the Rome Conference primarily due to the inclusion of the Singapore compromise, relating to the role of the Security Council.

All of the P-5 nations desired a strong role for the Security Council in regards to the initiation of investigations by the ICC, while the Like-Minded Group and the CICC were pushing for a distinct separation between the two. Singapore suggested the following compromise: instead of the ICC needing the approval of the Security Council to initiate every investigation, Singapore suggested that the Security Council could delay any investigation of the ICC if they had unanimous Council consent.[45] This compromise was amenable to several of the P-5 members (including China, Russia, and the UK), and eventually led to the UK's defection from the P-5 and its current status as a member of the Like-Minded Group.[46]

During the negotiations at the Rome Conference France also altered their position. Many observers believe their defection from the P-5 is also attributable to the concessions that were made by the Like-Minded Group. In particular, in order to gain French support of the final Statute, the Like-Minded Group agreed to include Article 124. This Article allowed for state parties to "opt out" of the war crimes provision for a period of seven years. With this concession in place, France went on to not only approve and sign the Statute; they were also one of the earliest ratifying states of the Rome Statute.[47]

In the end, the only permanent Security Council members to vote against the Rome Statute were the US and China. Russia voted in favor of the Statute and eventually signed it, but at this point in time the prospects of ratification seem dim. I have already discussed at length why the US decided not to vote in favor of the Statute so let me now turn to the other major objector, China. In China's case, one could speculate that they were simply unconvinced of the need for an international criminal court.[48] They appeared somewhat detached from the negotiations, as they are from many foreign policy issues, and seemed unmoved by moral necessity for a permanent ICC. As a result of China's refusal to approve the Statute, by the conclusion of the Conference only China and the US remained within the once powerful coalition of the P-5.

---

45 The Rome Statute, Article 16, embodies this compromise.

46 Bendetti and Washburn, "Drafting the ICC," 19-20 and Brown, "The Statute of the ICC," 63, both discuss the compromise and the support that it received.

47 France was the twelfth state to ratify the Rome Statute on June 9, 2000.

48 Bendetti and Washburn, "Drafting the ICC," 17.

The numerous defections are a prime example of the cooperative effort that occurred between states in order to obtain a successful vote. No one group of states received all that they desired, but they all received some concessions; and in the end the framework of an institution that could assist in the upholding of international humanitarian law was approved.

Unanswered Questions

If scholars are to employ an analysis of the ICC from a neoliberal institutionalist perspective, one question that they must address is whether or not this theory provides an accurate understanding of this cooperative arrangement? Initially it appears as if the answer is yes—but that is only an initial assessment. According to neoliberalism, the ICC formation process is a cooperative effort amongst self-interested, rational states, which desire a stronger system of international criminal justice. The PrepCom meetings and the Rome Conference are clear examples of cooperation among states. These events also establish the fact that cooperation and institution building can occur, despite the absence of hegemonic leadership. Therefore, at the most fundamental level, one can conclude that neoliberal institutionalism provides international relations scholars with at least an elementary understanding of the formation of the Rome Statute of the ICC. But does this analytical perspective provide scholars with anything beyond this elementary level? Does it detail a full account of the cooperative process or does it leave too many questions unanswered?

If we look closely at the Rome Conference and how the ICC finally received approval, it becomes apparent that there is a need to move beyond a simple neoliberal understanding of the Court's formation process. For example, this theory does not account for all of the actors involved in the negotiations. It also fails to account for the formation of state's interests. Finally, it fails to address the question of why now (1998). In short, neoliberal institutionalism, because of its foundational principles, simply cannot address these issues. Thus, in order to achieve a fuller understanding of the formation and function of the ICC, it becomes necessary to engage these unanswered questions so that future analysis may invoke a perspective that can account for these shortcomings.

Non-state Actors

The first question that neoliberal institutionalism fails to address concerns the actors involved in the formation process. One group of non-state actors that influenced the negotiation process was the NGO community. At the Rome Conference, the number of participating NGOs exceeded three hundred.[49] These

---

49 Bassiouni, *The Statute of the International Criminal Court,* 25-26.

NGOs established the Coalition for an ICC (CICC) and through the use of their collective power, were able to play a major role in the approval of the Rome Statute. The CICC aided the formation process in numerous ways: from publishing expert papers, to initiating informal meetings with delegates, to passing information along to the less represented states. The CICC undoubtedly played a critical role during the Rome Conference and greatly assisted the approval process of this Statute. Neoliberal institutionalism does not provide a sufficient basis for understanding the role of these NGOs and the CICC.

Along with the NGOs, many participants in the formation process believe that a large portion of the credit for success has to go to the individual leadership employed during the Rome Conference. As Roy Lee stated, "An effective negotiating body must have a competent presiding office to guide the proceedings, to induce compromises and to forge agreements."[50] It appears as if both the PrepCom meetings and the Rome Conference had outstanding individual leadership. And yet, if analyzed from a neoliberal institutionalist perspective, the individual leadership at the Conference would not be part of the analysis. This leaves the unanswered question of how much of a factor was the individual leadership during this process? If the proper leadership were not in place, would the Conference have been as successful as it was? In order to ascertain an answer to these questions, scholars must look beyond the neoliberal paradigm.

I should note that neoliberalism does not ignore non-state actors, such as NGOs and individuals. What it does advocate is a form of analysis that privileges nation-states and their interests. In this regard, neoliberal institutionalism tends to analyze non-state actors as secondary or complèmentary participants to the cooperation process. It is possible that scholars can achieve an elementary understanding of the ICC without understanding the role of the CICC, but if we want a fuller, richer analysis of the formation process, then it is necessary to study the role of non-state actors as more then secondary players. Neoliberalism does not account for a primary role of non-state actors and therefore fails to recognize an important piece of the puzzle. The result is an incomplete understanding of the success achieved at Rome and beyond.

Cognitive Factors

Along with this failure to account for the role of non-state actors, neoliberalism also fails to address the role of cognitive factors. Neoliberalism views the

---

[50] Lee, "Rome Conference Contributions," 19. This leadership would include the PrepCom Chair Adriann Bos, Chair of the Committee of the Whole for the Rome Conference Philippe Kirsch, and Chair of the Rome Statute Drafting Committee Cherif Bassiouni.

formation of the ICC as an interest-based process.[51] In other words, neoliberalism perceives nation-states as having self-interests that may or may not concur with other state's interests. But according to neoliberalism, the one fact that these states cannot escape is the interdependence that binds them together. Therefore, neoliberal theorists view cooperation as a necessity. In these types of negotiation situations, the deliberation or conflict that occurs between states is often over the institutional preference that states believe will best achieve their interest, not always over the overarching interest itself.[52] What is lacking in the neoliberal institutionalist form of analysis is an understanding of the origin of these overarching, complementary interests. For neoliberal institutionalists, states' interests are exogenously given; therefore an account of their origin is inconsequential.

A knowledge-based or ideational perspective would not suffer from this type of narrow perspective.[53] Cognitivists search for the ideas that shape the formation of international institutions and use these ideas as explanatory variables. According to the cognitivist position, the main flaw in neoliberal thinking is the fact that they believe that states' interests are exogenously given.[54] Such an analysis fails to adequately address the process of interest formation and the impact that this process has on regime formation.

For knowledge-based theorists, the construction of ideas is crucial and the acceptance of exogenously given interests by neoliberalism is considered a detriment to an understanding of global politics, not only methodologically, but also ontologically. If we are to adequately understand the formation and function of regimes, IR scholars must understand the dynamic nature of interests and the fact that changes in the ideational perspective of decision-makers can result in a change in policy. By engaging in this type of analysis, one might better understand why the construction of the ICC in the late 1990s has achieved such success, while it failed to form in the immediate post-World War II era. An analysis of ideational

---

51 Hasenclever, Mayer and Rittberger, *Theories of International Regimes,* defines interests as the central variable in neoliberal thought. They differentiate this idea from the power-based and knowledge-based schools of thought concerning regime formation.

52 The community of states overarching interest, at least in this case, is conflict management and the premise of international justice.

53 Hasenclever, Mayer and Rittberger, *Theories of International Regimes,* 136-210, provide a detailed discussion of knowledge-based theories. Readers should note that although cognitivists may not suffer from a narrow interest-based analysis, these theorists may suffer from their own narrow analysis. While neoliberals adhere to a strict understanding of regime formation through common interests, cognitivists look at regime formation as ideational. The problem is that such an analysis is also exclusionary and therefore, if used exclusively, this theory may suffer from the same problems I have cited for neoliberalism.

54 Hasenclever, Mayer and Rittberger, *Theories of International Regimes,* 136.

perspective at these divergent moments may enhance our understanding and exploration of regime formation in this issue-area.[55]

Why Now?

As I alluded to above, the neoliberal perspective also fails to address the question of why now. Historically there were several moments in time during which the formation of an international criminal court seemed plausible. In fact, in the immediate post-World War II era, the International Law Commission drafted a statute for the establishment of such a court.[56] However, the international community declined to act on that proposal and therefore, the community of states shelved the idea of forming a permanent ICC for another forty years.

It was not until 1989 that the initiative to form a permanent international criminal court re-emerged. The ILC began its work on drafting a Statute in the early 1990s and with continued support from a large portion of the UN General assembly, the ILC was able to parlay their work into the establishment of a Preparatory Committee, the convening of the Rome Conference, an approved Rome Statute, and finally the ascertaining of the requisite ratifications and a functioning ICC. The question that an analysis of the ICC formation process must attempt to address is why the establishment of the ICC was so successful in the 1990s, but failed to gain any support in the post-World War II era?[57]

Neoliberal institutionalism and its state-centric ontology can not address this question with any proficiency. If one analyzes this process from a neoliberal perspective, there is no reason to question why the court received such support in the 1990s, except to say that at this juncture in time the formation of an ICC simply meshed with exogenous, *a priori* state interests. An analysis of why these interests were formed at this particular period in time and what contextual and ideational factors contributed to this formation process is not accounted for by neoliberalism. The stringent interest-based perspective from which neoliberals work fails to problematize the origin of interests and therefore, cannot account for the transformation of interests that must have occurred between 1953 and 1989.

---

55 Chapter six and seven of this text contain an analysis of the ICC from an ideational perspective.

56 Bassiouni, *Statute of the ICC,* 10-15 and Leila Nadya Sadat, "The Evolution of the ICC: From The Hague to Rome and Back Again," in *The United States and the International Criminal Court: National Security and International Law,* ed. Sarah B. Sewall and Carl Kaysen (Lanham, MD: Rowman & Littlefield Publishers, Inc., 2000), 36-38, discuss the ILC's post-World War II actions at length. Chapter two of this text also contains a detailed analysis of this period of time.

57 Even prior to the post-WWII era, there were calls for the establishment of an ICC. Yet, it is not until the 1990s that the international community supports this initiative and moves to form such an institution.

Understanding American Opposition

The previous conclusions concerning neoliberals' explanatory power does not mean that this perspective fails to achieve any understanding of the formation process. One critical area of understanding, although not full understanding, that neoliberalism does assist with is the rationale for American opposition to the Rome Statute.

In general, neoliberal institutionalism views American opposition as the result of relative gains. Neoliberals do not discount the importance of relative gains—they simply view them as highly conditional. In the case of the United States, the neoliberal argument states that the American government, although sharing the same interest for international justice, did not approve of the Rome Statute because they believe that the intentions of other states, combined with their gains, will lead to greater threats to American interests. In other words, the US believes that the ratification of the Rome Statute would allow their state to possibly gain absolutely, but the relative gains made by other states is seen by the US as a threat to their sovereignty.[58]

This is an interesting and defensible argument, but to understand fully this aspect of US opposition, one would need to also undertake an analysis of the domestic system. Although Keohane does acknowledge the need for a two-level game, he never actually employs it in his systemic model of regime formation.[59] Neoliberal institutionalism does not account for interest formation in general, much less domestic interests. This lack of two-level analysis limits the scope of neoliberal theory and results in a more superficial analysis of US opposition. Therefore, a full understanding of American opposition to the Rome Statute requires the initiation of additional analytical perspectives.

Conclusion

This chapter has clearly shown that neoliberal institutionalism provides scholars with an elementary understanding of the Rome Statute formation process. This analytical perspective shows us that cooperation occurs because of a mutuality of interests among states and the selfish desire by these states to achieve these interests. This perspective goes on to describe how states understand that cooperation, as opposed to unilateral action, is the best way to achieve their goals.

---

[58] David Scheffer, "The US and the ICC," sees this threat primarily in the form of foreign states being able to bring US soldiers to trial at the ICC.

[59] Keohane, "Institutional Theory," 294, acknowledges the advantages of an analysis using Robert Putnam's two-level game, "Diplomacy and Domestic Politics: The Logic of Two-Level Games," but does not go so far as to incorporate it fully into neoliberal theory. Neoliberalism remains primarily a systemic analysis of international relations.

Moreover, in most instances, as long as all participants are achieving absolute gains, relative gains are insignificant. Thus, the theory of neoliberal institutionalism does adequately explain the ICC formation process and upholds the hypothesis that cooperation can occur either after or in lieu of hegemony.

As a result of this conclusion, one can consider neoliberal institutionalism a good starting point for understanding the formation of this institution; however several questions remain. 1) What was the role of NGOs in the formation process? 2) How important was the individual leadership in this process? 3) What are the sources of the interest negotiated in the formation process of the ICC? 4) Why is this institution forming now and not in 1951? 5) Aside from the relative gains problem, why is the US opposed to the Rome Statute?

These are crucial questions that must be addressed if this narrative is going to accomplish its goal of fully understanding the ICC formation process. Neoliberalism does not, indeed cannot, adequately address these issues on its own. Thus, by consulting other analytical perspectives I anticipate that my readers will ascertain a fuller and richer understanding of the formation process and enhance our understanding of the case and its impact on global politics.

Chapter 6

Making Sense of Regime Theory

> The contested state of contemporary International Relations makes it difficult to assess the relationship between its new and enduring theoretical concerns... Uncertainty breeds faddism, concepts come and go, and innovation is difficult to distinguish from variation. The study of international regimes, however, represents more than a transitory interest.
>
> Robert M.A. Crawford[1]

Foundations of Regime Theory

Regime theory has been a part of the international relations landscape for over two decades. This analytical perspective first emerged in the 1970s, but the first major contribution to this perspective came in the 1982 special issue of *International Organization.* In this issue, several esteemed international relations scholars, under the editorial guidance of Stephen Krasner, set out to define the concept of international regimes and assess their impact on global politics. Many scholars in the field scoffed at such an endeavor. They believed that the study of regimes was fruitless and lacking staying power. One of those critics, Susan Strange, characterized the study of international regimes in the following manner: "the study of regimes is, for the most part a fad, one of those shifts of fashion not too difficult to explain as a temporary reaction to events in the real world but in itself making little in the way of long-term contribution to knowledge."[2]

It is now over twenty years later and regime theory has not vanished from the pages of global politics scholarship. In fact, one could assert that over the past decade or so regime theory has enjoyed a sort of renaissance in the literature.[3] The current scholarly interest in both inter-governmental organizations and the idea of global governance has rejuvenated the field's interest in regimes. Thus, regime

---

[1] Robert M.A. Crawford, *Regime Theory in the Post-Cold War World: Rethinking Neoliberal Approaches to International Relations* (Brookfield, VT: Dartmouth Publishing Company, 1996), 2.

[2] Susan Strange, "*Cave! Hic Dragones:* A Critique of Regime Analysis," in *International Regimes,* ed. Stephen D. Krasner (Ithaca, NY: Cornell University Press, 1983), 337.

[3] A few examples of this renaissance are: Hasenclever, Mayer and Rittberger, *Theories of International Regimes;* Stokke, "Regimes as Governance Systems"; Oran R. Young, *Governance in World Affairs* (Ithaca, NY: Cornell University Press, 1999); Andrew Moravcsik, "the Origins of Human Rights Regimes: Democratic Delegations in Postwar Europe," *International Organization* 54 (2000): 217-252.

theory, contrary to Strange's assessment, continues to play an important role in international relations scholarship.

Robert Crawford's assessment of this analytical perspective, cited at the outset of this chapter, seems to hold the truth—regime theory is not a fad or some transitory interest; instead, it is an analytical perspective that can assist international relations scholars in their endeavor to better understand global politics. For the purpose of this text, regime theory may prove specifically useful in understanding the formation of the International Criminal Court and the evolving regime that is constituted by the success at and beyond the Rome Conference.

In order to understand how this analytical perspective is useful to an analysis of the ICC, we must first understand the construct of the perspective itself. This endeavor will not be an easy one. The primary problem is that regime theory is not a parsimonious theory. It has many different schools of thought and models of interpretation. The goal of this chapter is to examine these divergent schools of thought in an attempt to discover which one will best assist in this analysis of the ICC. However, prior to embarking on this quest, it is necessary to first define "international regimes" as a concept.

Avoiding Imprecision

Much like the non-parsimonious nature of the theory itself, a coherent definition of international regimes tends to elude international relations scholars.[4] Since the 1970s, international relations scholars have proposed several definitions of regimes. Keohane and Nye defined regimes as, "sets of governing arrangements that effect relationships of interdependence."[5] Oran Young defined them as, "recognized patterns of practice around which expectations converge…regimes are social structures."[6] In his more recent work, John Gerard Ruggie defined regimes as, "a set of mutual expectations, rules and regulations, organizational plans, energies, and financial commitments that have been accepted by a group of states."[7] Nevertheless, Stephen Krasner's 1982 definition captured the field's attention and remains the most widely accepted definition of this concept. Krasner defines international regimes as, "sets of implicit or explicit principles, norms,

---

4 Hasenclever, Mayer, and Rittberger, *Theories of International Regimes,* 8-14, exemplify this statement best by discussing the positive attributes of both a complex and a lean definition of international regimes.

5 Keohane and Nye, *Power and Interdependence,* 19.

6 Oran Young, "International Regimes: Problems of Concept Formation," *World Politics* 32 (1980): 332.

7 John Gerard Ruggie, *Constructing the World Polity: Essays on International Institutionalization* (New York: Routledge, 1998), 56.

rules, and decision-making procedures around which actors' expectations converge in a given area of international relations.[8]

He goes on to clarify this definition in the following manner: "Principles are beliefs of fact, causation, and rectitude. Norms are standards of behavior defined in terms of rights and obligations. Rules are specific prescriptions or proscriptions for action. Decision-making procedures are prevailing practices for making and implementing collective choices."[9]

As stated above, over the past twenty plus years, Krasner's description of regimes has emerged as the definition of choice for international relations scholars. Critiques of this definition surfaced, but to date, no one has been able to espouse a more preferable understanding of this concept.[10] Krasner's formulation of what an international regime is remains a constant. The question that remains is how to employ this definition in an attempt to understand the formation of an International Criminal Court? More specifically, should we consider the Rome Statute and the resulting institution an international regime?

Regimes versus Organizations

This question confronts the issue of whether a regime is simply another term for an international organization. According to Krasner's definition, a regime is "a set of norms, principles, rules, and decision-making procedures." No where in this definition does the premise of institutionalization appear. Formality, to some extent, exists in the process of establishing rules and decision-making procedures, but we should not mistake this for an international organization. An international regime can exist without the presence of an international organization (although it may eventually become embodied in an international organization). This is due to the fact that international regimes do not always possess the capacity to act on the norms and principles that form them. International organizations, on the other hand, can.[11] International organizations have the ability to respond to world events because of the formal institutionalization that exists within these entities. Thus, one can think of regimes as the underlying foundation of many international organizations, but they are not co-constitutive terms.

As a result, it is accurate to think of the formation of the Rome Statute as both a regime and a precursor to the formation of the more formal institution of the ICC. During the Rome Conference a group of actors converged around a set of

---

8 Stephen D. Krasner, "Structural Causes and Regime Consequences: Regimes as Intervening Variables," in *International Regimes,* ed. Stephen D. Krasner (Ithaca, NY: Cornell University Press, 1983), 2.

9 Krasner, "Structural Causes, Regime Consequences," 2.

10 Oran R. Young, "International Regimes: Toward a New Theory of Institutions," *World Politics* 39 (1986): 104-122, provides one of the more scathing critiques of Krasner's definition.

11 Hasenclever, Mayer and Rittberger, *Theories of International Regimes,* 10-11.

principles, norms, rules, and decision-making procedures within the issue-area of international humanitarian law. Was the construction of an international organization the result of the Conference? Yes, and that is why we can view the formation of the ICC as an excellent example of the regime formation process and the multiple steps that are necessary for a regime to become a formal institution. However, institutionalization is not a necessary evolution if one is to define the ICC as a regime. The Rome Statute can stand on its own as an international regime—institutionalization only strengthens its categorization.

Throughout the PrepCom meetings and the five-week Rome Conference, the international community converged around a set of principles, norms and rules. On the final day of the Conference, one hundred and twenty nations voted to explicitly support these principles. At this point a regime formed in the issue-area of humanitarian law. In many ways this regime is simply a more complex regime than several previous ones. The Hague Conferences, the Genocide Convention, and the Geneva Conventions, according to Krasner's definition, are all international regimes; however, they were more simplistic regimes with little capacity to act.[12] The international community's acceptance of the Rome Statute bundled these previous regimes into a more encompassing and formalized regime. What is important to remember is that according to the accepted definition of a regime, it does not have to be an international organization, despite the fact that in most issue-areas that is the ultimate goal. Therefore, the Rome Statute constitutes both a regime and an international organization.

Divergent Theories

With a working definition of international regimes in place, this narrative must now turn to a discussion of the regime formation process. The literature on regime formation lacks a central theoretical perspective. Instead of convergence around one explanatory perspective concerning regime formation, this literature reflects at least three different perspectives.[13] The three most influential of these competing perspectives are interest-based theories, power-based theories, and knowledge-based theories. All of these perspectives, or schools of thought, reflect a certain understanding of why and how regime formation occurs. They differ not only in

---

[12] Within the literature on environmental regimes, many conventions and treaties are termed regimes. Oran R. Young, "Rights, Rules and Resources in World Affairs," in *Global Governance: Drawing Insights from the Environmental Experience,* ed. Oran R. Young (Cambridge, MA: The MIT Press, 1997), 1-23, cites the 1979 Convention on Long-Range Transboundary Air Pollution and the 1985 Vienna Convention on the ozone, as typical environmental regimes. Neither of these is a formal international organization.

[13] Hasenclever, Mayer and Rittberger, *Theories of International Regimes,* discuss three perspectives with multiple subinterpretations. Young and Osherenko, "Testing Theories," examine four competing perspectives. Krasner, "Structural Causes, Regime Consequences," discusses five different causal variables of regime formation.

the central variable of their analysis, but also in regards to the ontological foundation of their perspective. In other words, these schools of thought employ different causal effects to explain three different understandings of the nature of international relations. In many ways, my discussion of international regimes reflects the field's meta-theoretical debates. The fundamental manner in which it differs is the fact that this discussion emphasizes the formation, resiliency, and effectiveness of regimes, instead of grand theory.

Along with this diversity in regime theory, there is also diversity within the three schools of thought. If you analyze them closely, one can see that the three perspectives each have several competing sub-interpretations. In an attempt to assess the relevance of these perspectives to the ICC case, I will center my discussion on the primary interpretation within each school of thought and limit my discussion of the sub-interpretations. This will allow me to compare and contrast these perspectives in a broad fashion, without losing sight of the ultimate goal—a better understanding of the ICC formation process. I begin with the power-based perspective and its emphasis on hegemony in regime formation.

Power-Based Theories

Power-based theories of regime formation are closely related to the realist/neorealist paradigm. This perspective on regimes emphasizes the relative power of self-interested states and the impact that cooperative behavior has on this power distribution. Although realists generally argue that inter-state cooperation is limited, the power-based regime theorists acknowledge the existence of regimes while remaining true to the realist assumption that power is the central variable in world politics.

Power-based or realist perspectives on international regimes focus on six guiding principles.[14] The first is that nation-states are the central actors in international politics. Second, power-based theories emphasize relative power capabilities within the cooperation process. States are not simply interested in absolute gains, but also take into account the relative capabilities of other actors within this process. Therefore, international regimes reflect the distribution and power within the international community. Third and closely related to the previous principle, states are sensitive to relative gains accrued, or possibly accrued, in a cooperative situation. A state will not take part in the regime formation process unless the relative gains accrued by that state are positive. Fourth, power-based theories are predicated on a rational modeling scheme. States

---

[14] Krasner, "Structural Causes, Regime Consequences," 11-17, Young, "International Regimes: Toward a New Theory of Institutions," 108-115, and Hasenclever, Mayer and Rittberger, *Theories of International Regimes,* 83-135, all discuss these six principles of power-based theories of regimes.

are viewed as rational actors who undertake a cost/benefit analysis, primarily focused on relative gains, prior to partaking in a cooperative endeavor. Fifth, envy of other state's power capabilities plays a major role in state action. Finally, power-based theories are pessimistic about international cooperation. This does not mean that they discount the possibility of cooperation altogether, but they are doubtful about the prospects for regime formation.

Power-based regime theory, although predicated on these core principles, has several sub-interpretations. These interpretations all embody the main hypotheses of power-based theory, but they emphasize different aspects of the theory. I will briefly discuss three of these interpretations.

Hegemonic Stability Theory

The first and most widely recognized sub-interpretation is the theory of hegemonic stability. This theory is one of the primary components of realism/neorealism and has found a useful niche within the regime theory literature. In general, this theory believes that regime formation, effectiveness, and resiliency are predicated on the presence and willful action of a hegemon.[15] Without the presence of a hegemon, at least within a specific issue-area, the formation and establishment of a regime is impossible.

This theory emerged from the work of economist Charles Kindleberger and was later applied to international relations, albeit in a broader manner, by Robert Gilpin.[16] The main hypothesis behind the original formulation of hegemonic stability theory is that only with the presence of an economic and political power can the global community achieve stability. If the hegemon acts as a unilateral, responsible leader, then the whole of the international community benefits because of the stability (which is viewed as a public good) that ensues.[17] One problem with Kindleberger's model is the issue of free riders. As Duncan Snidal points out, within a system predicated on hegemonic stability theory there is a tendency for smaller states to exploit the power of the larger states.[18] The hegemon's providing of the public good allows the smaller states to simply partake of the benefits without any cost to them.

---

15 Young and Osherenko, "Testing Theories," 248, define hegemon as "an actor possessing a preponderance of material resources."

16 Charles P. Kindleberger, "Hierarchy versus Inertial Cooperation," *International Organization* 40 (1986): 841-847. Robert Gilpin, *War and Change in World Politics* (Cambridge: Cambridge University Press, 1981), discusses his theory of hegemonic stability theory.

17 Charles P. Kindleberger, "Dominance and Leadership in International Economy," 242-254; and Charles P. Kindleberger, "Hierarchy and Inertial Cooperation," *International Organization* 40 (1986): 841-847.

18 Duncan Snidal, "The Limits of Hegemonic Stability Theory," *International Organization* 39 (1985): 579-614.

This critique gave rise to what Snidal calls a coercive leadership model.[19] The work of Robert Gilpin clearly embodies this model. According to Gilpin, the hegemon does provide for the public good, that is stability, but the hegemon does not provide this service free of charge.[20] Instead, the hegemon uses their superior power to prevent free riders from existing and to force smaller actors to contribute to the public good. In this alternative variant, the hegemon provides for the public good, but this source of stability comes at a cost to those who partake in it.

The obvious question is how does this theory apply to regime formation? The theory of hegemonic stability, when applied to regime theory, asserts two fundamental principles. One, a regime cannot form unless a hegemon is both present within the issue-area, and willing to establish a regime for that issue-area. Any attempt to establish a regime without the participation and leadership of the hegemon will result in failure. Two, if an international regime is established, it becomes imperative that the hegemon maintain its position of power and use that power in a capacity that benefits the regime. If power becomes more equally distributed amongst the members of the international community, the regime falters and collapses.[21] In other words, according to the hegemonic stability theory, the presence of a hegemon is necessary for formation, effectiveness, and resiliency of an international regime.

Power-Oriented Approach

Hegemonic stability theory is not the only interpretation of a power-based analysis of regimes. Stephen Krasner defines another position in his work on regimes.[22] Krasner's position, a power-oriented approach, deals directly with the formation process of regimes.[23] Unlike the hegemonic stability literature, which came to the issue of regimes via economics, Krasner confronts the concept of international regimes head on. According to Krasner, regimes form not as a result of coordinated efforts to solve problems of market-failure, but as a result of the distribution of national power capabilities.[24] In other words, regime formation is the direct result of the exercise of state power and occurs because powerful states wish to secure a larger portion of the gains, not facilitate cooperation.

---

19 Snidal, "Limits of Hegemonic Stability Theory," 582.

20 Gilpin, *War and Change,* 10-11.

21 Keohane, *After Hegemony,* 31-39 summarizes and critiques this theory.

22 Stephen Krasner, "Global Communications and National Power: Life on the Pareto Frontier," in *Neorealism and Neoliberalism: The Contemporary Debate,* ed. David A. Baldwin (New York: Columbia University Press, 1993), 234-249; and Krasner, "Sovereignty, Regimes and Human Rights."

23 Hasenclever, Mayer and Rittberger use the term "power-oriented approach" in *Theories of International Regimes,* 84, however its original point of origin is Krasner, "Global Communications, National Power," 243.

24 Krasner, "Global Communications, National Power," 235.

Krasner concurs with realist theory that relative power is the defining component of state action. The primary goal of states is to acquire a larger degree of benefits then the other actors in the system. Actors who feel that such action results in a favorable distribution of benefits (favorable to themselves) undertake regime formation. The way in which a state assures itself of relative gains is by employing the use of state power. Krasner espouses the idea that state power is manifest in at least three forms.

1. Power may be used to determine who can play the game in the first place.
2. Power may be used to dictate rules of the game—for instance, which gets to move first.
3. Power may be used to change the payoff matrix.[25]

Thus, the formation of regimes, although initiated as a way to establish stability, is a direct result of state power and interest. Krasner empirically details his power-oriented approach in the issue-areas of global communications and human rights. What Krasner concludes in both instances, is that regimes formed in order to maximize relative gains, not to facilitate cooperation and deal with problems of market-failure. Therefore, Krasner views power as a means of statecraft, which allows dominant actors to increase relative gains. But it is important to note that the power-oriented approach, although more directly related to the study of regimes than hegemonic stability theory, does not view regime formation with a high degree of optimism. Krasner is still a realist and as a result, he views any type of regime formation and resiliency with a large degree of skepticism.

Modern Realism

Joseph Grieco's modern realism is the final interpretation of power-based theory.[26] Grieco centers his analysis of regime formation on a critique of neoliberal institutionalism.[27] Modern realism, although in agreement with neoliberalism in many ways, chastises this theory for its emphasis on the rational egoist motives of nation-states.[28] According to Grieco, states are not rational egoists because when calculating the costs and benefits of cooperation, states do not simply account for their own gains. The primary concern for states is relative gains and their power position within the international system. So according to modern realism, the

---

25 Krasner, "Global Communications, National Power," 238.

26 Grieco, "Anarchy, Limits of Cooperation," and Grieco, "Understanding the Problem," serves as the foundational work of this theory.

27 See chapter four for an extensive discussion of this theoretical perspective.

28 Grieco, "Anarchy, Limits of Cooperation," 125-131.

maximization of absolute power is not a state's main concern; instead their main concern is their relative position of power within the system.[29]

Clearly modern realism shares many qualities with Krasner's power-oriented approach. States are the primary actors, relative gains are more important than absolute ones, and distributional issues are crucial. However, despite the similarities to Krasner's power-oriented perspective, modern realism and the power-oriented approach differ in one fundamental way—their understanding of outcomes. For Krasner, power is a means to a particular outcome. That is, states exercise their power in an attempt to benefit their situation. For Grieco, power is an end in itself. Modern realism views a state's relative power position as the end point that determines state action. If regime formation and international cooperation occur, it is the result of a balanced distribution of gains among the actors involved. This is because modern realists consider states to be "defensive positionalists" whose primary concern is with maintaining their relative power position in the self-help international system.[30] This makes any form of international cooperation extremely difficult and results in modern realism being even more pessimistic about regime formation then any of the other power-based theories.

Evaluation and Power-Based Theories

The use of power-based theories of regime formation, although helpful in some limited ways, does not benefit an analysis of the ICC on a grand scale. There are several problems that arise if one employs a power-based theory alone. The first is the lack of non-state actor analysis. According to all interpretations of power-based theory, states are the primary actors and the construction of international institutions rests solely on their actions. The process through which the international community formed the Rome Statute clearly does not accord with such a viewpoint. States may have been the final signatories and ratifying actors, but this does not account for the multiple non-state actors that contributed significantly to the formation process. The role of the CICC, along with the Conference's individual leadership, was both crucial components of the formation process. A power-based perspective simply would not account for these actors.

Second, the theory of hegemonic stability and Krasner's power-oriented approach both emphasize the necessity of hegemonic leadership in the formation process. According to this theory, without the presence of a hegemon international cooperation is not a plausible option. But as I described in chapter five, the one state that most scholars view as the hegemon, the United States, chose to vote against the Rome Statute. Despite this lack of hegemonic support, the Rome

---

[29] Waltz, *Theory of International Politics,* 126, and Grieco, "Anarchy, Limits of Cooperation," 127.

[30] Grieco, "Understanding the Problem of International Cooperation," 303.

Statute received a resounding affirmation both at and beyond the Rome Conference; and it is now a functioning international organization. This type of overwhelming global support, despite the lack of hegemonic leadership, does not uphold a power-based theory of the ICC.

Finally, the emphasis that both Grieco and Krasner place on relative gains fails to adequately capture the nature of the Rome negotiations. If major world powers, such as Germany, France, and the United Kingdom, were so concerned with relative gains, they probably would not have signed the Rome Statute. This Statute does not provide these states with an increase in relative power. If anything, it limits the power of all state parties because it limits the national sovereignty of these countries.[31] The one accurate prediction that a power-based theory provides us with concerns the lack of US support. It would appear as if the US is concerned with relative power losses and this is one of the primary reasons for their rejection of the Rome Statute.[32]

From this brief analysis of power-based theories, one can conclude that the use of this theoretical perspective would not provide us with an adequate understanding of the Rome Statute formation process. All of the interpretations that fall under the power-based rubric lack some essential analytical tool. Thus, they fail to account for or anticipate events, making it necessary that this analysis employ different models of regime formation. Without a broadening of our theoretical tool box, one cannot gain a full understanding of this institution and its formation process.

Interest-Based

The second perspective that I will discuss is the interest-based perspective. Scholars generally consider this school of thought to be the mainstream theory on regime formation.[33] As stated earlier, in many ways the competing regime theories parallel the meta-theoretical debates in international relations. Interest-based theory is generally equated with neoliberal institutionalism and the work of Robert Keohane, although alternative interpretations exist. Chapter four of this text discusses this theoretical model extensively; therefore, at this point I will briefly reiterate some of the main points of this theory and then discuss some of the alternative models of interest-based theory.

---

[31] Leonard, "Discovering the New Face of Sovereignty."

[32] It is important to remember that the US position is not anti-ICC, but anti-Rome Statute. This is due mainly to the fact that the Rome Statute remains outside of US veto power. Thus, the US cannot control the action taken by the ICC (as it is formulated within the Rome Statute), creating a situation of relative power loss for the US.

[33] Hasenclever, Mayer and Rittberger, *Theories of International Regimes,* 4 and 23.

Neoliberal Institutionalism or Functional Theory

Scholars generally equate neoliberal institutionalism with the work of Robert Keohane.[34] In his work on regime formation, Keohane hypothesizes that cooperation may occur if states share a common interest and these states believe that the only means to achieve their common goal is through cooperation. If these states, acting in a rational egoist mode, deduce that cooperation will benefit them, then cooperation will occur. This cooperation can occur absent of a hegemon and can result in gains by all participants. This is not to say that hegemonic leadership would not assist in regime formation or that relative gains do not matter. On the contrary, Keohane acknowledges the fact that hegemony can assist in the initiation of international cooperation and the persistence of regimes, but according to neoliberal institutionalism, it is not a necessary component of cooperation.[35] Keohane also acknowledges that relative gains matter to states, but he does not believe that they will act as a deterrent to cooperation. As long as all of the actors involved are accruing absolute gains and one state is not using its relative gains against another state, then cooperation is possible despite an inequity in gains.[36] Thus, "any claims being made about the impact of relative gains are highly conditional."[37]

States form international regimes as a way to facilitate international cooperation.[38] In other words, neoliberal institutionalism views the formation of international regimes as a vehicle for furthering cooperation among nation-states. They achieve this by supplying states with information and reducing uncertainty about outcomes, while allowing states to achieve their exogenously defined self-interests.[39] Thus, by forming an international regime, states have the ability to reduce costs and improve the benefits, or absolute gains, of the participants. Nevertheless, this does not mean that international cooperation between states is easily achieved. Keohane understands that regime formation is a difficult process because of the fact that state's interests are not harmonious. However, the prospect of a regime alters the incentive for cooperation, making the desire to cooperate more palatable to many states. In many ways Keohane's interest-based theory of regimes borrows quite a bit from the power-based realist models, but the prospect for regime formation is much greater in his functional model.

---

[34] The primary works of neoliberal institutionalism, as it pertains to regime formation, are: Keohane, *After Hegemony;* Axelrod and Keohane, "Achieving Cooperation"; and Keohane, "Institutional Theory, Realist Challenge."

[35] Keohane, *After Hegemony,* 50-51.

[36] Keohane, "Institutionalist Theory, Realist Challenge," 274-278.

[37] Keohane, "Institutionalist Theory, Realist Challenge," 277.

[38] Keohane, *After Hegemony,* 49-64.

[39] Keohane, *After Hegemony,* 97.

Problem-Structural Approach[40]

The University of Tubingen in Germany serves as the origin of the problem-structural approach of regime formation.[41] The underlying assumption of this approach is that if one wants to understand the formation of international regimes, then a closer analysis of the specific issue-area in question is necessary.[42] The problem-structural approach considers the specifics of a particular issue-area to be one of the major components of regime formation. Therefore, the problem-structural approach advocates beginning any analysis of regime formation with a detailed analysis of issue-areas—not the specifics of different issue-areas but the specifics of the concept "issue-area."

Efinger and Zurn, building on Keohane's 1984 definition[43], define an issue-area as: "consist[ing] of one or more, in the perception of the actors inseparably connected objects of contention and of the behavior directed to them. The boundaries of issue-areas are determined by the perception of the participating actors."[44]

According to the problem-structural approach, the characteristics of certain issue-areas determine how or whether cooperation can occur. Unlike Keohane's functional theory, which emphasized the common interests among states, problem-structural theory centers on the conflictual nature of global politics. The study of regime formation is a study of conflict management, which is the primary goal of international regimes, and the type of issue-areas that are most "regime conducive."[45] The result of this research is a conflict typology that distinguishes between consensual and dissensual conflicts.[46]

---

[40] Due to the fact that a large content of this theories literature is written in German, this section relies heavily on the summary by Hasenclever, Mayer and Rittberger, *Theories of International Regimes,* 59-68, and Rittberger, "Research on International Regimes in Germany," 13-16.

[41] Some of the primary advocates of this approach are: Manfred Efinger and Michael Zurn, "Explaining Conflict Management in East-West Relations: A Quantitative Test of Problem-Structural Typologies," in *International Regimes in East-West Politics,* ed. Volker Rittberger (London: Pinter, 1990), 64-89; Volker Rittberger, "Research on International Regimes in Germany: The Adaptive Internationalization of an American Social Science Concept," in *Regime Theory and International Relations,* ed. Volker Rittberger (Oxford: Oxford University Press, 1993), 3-22.

[42] Hasenclever, Mayer and Rittberger, *Theories of International Regimes,* 59-60.

[43] Keohane, *After Hegemony,* 61.

[44] Efinger and Zurn, "Explaining Conflict Management," 68.

[45] Rittberger, "Research on International Regimes in Germany," 14.

[46] Rittberger, "Research on International Regimes in Germany," 14-16, and Hasenclever, Mayer and Rittberger, *Theories of International Regimes,* 62-65, provide further explanation on the conflict typology.

Dissensual conflicts are those conflicts in which actors disagree on what is collectively desirable. These conflicts could be conflicts about means (actors share a common goal but disagree on how to achieve it), or conflicts about values (actors do not share common beliefs concerning the legitimacy of a possible cooperative action).[47] Due to the fact that conflicts about values leave little room for negotiation and compromise, problem-structuralists believe that the possibility of regime formation in these situations is limited; whereas, in conflicts about means there is an opportunity for actors to compromise.

Consensual conflicts are those conflicts in which "actors are confronted with a situation of scarcity in which every actor desires the same valued object but cannot be satisfied fully because there is not enough for everybody."[48] Two types of consensual conflict are conflict of interests about relatively assessed goods and conflict of interest about absolutely assessed goods. Due to the fact that relatively assessed goods (those goods whose value is not independent of other actor's goods) promote greater competition amongst actors, the promotion of conflict management is low. However, conflicts of absolutely assessed goods hold a very high propensity for regime formation because of the independent nature of each actor's goods.

The conclusion that problem-structuralists draw from this research is that there is a "considerable amount of variation in the outcome of interstate interactions."[49] Without accounting for the different forms of conflict that are endemic to certain issue-areas, no complete understanding of regime formation is possible. Therefore, although interest-based in its orientation, the problem-structural theory is attempting to initiate a more complex model for understanding cooperation, or more appropriately conflict management.

Evaluating the ICC with Interest-Based Theories

As I discussed at the end of chapter five, interest-based theories are not sufficient for understanding the formation of the ICC. Both Keohane's functionalist approach and the German school of regime formation fail to adequately account for at least two important factors. The first, which accords with power-based theories, is the fact that an interest-based analysis is state-centered. If an analysis of the ICC were to be undertaken using an interest-based theory, the primary focus would be on nation-states. Although states are important actors in the negotiation process, they were certainly not the only influential actors. Some of the participants at the Rome Conference have stated that without the assistance of NGOs, epistemic communities, and individual leadership, the Rome Statute would

---

47 Rittberger, "Research on Regimes in Germany," 14-15, and Hasenclever, Mayer, and Rittberger, *Theories of International Regimes,* 63.

48 Rittberger, "Research on Regimes in Germany," 14.

49 Rittberger, "Research on International Regimes in Germany," 16.

never have come to fruition. Therefore, the interest-based emphasis on state actors leaves scholars lacking in understanding.

The second factor that interest-based theories lack is an adequate understanding of interest formation. In particular, neoliberal institutionalism simply accepts state's interests, which guide the actions of the states, as exogenously given. There is no attempt by the interest-based theorists to understand how the interests were formed. A discussion concerning the cognitive aspect of regime formation is left aside as this theory simply accepts state's interests as given.[50] This type of analysis, although simplistic and probably more cogent then other theories, fails to truly understand why state's engage in cooperative efforts. There is a necessity to understand how interests form, because it is these common interests that move actors toward cooperation and regime formation.[51] As a result, I would conclude that interest-based theories are too simplistic and therefore, they fail to obtain a comprehensive understanding of a very complex process.

Knowledge-Based Theories

The final school of thought that I will analyze is the knowledge-based or cognitive theory of regime formation. This theoretical perspective differs drastically from the previous two in that cognitivists believe that an analysis of regime formation must question the origin of interests.[52] According to cognitivist theory, the central component of any analysis of regime formation is the ideas and knowledge that shape interests. Interests are the "expression of the actors' values."[53] Thus, cognitivist theory asserts an intersubjective ontology; one that they premise on

---

50 Some scholars, most notably Hasenclever, Mayer and Rittberger, "Theories of International Regimes," 68-82, would include the work of Oran Young in the interest-based school. But I would argue that the pronounced emphasis that Young places on cognitive aspects of regime formation place him in a category all his own. Young proposes a much more multivariate model then the three discussed in this chapter and it is his model that I will discuss in the next chapter.

51 Effinger and Zurn, "Explaining Conflict Management," 68, do acknowledge the importance of perceptions. However, the origin of these perceptions are never fully pursued, thus placing them in a category much like Keohane's exogenously given interests.

52 Interest-based theories in particular explain regime formation by understanding exogenously given interests, where as knowledge-based theories with attempt to understand the formation of interests. Hasenclever, Mayer and Rittberger, *Theories of International Regimes,* 136-139, explain the theoretical foundations of a cognitivist approach.

53 Ernst B. Haas, *When Knowledge is Power: Three Models of Change in International Organizations* (Berkeley, CA: University of California Press, 1990), 2.

interpretation and preference.[54] This type of analysis takes to task both power-based and interest-based theories over issues of rationality and actor involvement.

As will become apparent, this type of regime analysis is the most divergent from traditional meta-theories of international relations. In many ways this theory encompasses the literature of the critical theorist and the post-internationalist movement. The main authors of the knowledge-based perspective are: Robert Cox, Thomas Franck, Ernst and Peter Haas, Friedrich Kratochwil, John Gerard Ruggie, and Alexander Wendt. But as with the earlier schools of thought, a knowledge-based approach is also subject to multiple interpretations. In this case there are two distinct interpretations: weak cognitivists and strong cognitivists.[55] The primary difference between these two perspectives is the distance that they place between themselves and the other two theories of regime formation. Weak cognitivists act almost as a supplement to interest-based regime theory, while strong cognitivists vehemently oppose all previous conceptions of regime formation.

Weak Cognitivism

Weak cognitivism, as Adler and Haas put it:

> Begin[s] where neoliberal institutional approaches leave off; namely we relate institutions to the dynamic interaction between domestic and international political games, and we describe these games not only in terms of material interests but also as part of the bargaining and negotiation that take place among different epistemic understandings and practices "carried" by epistemic communities and later by policymakers as well.[56]

In many ways this approach is a supplement to neoliberalism, but the primary difference resides in the emphasis that they place on ideas. According to weak

---

54 "Constructivism" serves as the ontological underpinnings of knowledge-based theory, but readers should note that constructivism is not a theory it is an ontology. It analyzes the nature of things and how they are related, while leaving the epistemological theorization to the philosophers. According to constructivism, the world is what we make of it; everything is socially constructed and this construction is done primarily through language and the establishment of rules. What cognitivists are analyzing is the social construction of these rules, or regimes. Vendulka Kubalkova, Nicholas Onuf and Paul Kowert, ed. *International Relations in a Constructed World* (Armonk, NY: M.E. Sharpe Press, 1998), provide an excellent description of constructivism. For a constructivist account of the ICC, see Leonard, "Discovering the New Face of Sovereignty."

55 Hasenclever, Mayer and Rittberger, *Theories of International Regimes,* 136-210, serve as the origin of this terminology.

56 Emanuel Adler and Peter M. Haas, "Conclusion: Epistemic Communities, World Order, and the Creation of a Reflective Research Program," *International Organization* 47 (1992): 369.

cognitivists, it is ideas (often ascertained from epistemic communities) that shape actors' interests. Interests are not exogenously given; therefore, there is a need to move beyond Keohane's contractualist model.

In order to understand the weak cognitivism position, one must look at the three core assumptions of this approach.[57] First, the weak cognitivist approach centers on the role of interpretation. According to this perspective, prior to the formation of an international regime, actors must assess the situation and determine what they consider the proper action. This assessment is an interpretive endeavor that is not necessarily predicated on some objective form of exogenously given interests. This interpretation is an intersubjective exercise that depends on the information available to the actors involved. Therefore, the knowledge available to actors is crucial to the regime formation process, because it helps to shape their interests and diminish uncertainty.

The second and closely related assumption of weak cognitivism is that decision-makers tend to rely more and more on the information they obtain from epistemic communities. Weak cognitivists do not see contemporary international actors as isolated decision-making entities. These actors have the opportunity to receive a plethora of information from any number of experts within that issue-area. As a result, these epistemic communities play a major role in regime formation.[58]

Peter Haas defines an epistemic community as "a network of professional experts with recognized expertise and competence in a particular domain and an authoritative claim to policy-relevant knowledge within that domain or issue-area."[59] These communities share a set of normative beliefs, shared notions of validity, and a common policy agenda. Their role in the regime formation process is to provide information to the decision-makers in an attempt to avoid uncertainty. Their impact, from a weak cognitivist perspective, is that this dissemination of information helps to shape actors' interest. Epistemic communities provide actors with the information that they (international actors) must then interpret and use in the bargaining process. Weak cognitivists assume that this reduction in uncertainty will lead to greater cooperation. Therefore, one could deduce that without epistemic communities the possibility of international cooperation would decrease dramatically.[60]

---

57 Hasenclever, Mayer and Rittberger, *Theories of International Regimes,* 140-142, supply us with an excellent summary of the weak cognitivist's ideas. Ernst Haas, *When Knowledge is Power;* Adler and P. Haas, "Conclusions: Epistemic Communities"; and Peter M. Haas, "Introduction: Epistemic Communities and International Policy," *International Organization* 46 (1992): 1-35, serve as the origination of most of these assumptions.

58 P. Haas, "Introduction: Epistemic Communities," 2-3.

59 P. Haas, "Introduction: Epistemic Communities," 3.

60 Adler and P. Haas, "Conclusion: Epistemic Communities," 388-390. But it is important to note that not all weak cognitivists share this idea. Young, *Governance in World Affairs,* 65-66, asserts that some types of uncertainty often lead to cooperation. It is the thickening

The primary method of achieving this increased cooperation is through "learning." The third assumption of the weak cognitivists' position, which states that in order to achieve regime formation there must be some level of intersubjectively shared meanings among the actors, embodies this process. This base level of agreement may simply be a mutual understanding of the problem and how it relates to global affairs.[61] However, it is essential that this consensual knowledge exist because this is the basis for learning and policy coordination.

As Peter Haas describes it, "governments and organizations may be said to learn through the evolution of consensual knowledge."[62] If this evolution of consensual knowledge leads to behavior changes by international actors, then learning has occurred. Governments and organizations must build upon the consensual base that Haas cites as crucial to policy coordination, so that when learning occurs the possibility of cooperation among international actors is greatly increased.[63]

In analyzing the primary attributes of a weak cognitivist position, one can see the close interrelationship of the aforementioned assumptions—interpretation, use of expert knowledge, and the need for intersubjectively shared meanings all feed off of one another. Nevertheless, it is apparent that each of these assumptions necessitates the functioning of epistemic communities. According to the weak cognitivist position, actors' interests, shared meanings, and learning processes all rely on the expert information that epistemic communities provide. Without a proper analysis of these communities no real understanding of regime formation is possible. These types of analyses would only account for the actions of actors with exogenously given interests or interests imposed by a hegemon. Thus, the previous forms of regime theory would not account for learning and non-state actors, and this is the major contribution of a weak cognitivist position.

There is another interpretation of cognitivism that declares that a proper analysis of regime formation needs to do more than simply supplement the neoliberal position. Instead of filling in the gaps left by neoliberalism, this group of scholars hopes to completely undermine the neoliberal and realist positions in an attempt to initiate a radically new understanding of regime formation.

---

of the "veil of uncertainty," concerning actors interests and future positions, that often times allows for a successful institutional bargaining process.

[61] P. Haas, "Introduction: Epistemic Communities," 29-30, describes the importance of consensual knowledge to the learning process.

[62] P. Haas, "Introduction: Epistemic Communities," 30.

[63] Note that learning does not always lead to policy coordination. Cooperation is a function of whether actors, in coordination with epistemic communities, see a need for it. P. Haas, "Introduction: Epistemic Communities," 30.

Strong Cognitivists[64]

The strong cognitivist position attacks both the epistemology and ontology of previous theories of regime formation. In general, these scholars question the use of rationalist theorizing concerning international regimes. The formation of international regimes is not a result of rational cost/benefit analysis; therefore, a positivist epistemology of understanding is insufficient.[65] Strong cognitivists view the formation of regimes as part of a social process and believe that an analysis of this type of process necessitates a more normative understanding of the world—one that is predicated on social discourse and rules. John Ruggie and Friedrich Kratochwil speculate on the use of more "interpretive epistemology," such as Ernst Haas' "evolutionary epistemology" or Robert Cox's "historical materialist epistemology."[66] The primary reason for shunning the positivist epistemology of previous theories is the contradiction that exists between rationalism and regime theory ontology.

According to strong cognitivism, the ontology of international regimes is based on intersubjective meanings. If we are to understand regime formation, we must understand the nature of intersubjectivity and, as stated above, positivism cannot do this. Strong cognitivists view the ontology of international regimes as ideational causation or social construction.[67] If international relations scholars employ this type of ontology, the basis for the formation of regimes becomes social ideas that then define actors' interests, and often result in international cooperation. This cooperation, along with regime formation, is simply another component of a socially constructed world. Knowledge is the primary constitutive component of both states and states' interests, which leads strong cognitivists to study the role of states in international society and problematize their existence. Therefore, this perspective views regimes as not only regulative institutions, but also as constitutive ones because they "create a common social world by fixing the

---

[64] The strong cognitivist approach is very complex and has several different interpretations. A summarization of all these interpretations, due to the complex nature of the subject, is beyond the scope of this text. Therefore, I will center on a broad interpretation of strong cognitivism, with a particular emphasis on the work of John Gerard Ruggie. For a complete description of strong cognitivism, see Hasenclever, Mayer and Rittberger, *Theories of International Regimes,* 154-210.

[65] Robert W. Cox, "Towards a Post-Hegemonic Conceptualization of World Order: Reflections on the Relevancy of Ibn Khaldun," in *Governance Without Government: Order and Change in World Politics,"* ed. James N. Rosenau and Ernst-Otto Czempiel (Cambridge: Cambridge University Press, 1992), 135; and Ruggie, *Constructing the World Polity,* 96-97.

[66] Ruggie, *Constructing the World Polity,* 96.

[67] John Gerard Ruggie, "The Social Constructivist Challenge," *International Organization* 52 (1998): 865-869.

meaning of behavior."[68] But they do not consider the relationship between regimes and society as a one-way street. The two entities are actually co-constitutive in that although regimes construct the social world, society also helps to shape and define regimes. Therefore, within a strong cognitivist perspective, states are seen as simply actors within a society that is co-constituted with social institutions.

We can assert that strong cognitivism is simply an expansion of the weak cognitivist perspective. Obviously in the construction of ideas epistemic communities will play a role in the learning process and learning will play a role in the regime formation process. But the primary difference between these two perspectives is the place of knowledge in the international system. For weak cognitivism, knowledge needs to be understood because of its impact on state interests and the formation of these interests. For strong cognitivism, knowledge and ideas need to be understood because they are considered the building blocks of society. Knowledge and the social acceptance of this knowledge constitute both international regimes and states (along with everything else). Thus, as Hasenclever, Mayer and Rittberger explain:

> Strong cognitivists…advocate a sociological turn in the study of international regimes…to reflect their basic insights that knowledge not only affects states' interests but is constitutive of their identities: states as the central actors in international relations do not merely hold a certain stock of knowledge…which influences their choices in specific situations, but they *are* states…only by virtue of a shared knowledge which spans international relations as a social space.[69]

Evaluating the ICC with Knowledge-Based Theories

Knowledge-based theories appear to be the most conducive to an analysis of the ICC. These theories explore the origins of states' interests, the process of learning, and the role of epistemic communities, such as the NGO Coalition for an International Criminal Court (CICC). Such analysis appears to lead to a more fruitful discussion of the Rome Statute's formation process and possibly provides international relations scholars with a better paradigmatic tool for understanding the origins of international regimes.

As the last chapter explained, the formation of the Rome Statute was highly contingent on the role of NGOs and their ability to provide states with knowledge.[70] An observer of these negotiations could argue that the primary reason for the overwhelming success of the Rome Conference was ideational

---

68 Hasenclever, Mayer and Rittberger, *Theories of International Regimes,* 163.

69 Hasenclever, Mayer and Rittberger, *Theories of International Regimes,* 138.

70 William R. Pace and Mark Thieroff, "Participation of Non-Governmental Organizations," in *The International Criminal Court: The Making of the Rome Statute—Issues, Negotiations, Results,* ed. Roy S. Lee (The Hague: Kluwer Law International, 1999), 391-398, discusses the importance of the CICC to the negotiation process.

causation initiated by the CICC. One could also assert that certain states' behavior patterns changed during the negotiations, thus possibly showing the results of a learning process.[71] Most importantly, this perspective allows scholars to go beyond the superficial analysis of neoliberals, which deem interests as exogenously given. Thus, a knowledge-based analysis provides us with a more complex understanding of what occurred prior to, during, and after the Rome Conference. It allows us to address the socially constructed nature of both international norms and states' interests, and the role that epistemic communities played in this process. Thus, with all of the benefits that knowledge-based theory provides scholars, is it reasonable to assert that this theory is the best analytical tool?

Knowledge-based theories of regime formation still suffer from one of the same problems as the other two perspectives—they are exclusionary. In particular, knowledge-based theories center on ideational causation and the role of epistemic communities, thus blocking out other forms of causation, such as hegemonic power, bargaining processes or leadership. An example of how this exclusionary thinking limits a knowledge-based analysis is the case of Russia and its recent signing of the Statute.[72] In this case, a knowledge-based theory attempts to explain the Russian signature as ideational, when in fact it may be the result of a bargaining process that occurred after the Rome Conference. Russia simply wanted greater clarification on the rules of procedure and evidence, and when this occurred during the June 2000 PrepCom meeting, Russia decided to sign. Was this learning or institutional bargaining? I would argue that it was probably more in accordance with Keohane's institutional bargaining theory and not a cognitivist perspective.

Another major factor that is left out of the cognitivist perspective is the role of leadership. For cognitivists, leadership is found within epistemic communities (or transnational advocacy networks) and their expertise on the issue-area. Although this may be a fundamental part of the ICC formation process, it is still necessary to account for individual leadership and the role that it played. Many in attendance at Rome argue that without the individual leadership present at the Conference, the participants would never have approved the Rome Statute.[73] Knowledge-based theories do not account for this aspect of the formation process. Knowledge-based theories, as with the previous two schools of thought, remain exclusionary and as a result, lack a complete understanding of the formation process.

---

71 State behavior changed both during and after the Rome Conference. One example of this learning process is the evolutionary process of countries like Mexico and Russia—from pre-Rome opposition to post-Rome signatories.

72 Russia, although voting in favor of the Statute in Rome, had their reservations about the Statute however, with the clarification on the rules of procedures and evidence, Russia decided to sign the Statute on September 13 2000.

73 Bassiouni, *Statute of the ICC;* Bendetti and Washburn, "Drafting the ICC"; and Lee, "Rome Conference Contributions," both espouse this position.

Conclusion

The primary goal of this chapter was to describe the three primary schools of thought in regime theory. What I discovered was that each perspective contributes to an analysis of the ICC, but each, if taken exclusively, also fails to achieve a full understanding of the regime. As a result, the conclusion that one can derive from this chapter is that no single theory of international regimes is sufficient. They each provide scholars with some crucial piece to the puzzle of understanding, but none can claim prominence over the others. This is especially true in an analysis of the ICC. From the brief analyses undertaken using each theory, I discovered that a knowledge-based theory provided the best understanding of the ICC formation process, but this perspective did not present scholars with a definitive understanding of this regime.

Thus, even though a cognitivist perspective is beneficial to this analysis, it certainly is not complete. This chapter has shown us that regime theory, in its traditional paradigmatic forms, is an insufficient form of analysis. What IR scholars need is a more complete form of analysis that not only includes all of the bivariate explanations of regime formation that this chapter discusses, but also goes further to include other factors. Oran Young and Gail Osherenko proposed such a model in 1992.[74] They termed it a multivariate model of regime formation and it is this model that I employ in the next chapter.

---

[74] Young and Osherenko, "Testing Theories," 238-243.

Conclusion

[illegible] As a result, [illegible] This is particularly [illegible] the best [illegible] signal.

Thus, [illegible] This chapter has shown us that [illegible] and it is this model that I employ in the next chapter.

[illegible]

Chapter 7

Complexity Leads to Understanding

> We are now convinced that it will not do to confine scholarly attention in this field to a search for bivariate relationships governing the process of regime formation. Those who proceed in this manner will not only find that most of their hypotheses are disconfirmed, but they will also fail to develop a clear picture of the complex process of regime formation.
>
> Oran R. Young and Gail Osherenko[1]

Introduction

The preceding chapter discussed the traditional way of approaching regime formation. In that chapter I discussed the three primary schools of thought and briefly analyzed the ICC from these different perspectives. In my final analysis, I discovered that all of these perspectives, as autonomous entities, were clearly insufficient primarily due to their narrow scope. Hasenclever, Mayer and Rittberger also recognized this problem. In their concluding chapter they argue that an "inter-paradigmatic division of labor" is desirable, but they doubt its feasibility.[2]

Despite their reservations, the quest for a sufficient understanding of the ICC formation process must now turn to a more complex understanding of regime formation—an inter-paradigmatic theory that embodies all of the previous hypotheses and allows them the opportunity to interact. There is no need to construct such a model, for it already exists. It is a more complex model then the bivariate models discussed in the last chapter and its employment should assist my project in its attempt to understand the formation of the ICC.

Oran Young and Gail Osherenko refer to the traditional approaches to regime formation as single-factor accounts or bivariate approaches.[3] These types of analysis deal only with one hypothesis for the formation of regimes—either power, interests, or knowledge. The problem is that the formation of the ICC is not explainable or understandable by only one hypothesis. Scholars can only fully explain the formation process, as encapsulated in the PrepCom meetings and the Rome Conference, through the use of a much more complex, inter-paradigmatic model. In short, the need is for a multivariate model of regime formation.

---

1 Young and Osherenko, "Testing Theories," 239.

2 Hasenclever, Mayer and Rittberger, *Theories of International Regimes,* 211-212.

3 Young and Osherenko, "Testing Theories," define both of these terms.

The Multivariate Model of Regime Formation

In the early 1990s, the Institute of Arctic Studies at Dartmouth College, along with funding provided by the Ford Foundation, undertook a study of environmental regime formation. The goal of this project was to test the adequacy of the traditional theories of regime formation.[4] The project analyzed five environmental-based cases, all of which dealt with issues related to the Arctic region. After applying each theory to the different cases, the project's conclusion was that single-factor hypotheses of regime formation are inadequate in their analyses.[5] As Young and Osherenko stated:

> [I]t now seems apparent that regime formation is a complex process that does not lend itself well to analyses that focus on single factors and seek to formulate propositions taking the form of necessary conditions. At this stage in our search for understanding, we need to devote considerable time and energy to what we called substitution effects and interaction effects…[6]

Young and Osherenko did not stop at this conclusion, instead they pressed forward in an attempt to rectify this problem. The result is their multivariate model of regime formation.

The multivariate model of regime formation is much more complex then the schools of thought discussed in the previous chapter. In fact, what Young and Osherenko's model accomplishes is to combine the traditional schools of thought, while adding the cross-cutting factors of leadership and context, to achieve a more plausible model for understanding regime formation. It is, according to Young and Osherenko, the interaction amongst these different variables that provides scholars with the fullest explanation and understanding of regime formation.[7] No longer do we need to direct our attention to one explanatory variable. According to the conclusions of the Arctic regime project, such bivariate analysis only limits our ability to understand the formation process.[8] Thus, the multivariate model provides scholars with a complexity that is nonexistent in the bivariate models and as a result, proves beneficial to this study of the ICC and its formation process.

The model consists of two independent variables: social driving forces and cross-cutting factors. The social driving forces (power, interest and knowledge

---

4 Young and Osherenko, "Testing Theories," 224-228, also added contextual factors to the traditional hypotheses of regime formation and tested them.

5 Young and Osherenko, "Testing Theories," 238-240 and 247-248.

6 Young and Osherenko, "Testing Theories," 247.

7 Young and Osherenko, "Testing Theories," 241-243.

8 The first portion of Young and Osherenko, "Testing Theories," 221-238, discusses the testing of the traditional theories on environmental case studies. The result of this analysis was that none of these traditional theories provide scholars with a definitive understanding of the formation process.

factors) impact the institutional bargaining process in a direct manner. There is no pre-determined proportionality of influence on the bargaining process and the amount of influence that each factor exerts on the process is unique to the regime. The key is that this model demands that its users look at all three factors when analyzing regime formation. No one factor provides an adequate understanding of the bargaining process.

The second independent variable, cross-cutting factors (leadership and context), also impact the institutional bargaining process, but in an indirect manner. These factors act to determine how actors exercise their power and the ability of these actors to use knowledge factors in the process. They often establish and maintain the rules of the bargaining process and they establish the global environment within which negotiations take place. But in the end, these cross-cutting factors of have only an indirect, albeit an important, influence on the regime formation process.

The Complexity of the ICC Negotiations

Chapter five brought to light that the negotiation process surrounding the Rome Statute was a very complex one. It involved multiple actors, with multiple viewpoints, interacting amongst a whole host of contextual factors. That chapter concluded by arguing that neoliberal institutionalism, as an explanatory paradigm, was insufficient in its analysis of the ICC formation process. This theory's attempt to understand how and why the Rome Statute received such overwhelming support was lacking in several areas. The unanswered questions that were left at the end of this analysis serve as a reminder of its inadequacy.

First, it was determined that neoliberalism did not account for the presence and impact of non-state actors. The state-centric nature of this paradigm, although beneficial in some limited fashion, chained the analysis to only one primary actor—the nation-state. However, as this analysis discovered, the Rome Conference involved a plethora of non-state actors and it is their impact that scholars must also assess.

Second and closely related to the first, neoliberalism accepted the formation of states' interests as an exogenously determined factor. This paradigm never questioned the origin of these interests. Neoliberal institutionalism simply accepted these interests as exogenously given and discussed them only in terms of their impact on the negotiating process, not on the cognitive aspect of their formation process. In order to properly understand the formation of a regime, it is important that scholars also understand the interest formation process, not just their effect.

Finally, the limited scope of neoliberalism did not allow for a more complete assessment of contextual factors. Although not ignoring exogenous factors, an analysis of only shocks and crises does not account for a more broadly based understanding of the global context and what impact this might have on the bargaining process. Neoliberalism provided a superficial answer concerning the question of why the international community formed the ICC in 1998 and not the early 1950s; but superficiality is not the goal of this analysis.

It is due to these unanswered questions that this narrative now turns to the multivariate model of regime formation. Clearly this analytical framework provides a more complex and complete analysis. Ultimately, I hope that this model will address all of the previously unanswered questions and provide international relations scholars with an adequate lens for examining future regime formation processes.

Interest-based Factors

The interest-based perspective focuses on the role of states and states' interests in the regime formation process. It is undeniable that nation-states played a major role in the formation of the Rome Statute. In fact, it was a nation-state, Trinidad and Tobago, that resurrected the idea of a permanent international criminal court in 1989, it was the affirmative vote of one hundred and twenty nations in Rome that gave this idea a realistic form, and its is the ratification by ninety-nine states that have breathed life into this institution. Thus, one cannot deny the role of nation-states in the formation process or the process of creating a properly functioning Court. In short, without state support there would be no International Criminal Court.

The interest-based portion of the regime formation process model provides us with an understanding of the participating states' interests. As shown in chapter five, interest-based theories bring to the table the negotiating positions of the Like-Minded states, the Non-aligned movement, the P-5, and the rationale for US opposition. Each of these groups of states had their own agenda, and in the end it took complex negotiations amongst these states to achieve a successful treaty conference.

The Like-Minded states were the most ardent supporters of a strong and independent Court. Out of all of the states involved in the negotiation process, it was this group that pursued the goal of an ICC most vigorously. The Like-Minded states centered their platform on six guiding principles. 1) The need for an independent prosecutor. 2) The desire to form a Court that is independent from the United Nations Security Council. 3) The ability of the Court to have the final word on admissibility of evidence. 4) To provide the Court with inherent jurisdiction that would cover all core crimes. 5) To call for the full cooperation by all states with the ICC. 6) The commitment to a successful treaty conference in Rome.[9]

Countering the Like-Minded states supportive position was the P-5, led by the United States. This group of states, although not against the formation of an international criminal court, opposed the creation of a court as provided for in the Rome Statute. They cited seven major problems with the Rome Statute that needed to be rectified prior to their acceptance of this treaty. 1) The Court should not have any jurisdiction over non-party states. 2) The need to eliminate any semblance of an independent prosecutor. 3) The core crimes must not include the crime of aggression. 4) There must be an opt-out clause contained in the Statute. 5) The description of crimes must not include any reference to terrorist acts or drug crimes. 6) The Statute must contain a reservation clause. 7) The need to tie the Court closely to the Security Council, thus providing the Security Council with veto power over the Court.[10]

The final group of states, the Non-aligned movement, had the least impact on the negotiation process. This is primarily due to the fact that by the time the Rome Conference concluded the majority of these states had joined either the Like-Minded Group or a more regionally oriented group. At the outset of the negotiations, this group wanted the inclusion of two main principles. 1) The inclusion of nuclear weapons on the list of prohibited weapons. 2) The elimination of all control over the Court by the United Nations Security Council.[11]

As shown in chapter five, an interest-based analysis takes into account all of these positions and states' interests. Ultimately, this perspective views the formation of the Rome Statute as a result of state negotiation and cooperation. In assessing the success of the Rome Conference this perspective predicates its findings on the overlapping of states' interests that eventually culminated in a compromised institution that benefits all the participating actors. This type of analysis does provide us with a foundational understanding of what occurred prior to Rome and to some extent, during the Rome Conference. In particular, this perspective discusses the importance of cooperation among states as a method for obtaining a conflict management institution, it upholds the premise that most states are primarily concerned with absolute gains, and it correctly depicts these actors as rational egoists. Thus, one can conclude that an interest-based perspective analysis of the ICC does provide some insight into understanding the process. However, this theory's beneficial analysis does not equate into a complete understanding of the formation process.

---

9 Bendetti and Washburn, "Drafting the ICC," 21 and Pace, "Relationship Between the ICC and Non-Governmental Organizations," 206, contain this list. Chapter five contains a more detailed analysis of the states' positions.

10 Scheffer, "Development at Rome," and "United States and the ICC," provided a more detailed description of these disputed points.

11 Bendetti and Washburn, "Drafting the ICC," 31.

As stated earlier, an interest-based analysis leaves too many unanswered questions. Its state-centric perspective, although necessary for understanding the process, limits the scope of the analysis. Simply studying rational states and their exogenously given interests is not enough. To truly understand the formation process of the ICC, this study must encompass all of the components of a multivariate model of regime formation. [12]

Knowledge-based Factors

Use of a knowledge-based or cognitive approach to regime formation addresses two of the previously unanswered questions left from the discussion of interest-based theories—the importance of non-state actors and the importance of interest origins. As a result, the use of this component as a supplement to an interest-based approach provides us with a more complete and richer understanding of the ICC and its formation process.

Interest-based theories provide scholars with an understanding of the role of states and state interests. In the case of the ICC, states did play an important role in the negotiating process, but they were by no means alone in that process. In order to properly understand the process, this study must look beyond states to the role of non-state actors. Oran Young describes this realm of non-state actors as a "second social system"; a system that has formed around the more traditional society of states and is often described as *global civil society*.[13] The necessity to study this second social system lies in the fact that a plethora of political actors, beyond just nation-states, are addressing today's transnational problems. Non-state actors are assisting states in the regime formation process and as a result, becoming actors of significance within the cooperation literature. An analysis concerning the formation of the ICC necessitates the study of one group of non-state actors in particular, non-governmental organizations.

NGO Influence

Abram Chayes and Anne-Marie Slaughter stated the significance of the NGO community on the ICC negotiations most poignantly when they concluded that, "Without the NGO community, the ICC treaty might not have been concluded."[14]

---

12 Chapter five provides us with a more detailed analysis of how an interest-based theory assists and hinders our understanding of the ICC.

13 Young, *Governance in World Affairs,* 9.

14 Abram Chayes and Anne-Marie Slaughter, "The ICC and the Future of the Global Legal System," in *The United States and the International Criminal Court: National Security and International Law,"* ed. Sarah B. Sewall and Carl Kaysen (Lanham, MD: Rowman & Littlefield Publishers, Inc., 2000), 241.

Cherif Bassiouni reiterates this point when he stated "Non-governmental organizations, and particularly the 'NGO Coalition for an ICC' played an important and useful part in the process."[15] It is clear that the role of NGOs in the negotiation process was significant. The questions that this narrative must now address are: what exactly was the role of the NGO community and how crucial was their presence to the formation of the Rome Statute?

One can view the NGO presence, both prior to and during the Rome Conference, as an example of the changing nature of world politics and international treaty negotiations. Recently, NGOs have begun to take a much more influential role in the treaty formation process. Former UN Secretary-General Boutros Boutros-Ghali recognized this fact and in 1996, in a statement concerning the interaction between NGOs and the United Nations, Boutros-Ghali stated that:

> Until recently, the notion that the chief executive of the United Nations would have taken this issue seriously might have caused astonishment. The United Nations was considered to be a forum for sovereign states alone. Within the space of a few short years, however, this attitude has changed. *Nongovernmental organizations are now considered full participants in international life.*[16]

This rise to prominence has affected many issue areas and many treaty negotiations. The importance of NGO input surfaced during the drafting of the Land Mine Convention, the Antarctic Treaty Consultative Meeting, the Framework Convention on Climate Change, and numerous others. The community of states now often invites the NGO community to sit at the negotiating table with the delegates, participate in meetings, and assist in the overall negotiating process.[17] The Rome Conference is simply another example of the growing influence of NGOs and the importance of their presence during the negotiation process.

The influence of the NGO community on the ICC formation process took root on February 25, 1995. It was on this date that a group of NGOs, who were monitoring the UN debate on the ILC's Draft Statute for an International Criminal Court, decided to form the NGO Coalition for an International Criminal Court (CICC). The primary goal of the CICC was to "advocate the establishment of an

---

15 Bassiouni, *Statute of the ICC,* 25.

16 Boutros Boutros-Ghali, "Foreword," in *NGOs, The UN and Global Governance,* ed. Thomas G. Weiss and Leon Gordenker (Boulder, CO: Lynne Rienner Publishers, 1996), 7. (Emphasis was added.)

17 Leon Gordenker and Thomas G. Weiss, "Pluralizing Global Governance: Analytical Approaches and Dimensions," in *NGOs, The UN and Global Governance,* ed. Thomas G. Weiss and Leon Gordenker (Boulder, CO: Lynne Rienner Publishers, 1996), 17-51; and Maryann K. Cusimano, Mark Hensman, and Leslie Rodrigues, "Private-Sector Transsovereign Actors—MNCs and NGOs," in *Beyond Sovereignty: Issues for a Global Agenda,* ed. Maryann K. Cusimano (Boston: Bedford/St. Martin's Press, 2000), 255-283, clearly and cogently detail the NGO "phenomenon."

effective and just international criminal court."[18] At this time the group was made up of two dozen or so NGOs. By the time the Rome Conference convened, the CICC included over eight hundred organizations from every corner of the globe.[19] The sheer magnitude of this coalition made it impossible for the international community of states to ignore them and throughout the negotiation process their presence and influence was undeniable. As a result, if we are to understand the formation process of the Rome Statute we must first understand the platform and the role that the CICC played in this process. As the text will explain, the CICC's influence on the institutional bargaining process may have been greater than any state-oriented group.

According to the CICC's official statement:

> The main purpose of the NGO Coalition for an International Criminal Court is to advocate for the creation of an effective, just and independent International Criminal Court. The Coalition brings together a broad-based network of over 1,000 NGOs, international law experts and other civil society groups. The multi-track approach of the Coalition involves: promoting education and awareness of the ICC and the Rome Statute at the national, regional and global level; supporting the successful completion of the mandate of the Preparatory Commission and facilitating NGO involvement in the process; promoting the universal acceptance and ratification of the Rome Statute, including the adoption of comprehensive national implementing legislation following ratification; and expanding and strengthening the Coalition's global network.[20]

The CICC is clearly a strong advocate for the formation of a strong, independent, and fair Court that has the ability to pursue justice wherever it is deemed necessary. They sought to achieve this goal by constructing a Statute that embodies the ideas of universal jurisdiction, an independent prosecutor, independence from the UN Security Council, complementarity, jurisdiction over internal conflicts or civil wars, state-party cooperation, and respect of the rights of the accused.[21] As one can see, this list is closely related to that of the Like-Minded

---

[18] Pace and Thieroff, "Participation of Non-Governmental Organizations," 391. William Pace served as Convenor of the CICC and is Executive Director of the World Federalist Movement—Institute for Global Policy, which serves as secretariat for the Coalition. Therefore, any statements taken from William Pace can be viewed as indicative of the CICC platform.

[19] Pace, "Relationship Between the ICC and Non-Governmental Organizations," 200. At the Rome Conference there were two hundred and thirty five NGOs that were accredited by the General Assembly to act as official participants.

[20] The official CICC website: <http://www.iccnow.org> and every issue of *The International Criminal Court Monitor* lists this statement.

[21] I have compiled this list from several different NGO sources. These include: Lawyers Committee for Human Rights, "Major Unresolved Issues," and Human Rights Watch, *Justice in the Balance: Recommendations for an Independent and Effective International Criminal Court* (New York: Human Rights Watch, 1998), 2-3. I believe it is fair to say that

Group. As a result, a natural alliance developed between these two groups, but the roles that these two groups played were very different.

The Like-Minded Group was literally the authors of the Statute. It was their vote that was counted at the end of the Rome Conference and their domestic legislatures that must ratify the Statute. The NGO community, due its lack of formal sovereign statehood, did not have a vote nor would it have a seat amongst the party states upon ratification. Thus, the role of the NGO community would have to take on a different form, a form that is in many ways a complementary one to the role of nation-states.

Throughout the negotiation process the CICC engaged in numerous activities. These included but are not exclusive to:

- Convening sectoral caucuses (Women's Children's, Faith, Peace, and Victims'), national and regional networks, and issue working groups.
- Maintaining a World Wide Web site and email lists to facilitate the exchange of NGO and expert documentation and information concerning the ICC negotiations and the ad hoc Tribunals and to foster discussion and debate about substantive issues.
- Facilitating meetings between the Coalition and representatives of governments, UN officials and others involved in the ICC negotiations.
- Promoting education and awareness of the ICC negotiations at relevant public and professional conferences—including UN conferences, committees, commissions and preparatory meetings.
- Producing newsletters, bulletins, media advisories, reviews and papers on all aspects of efforts to establish the ICC.[22]

In general, the CICC acted as a consultant to the Conference participants. They assisted in the acquisition of knowledge by state delegates and the dissemination of this knowledge to the larger global community. The information that they provided was not simply objective data, but the interpretation that the CICC wished to convey to the participating states. This type of information was accepted by many states because of the expertise that the CICC has within this issue-area. In short, the CICC acted as an epistemic community, and that is why I also include a discussion of the CICC in the knowledge-based section of this model.

Discovering the Origin of Interests

Peter Haas defines epistemic communities as:

---

most organizations involved in the CICC would adhere to this list, but this is not to say that there couldn't be some disagreement concerning certain issues.

22 *The International Criminal Court Monitor* (any issue) or <http://www.iccnow.org>.

> Networks of knowledge-based communities with an authoritative claim to policy-relevant knowledge within their domain of expertise…they are a group of professionals, often from a number of different disciplines, who share the following set of characteristics:
>
> 1. Shared consummatory values or principles beliefs…
> 2. Shared causal beliefs or professional judgement…
> 3. Common notions of validity…
> 4. A common policy enterprise…[23]

An epistemic community is often associated solely with natural scientists. But as Haas explains, such a distinction is not necessary. Epistemic communities are not restricted to the natural sciences or to the methodologies employed within these disciplines. According to Haas:

> Epistemic communities need not be made up of natural scientists; they can consist of social scientists or individuals from any discipline or profession who have a sufficiently strong claim to a body of knowledge that is valued by society. Nor need an epistemic community's causal beliefs be based on the methodology employed in the natural sciences; they can originate from shared knowledge about the nature of social or other processes, based on analytic methods or techniques deemed appropriate to the disciplines or professions they pursue.[24]

If we place this definition of epistemic communities within a knowledge-based theory of regime formation, their role becomes crucial to the formation process. Epistemic communities act primarily as disseminators of information. They provide state actors with a wide array of information on a particular issue-area, thus minimizing the uncertainty that these state actors possess.[25] The ultimate outcome of this interaction, between epistemic communities and state actors, is learning. The process generally proceeds with states initially identifying epistemic communities within a particular issue-area. Once identified, states then seek the advice or knowledge that these experts have or epistemic communities can seek out the decision-makers and provide them with the information they have. If the international community of states accepts this consensual knowledge, then they

---

[23] Peter M. Haas, "Epistemic Communities and the Dynamics of International Environmental Co-Operation," in *Regime Theory and International Relations* ed. Volker Rittberger (Oxford: Clarendon Press, 1993), 179-180.

[24] P. Haas, "Introduction: Epistemic Communities," 16.

[25] According to P. Haas, "Introduction: Epistemic Communities," 21, it is under conditions of uncertainty that state decision-makers are most likely to turn to epistemic communities. This provides decision-makers with an increased understanding of the issue-area, as provided and interpreted by the epistemic community.

apply it to the regime formation process and the more simplistic consensual knowledge becomes organizational learning.[26]

During the negotiations on the Rome Statute this general process appears to have existed. The formation of consensual knowledge occurred with the establishment of the CICC in February of 1995. The establishment of this organization signified the acceptance of the fact that a permanent, independent, and strong ICC was necessary and that the appropriate professional/expert community advocated this position. This event provided the issue-area of humanitarian law with one dominant epistemic community, while the presence of competing bodies of knowledge, outside of certain nation-states, was minimal. As a result of this hegemonic consensual knowledge, the CICC was able to ascertain a highly influential position.

With the presence of consensual knowledge in place, the movement to organizational learning became much easier. The CICC was able to act as a disseminator of information to both state participants and the international community at large. During the PrepCom meetings, the CICC secretariat arranged numerous meetings with state officials.[27] The purpose of this contact was to place the information that this epistemic community had into the national policymaking arena.

This personal contact did have a profound effect on the negotiating process and assisted in the formation process of a draft treaty.[28] Eventually the CICC even discovered an ally in their fight for a strong and independent Court, the Like-Minded states. With both the definitive epistemic community within this issue-area and a group of influential states accepting this body of consensual knowledge, the quest for institutionalization of this knowledge became more plausible.

Although important during the PrepCom phase of negotiations, the CICC's real influence was felt during the Rome Conference. The CICC undertook a number of roles during the Rome Conference. These included: the creation of monitoring teams to cover the negotiations surrounding different aspects of the Statute, assisting the developing and transitional states with information gathering,[29] the convening of both regional and sectoral caucuses, translating documents, issuing

---

[26] Peter M. Haas and Ernst B. Haas, "Learning to Learn: Improving International Governance," *Global Governance* 1 (1995), 259-262, define consensual knowledge as "structured information about causes and effects…that enjoys general acceptance as true and accurate among members of the relevant professional community." Organizational learning is "the process by which the learning becomes ingrained in IOs."

[27] Pace and Thieroff, "Participation of Non-Governmental Organizations," 392.

[28] Bendetti and Washburn, "Drafting the ICC," 21-23.

[29] The need to assist the developing nations with information gathering was due to the small number of delegates that these states had at the Rome Conference compared with the large number of meetings that were occurring at one time. These states simply did not have enough delegates to cover all of the meetings, so the CICC assisted them in obtaining all of the information they needed from the meetings they could not attend.

reports to both NGOs and governments, organizing three news teams so that the Conference would have both daily print and electronic news coverage,[30] holding regular press briefings, meeting weekly with the Conference Chair, meeting daily to hold strategy sessions, meeting with government delegates and group coalitions (such as the Like-Minded Group), providing expert analysis and advice to the participating delegates, and publishing "virtual votes" on certain proposals and articles of the Statute.[31]

In general, the CICC provided information to state delegates and the international press, they attended meetings in an attempt to assist smaller states in obtaining all of the relevant information, they held weekly meetings with the Conference Chair, and they met regularly with numerous government groups and delegates. Undoubtedly, the CICC acted as an epistemic community and it is through this role that they assisted in the interest formation process of many states.[32]

As stated earlier, one counter argument to this classification is that epistemic communities must be natural scientists because they provide purely objective information. However, as Haas explains, the information provided by epistemic communities is rarely purely objective or simply raw data. Epistemic communities tend to provide information that is "the product of human interpretations of social and physical phenomena."[33] The information provided by the CICC was no different. This information provided delegates with a positive perspective on the ICC. This is logical given the fact that the ultimate goal of the CICC was a strong and independent Court. Thus, one can conclude that the information that the CICC was disseminating to the participating states was helpful in the formation of interests that were pro-Rome Statute.

Because of the high profile status of the CICC at the Conference, one could conclude that this epistemic community clearly influenced the interests of decision-makers. In turn, the most highly influenced states, such as the Like-Minded Group, then influenced the decision-makers in other states and the result is a convergence of interests and the adoption of the Rome Statute by an overwhelming number. Therefore, the CICC, acting as an epistemic community, did have a major influence on the formation of states' interests and assisted in the movement of consensual knowledge to organizational learning.

---

[30] The CICC published two print papers, *Terra Viva* and *On-the-Record,* and one online news service, *CICC Monitor.*

[31] Pace, "Relationship Between the ICC and Non-Governmental Organizations," 202-203; and Pace and Thieroff, "Participation of Non-Governmental Organizations," 392-395.

[32] As I will show later in this chapter, one can also claim that the CICC acted as a part of a transnational advocacy network (TAN).

[33] P. Haas, "Introduction: Epistemic Communities," 4.

Power-based Factors

Upon a superficial analysis of the ICC negotiations, it would appear as if power-based factors played a very insignificant role. The one nation-state with a plausible claim on global hegemony refused to approve the Court and continues to fight vehemently against the Rome Statute. Thus, the premise that a hegemon is necessary, or at least beneficial, to the regime formation process does not appear to hold true in this case. But this does not mean that power-based factors did not have a significant influence on the negotiating process or the final document.

As stated earlier, the US position on the Rome Statute remains one of opposition. Despite President Clinton's last minute signing of the Statute, the current US position on the Rome Statute is that it is fatally flawed.[34] This is the primary justification for the Bush administration's move to "unsign" the Statute in May 2002 and promote such anti-ICC policies as the "Hague Invasion Act."[35]

According to US officials, the primary defect of the Rome Statute concerns the jurisdiction of the Court. Due to the fact that the Court can try nationals of non-party states, the US believes that the Court not only opens itself up to politicization, but it also undermines a basic principle of international law—sovereignty. In particular, the US is concerned with the exposure of its armed forces.[36] Rectification of this issue is a must if the US is ever going to ratify the Treaty, but such a prospect seems doubtful.[37]

It is quite evident that the US is opposed to the Rome Statute and during the Conference they fought vehemently to produce a very different document. Does this mean that power, as defined by the power-based theorists, had no impact on the institutional bargaining process? Absolutely not. The US had a very profound impact on the final Rome text, and much of their impact was a result of their perceived hegemonic status.

As elaborated in both this chapter and chapter five, there were several different contingents at the Rome Conference, each with their own agenda. The Like-Minded Group of states, along with the CICC, were in favor of a strong and independent Court.

The Non-aligned movement supported a Court as long as it included a ban on nuclear weapons and was totally independent of the Security Council. The P-5, or more accurately the US, wanted a much more limited Court in terms of jurisdiction

---

[34] President Clinton did sign the Rome Statute on December 31, 2000, but he did not endorse ratification of the Statute. He stated that the bill would not reach Congress unless US concerns, which I discussed earlier in this text, were sufficiently addressed by the PrepCom.

[35] The official title of this act is the American Servicemembers Protection Act.

[36] David J. Scheffer, "Evolution of U.S. Policy Toward the International Criminal Court," speech delivered at American University, Washington D.C., September 14, 2000.

[37] Chapter two and five contain a more detailed analysis of US opposition to the Statute.

and independent prosecutorial powers. The end result was a treaty that no single group of participants can claim fit their original demands.

Philippe Kirsch described the formation process as "easily the most complex international negotiations I have ever been involved in."[38] This complexity was due to the tremendous number of issues that had to be dealt with during the five-week Conference and the conflicting positions on these issues.[39] The US established its position on the draft text early in the Conference and attempted to use its power to influence the proceedings; and in many facets of the negotiation process they were very successful. The other participants, including the CICC, understood that without the approval of the US delegates, the ICC Statute could become another League of Nations. For advocates of an international criminal court, the fear was that without the support of the sole superpower the legitimacy and enforceability of the Statute would be severely diminished. But if the negotiations were able to garner the support of the US government, this would result in a massive step towards a well-functioning and enforceable treaty. As a result, the participating delegates made numerous concessions to the US during the Conference in order to make the Statute more attractive to the lone superpower.

US power was the determining factor in several facets of the final Statute. The major compromise occurred on the question of jurisdiction. The Like-Minded Group and the CICC had been pushing for a Court with universal jurisdiction.[40] They wanted a completely independent prosecutor who would possess the power to initiate investigations of the core crimes no matter what the individual or the states' relationship to the Court. The US viewed such a broad reaching Court as simply unacceptable. The final result was a Court with limited jurisdiction. The ICC has jurisdiction over cases in which the crime was committed on a party state's territory or the accused is a national of a party state.[41] This compromise does not favor the Like-Minded Group or the United States, but it clearly resulted from a perceived need to placate the US and entice them into supporting/signing the Statute. Therefore, we can consider this compromise the result of US power and the perceived need to accommodate the global hegemon.[42]

Other concessions were also made in an attempt to accommodate the US position. The delegates agreed to strengthen the principle of complementarity, a

---

[38] Cited in Lawrence Weschler, "Exceptional Cases in Rome: The United States and the Struggle for an ICC," in *The United States and the International Criminal Court: National Security and International Law,* ed. Sarah B. Sewell and Carl Kaysen (Lanham, MD: Rowman & Littlefield Publishers, Inc., 2000), 85.

[39] Weschler, "Exceptional Cases in Rome," 85, places the size of the draft document at over two hundred pages, with one hundred and twenty articles, and thirteen hundred brackets or unresolved issues from the PrepCom meetings.

[40] Bendetti and Washburn, "Drafting the ICC," 20-21.

[41] Rome Statute of the ICC, Article 12.2.

[42] As Weschler, "Exceptional Cases in Rome," 106, explains, the CICC was particularly distraught over this compromise.

role was maintained for the Security Council, protection was granted for national security information, a large number of due process clauses were included, clear and comprehensive definitions of the core crimes were approved, among others.[43] It is plausible to assert that these compromises came about primarily because of US power. This is not a position that many of the delegates savored. As one of the Korean delegates stated, "It's as if we're being forced to choose [between] a court crippled by American requirements…or a Court crippled by lack of American participation."[44] But the perceived hegemonic status of the US made it necessary for other actors to try and accommodate them. Many delegates were under the assumption that without US support the Court would simply be another League of Nations. It is for this reason that power-based factors do play a part in our understanding of the Court's formation process.

The Importance of Leadership

The preceding sections of this chapter have discussed the direct effects of the social driving forces of Young and Osherenko's regime formation model. I have discussed these factors as representing interactive forces in which no one factor is the sole explanatory or causal factor.[45] However, these social driving forces are not the only factors involved in the regime formation process. Young and Osherenko also discuss the role of two cross-cutting factors, leadership and context. According to the multivariate model, an analysis of regime formation is incomplete without an analysis of these factors and the indirect effect they have on the institutional bargaining process.[46]

The first cross-cutting factor I will discuss is the idea of leadership. Leadership is a crucial component to any institutional bargaining process. Therefore, a proper understanding of leadership is a key ingredient to a complete analysis of the Rome negotiations. According to Oran Young:

> Leadership…is a critical determinant of success or failure in the processes of institutional bargaining that dominate efforts to form international regimes or, more generally, institutional arrangements in international society…Thus, the presence of

---

43 Scheffer, "Development at Rome," 1-2, describes the objectives that the US felt it achieved during the Rome Conference.

44 Weschler, "Exceptional Cases in Rome," 103, quoting Kak-Soo Shih, Korean delegate to the Rome Conference.

45 Young and Osherenko, "Testing Theories," 241-243, discuss the importance of understanding regime formation as part of an interactive process among these social driving factors.

46 Young and Osherenko, "Testing Theories," 240.

> leadership is a necessary condition, but not a sufficient one, for success in reaching agreement on the terms of constitutional contract in international society.[47]

The purpose of this section will be to evaluate the role that leadership played during the ICC formation process and whether Young's assessment of leadership, as a critical component in the regime formation process, is a correct one. However, before undertaking such an endeavor, it is important to first define leadership as a concept and understand the nature of its role in institutional bargaining.

Within the regime formation literature, leadership is defined as, "the actions of individuals who endeavor to solve or circumvent the collective action problems that plague the efforts of parties seeking to reap joints in processes of institutional bargaining."[48] Leadership does not refer to the actions of states, international institutions, or non-governmental organizations. Leadership is centered on the individual and the efforts of these individuals to move the negotiating process forward. Thus, I will not consider the previously discussed social driving forces as part of a leadership role. In particular, one could construe the role of hegemony as a form of leadership, but the embodiment of leadership in a state is not considered a form of leadership in the multivariate model. Instead, Young and Osherenko distinguish between three forms of leadership: structural leadership, entrepreneurial leadership, and intellectual leadership.[49]

Structural leadership occurs with an individual, acting in the name of a strong state party, who attempts to use their bargaining leverage within that issue-area to formulate a positive outcome. In other words, this individual uses their structural power, often in the form of material resources, to gain an agreement that would benefit them.[50] This form of leadership is closely related to a power-based approach to regime formation, only at the individual level. As we will see, this type of leadership had the most insignificant bearing on the ICC negotiations and as a result, I will discuss it in only a limited capacity.

The second form of leadership is entrepreneurial leadership. This type of leadership centers on an individual's negotiating skills and their ability to present a mutually beneficial treaty to the participating parties.[51] In order for an entrepreneurial leader to be successful, there must be a bargainer's surplus, which only exists when parties can achieve joint gains through a cooperative exercise. Entrepreneurial leaders will assist in the regime formation process by engaging in four activities. 1) The leaders will act as agenda setters for the institutional bargaining process. 2) They will attempt to popularize the issue in question,

---

47 Oran R. Young, "Political Leadership and Regime Formation: On the Development of Institutions in International Society," *International Organization* 45 (1991), 281 and 302.

48 Young, "Political Leadership and Regime Formation," 285.

49 Young, "Political Leadership and Regime Formation," 287-302.

50 Young, "Political Leadership and Regime Formation," 288-293.

51 Young, "Political Leadership and Regime Formation," 293-298.

making sure to draw as much international attention to the issue as possible. 3) These leaders will have to construct policy options that will help move the bargaining process forward, thus avoiding any stalemates within the regime formation process. 4) They will have to act as brokers for the parties involved. This will entail garnering support for certain options and using that support to reach a successful conclusion to the bargaining process.[52] This type of leadership is absolutely crucial to the formation of an international regime and as we will see, such entrepreneurial leaders played a critical role in the ICC negotiations.

The third type of leadership is intellectual leadership. This type of leadership is predicated on the power of ideas and the use of these ideas to construct knowledge and policies within the institutional bargaining process.[53] This form of leadership is closely related to the knowledge-based theory of regime formation and can be thought of as the individual embodiment of this theory. Through the power of knowledge and ideas, these leaders shape the actors' cognitive understanding of an issue and as a result, assist in the interest formation process of the participating parties. This form of leadership can have a major influence on the proceedings and is often used by entrepreneurial leaders to benefit their attempts to complete a successful bargaining process.

In terms of the ICC negotiations, the most prominent and influential forms of leadership were entrepreneurial leadership and intellectual leadership. We can see the impact of entrepreneurial leadership in both the pre-Rome negotiations and during the Rome Conference itself. The two most prominent entrepreneurial leaders were Adriaan Bos, Chairman to the Ad Hoc Committee and the Preparatory Committee of an International Criminal Court, and Philippe Kirsch, Chairman of the Committee of the Whole of the Rome Conference.

Entrepreneurial Leadership

Adriaan Bos was the driving entrepreneurial leader during the PrepCom meetings and the initiator of several key decisions during this preparatory period. As Chairman of the Bureau of the Preparatory Committee, Bos was expected to move negotiations forward in an attempt to establish a draft Statute to be presented at a diplomatic conference.[54] This would be no easy task. The Committee had to find a way to incorporate the numerous state proposals into the International Law Commission's (ILC) Draft Statute, while still making progress towards a final Statute that would be used in Rome. In order to accomplish this task, the Bureau, under the leadership of Bos, decided to use the ILC draft as the basis for the negotiations and insert the proposals into this text. This was done through the use of brackets next to the Statute's articles, showing the different proposals in a fairly

---

52 Young, "Political Leadership and Regime Formation," 294.

53 Young, "Political Leadership and Regime Formation," 298-302.

54 UN General Assembly, Resolution 5046 (L), fiftieth session, UN Doc A/50639 (1995).

clear manner. This method maintained the structure of the ILC draft and allowed for the committee to formulate changes around an existing framework.[55]

Bos also undertook several activities that gave the Rome Conference a better chance of success, while maintaining a relatively egalitarian atmosphere amongst the delegates. The first significant action taken by Bos and the Bureau was the establishment of trust funds for the purpose of encouraging lesser-developed nations to participate in the ICC negotiations. The result of this action was a more multilateral conference in which all nation-states had the opportunity to send delegates.[56]

Bos and his Committee also prepared studies on several of the more contentious issues. In particular, the Bureau addressed both the issues of financing the Court and the final clauses of the Statute.[57] They established studies on these issues in an attempt to avert unnecessary squabbling during the Rome Conference. This tactic would become crucial considering the time constraints that the Conference imposed on the delegates.

Another decision that the Bureau undertook was the decision to appoint coordinators to oversee the negotiations on different aspects of the draft statute.[58] Due to the complexity of the draft statute and the need to address so many different key issues, Bos and his committee saw the need to parcel out the workload not only for the PrepCom meetings, but also during the Rome Conference. This allowed for multiple meetings on multiple issues, thus allowing the Conference to make progress in a more timely fashion. Without this type of organization, the Rome Conference would have crumbled under the weight of the draft statute.

Bos also made sure that a post-Conference plan was in place. The Bureau members recognized the fact that even if the Rome Conference ended in success the process for establishing a permanent ICC would not be complete. The Bureau deemed it necessary to establish a preparatory commission that would act on post-Conference issues. This action proved essential since the Rome Conference failed to completely address numerous issues.[59]

The final and most important act of Bos and his committee was the decision to hold one last preparatory meeting in May 1998. The purpose of this meeting was

---

55 This method differed from the traditional method of compiling the proposals according to subject matter, which often places the emphasis on the proposals and not the Statute. Lee, "Rome Conference Contributions," 8.

56 Roy S. Lee, "Creating an International Criminal Court—Of Procedures and Compromises," in *Reflections on the International Criminal Court,* ed. Herman A.M. von Hebel, Johan G. Lammers and Jolien Schukking (The Hague: T.M.C. Asser Press, 1999), 143.

57 Lee, "Rome Conference Contributions," 9-10.

58 Lee, "Procedures and Compromises," 145-146.

59 The role of the post-Conference PrepCom is to address such issues as the definition of aggression, the relationship of the Court with the UN, and the rules of evidence and procedures.

to establish a point-by-point strategy on how the Conference should progress. The result was the Courmayeur Plan.[60] This plan determined that Parts I and III of the Statute (Establishment of the Court and General Principles of Criminal Law) should be discussed first because they were more amenable to a majority of the participants. Bos and his committee hoped that this agenda would establish some momentum at the outset, thus providing a foundation for cooperative Conference.

The Courmayeur Plan also stipulated that the plenary would only meet the first week of the Conference and that the majority of work would occur under the tutelage of the appointed coordinators during the working group meetings. Although this plan did not work as effectively as anticipated, and ultimately some divergence from the schedule was necessary, it was still important because it established the framework within which the Conference would work, thus alleviating the need to address this issue during the first week in Rome.

Another entrepreneurial leader of the ICC negotiations was Philippe Kirsch, Legal Advisor of the Canadian Department of Foreign Affairs and International Affairs and Chairman of the Committee of the Whole during the Rome Conference. Philippe Kirsch took over the role of Conference Chair in early-June of 1998. Sadly, this was due to the untimely illness of Adriaan Bos who was unable to continue in this role during the Conference.[61] Kirsch brought a high-pressure style to the negotiations and it showed in the way that he pushed delegates and working groups towards a consensus. Kirsch realized the need to progress at a rapid pace; five weeks did not appear to be long enough to draft an acceptable Statute. By the beginning of the fourth week Kirsch's leadership style began to shine. It was at this point that, according to reporter Lawrence Weschler:

> [Kirsch] expertly gaug[ed] the growing sense of anxiety in the hall [and] launched a series of calibrated interventions—working drafts on major issues in which he attempted to narrow the contours of the sprawling debate, bracketing out extreme positions that weren't any longer likely to elicit consensus, narrowing the options on any given contentious matter to three or four options, floating various compromises, narrowing the options still further… By the middle of the fourth week, a range of possible outcomes was beginning to arc into view.[62]

Kirsch now began to truly exhibit the qualities of an entrepreneurial leader. He was acting as an agenda setter, a popularizer, an innovator, and a broker.[63] On Sunday, July 5th, Kirsch called a meeting of twenty-eight delegates. The purpose

---

[60] Bassiouni, *Statute of the ICC,* 27-28 and Bendetti and Washburn, "Drafting the ICC," 28-2, discusses the Courmayeur Meeting and the resulting plan.

[61] Bassiouni, *Statute of the ICC,* 28.

[62] Weschler, "Exceptional Cases in Rome," 89. Weschler is a writer for *The New Yorker* and attended the Rome Conference.

[63] Young, "Political Leadership, Regime Formation," 294, lists these four qualities as the methods used to help participants obtain the bargainer's surplus.

of this meeting was to distribute an informal "package deal" paper as an attempt to identify areas of compromise and dissension.[64] This meeting provided Kirsch with the information he needed to narrow the options available and put together a more comprehensive package paper. Then, in a brilliant technical move, Kirsch convened a meeting of the committee of the whole in which the paper was discussed at length. But instead of allowing states to simply debate the issues, Kirsch proceeded to ask state delegates specific questions. This method not only saved valuable time, but it allowed for a greater specificity on the issues in question and provided Kirsch with a "virtual vote" on the preliminary work of the Conference.[65]

Heading into the final week of the Conference, it became apparent to Kirsch and his committee that certain issues were favorable to a majority of the participants and others were not. Clearly some brokering between parties was necessary and not everyone would get everything they desired. As Kirsch described this process:

> The trick is to emerge with a strong Statute with incentives enough that down the line currently reluctant governments may yet want to join on. Because later on it will be far easier to get governments to change their minds than it will be to change the statute itself. And, anyway, no government is going to want to join onto a useless statute.[66]

It was now apparent that the only way to ascertain a successful Conference would be to propose the Statute as a take it or leave it package deal.[67] On the final day of the Conference, Kirsch and his committee delivered a final Bureau text to the delegates. They mandated that this text be approved in its totality or not at all. As described in chapter two, this method worked brilliantly by preventing any proposal of amendments; and the result was a resounding approval of the Rome Statute.

Much of the credit for this successful negotiation process has to go to Philippe Kirsch and his leadership style. He recognized both the time restraints and the fragile nature of the issues in question, and as a result, Kirsch established the right agenda, employed the proper negotiating techniques, and brokered the right deals. Without this type of entrepreneurial leadership I do not believe that this regime formation process would have been as successful. The starting points of discussion were too broad, the differences of opinion too deep, and the time frame too limited. But somehow Philippe Kirsch and his committee made it work and much of the credit for the widely supported final document has to go to him.

---

64 Bendetti and Washburn, "Drafting the ICC," 29.

65 Bendetti and Washburn, "Drafting the ICC," 30.

66 Weschler, "Exceptional Cases in Rome," 104.

67 Cherif Bassiouni, Chairman of the Drafting Committee, stated that if such a tactic was not employed it would have surely meant the collapse of the Conference. Bassiouni, *Statute of the ICC,* 31.

Intellectual Leadership

Kirsch and Bos were not the only entrepreneurial leaders in this process. Cherif Bassiouni also acted in this role, but he blended entrepreneurialism with intellectual leadership. Bassiouni was the Vice-Chair of the PrepCom and the Chairman of the Rome Conference Drafting Committee. Acting within these roles provided Bassiouni the opportunity to serve as an entrepreneurial leader to the Conference participants. Bassiouni guided the drafting of the final Statute by working his committee almost round the clock the last week.[68] His guidance assisted in the final drafting process and resulted in a text that most of the participants found amenable.

But Bassiouni's real role may have been his intellectual leadership. This role stems from Bassiouni's extensive research on the issue of a permanent ICC and his work as both an NGO activist and a DePaul University Law School professor.[69] Bassiouni is a well-respected expert on this subject; therefore, his ability to lead through ideas was not surprising. Clearly Bassiouni's role as intellectual leader preceded his role has entrepreneurial leader, and in many ways may have allowed him to ascertain this position. Nevertheless, it is safe to assert that Bassiouni did fit the uncommon role of both intellectual and entrepreneurial leader.[70]

If we were to search for a pure intellectual leader, the obvious place to start would be within the NGO Coalition for an International Criminal Court. The primary designer of, and acting Convenor for, the CICC was William Pace. We can see Pace as one of the foremost intellectual leaders of this formation process. His dedication to the formation of the CICC and then the unprecedented success of this organization shows the signs of successful leadership. Bendetti and Washburn described Pace's leadership qualities as follows:

> He brought a sharp and flexible mind, foresight, well-developed political skills, fund-raising talent, and a zest—if not always a complete capacity—for management. Although sometimes he did not hold back the expression of his personal views, his integrity, commitment, and fairness in action kept even those who disagreed with him inside coalition.[71]

As cited earlier in this chapter, much of the ideational influence that occurred during the ICC negotiations was the result of the CICC's work. This organization

68 Bendetti and Washburn, "Drafting the ICC," 29.

69 Bassiouni has been writing explicitly on the subject of an ICC since at least the mid-eighties. See the bibliography for a partial listing of his publications on this subject.

70 Young, "Political Leadership, Regime Formation," 300-301, cites the fact that when these two roles do come together, scholars must certainly view it as an "uncommon instance."

71 Bendetti and Washburn, "Drafting the ICC," 9. Bendetti and Washburn also attribute the success of the CICC to Pace's "fundamental insight."

helped shape state's interests and form the cognitive framework of the regime formation process. Due to William Pace's central role in the formation and maintenance of the CICC, I believe it is accurate to call his leadership both intellectual and influential.

According to Oran Young, the establishment of an effective international regime usually requires the "interplay of at least two forms of leadership."[72] In the case of the ICC, individual leadership was undertaken in both an entrepreneurial and an intellectual capacity. The presence of these individuals made the formation of this regime much easier and could be considered as a necessary component to the success achieved at Rome. In terms of negotiating procedures, bargaining skills, and cognitive interest formation, the individuals discussed above provide outstanding leadership in a difficult situation. This cross-cutting factor proved a crucial part of the formation process and we could not have ascertained a complete understanding of the ICC without an analysis of individual leadership.

Contextual Factors

The final factor of Young and Osherenko's multivariate model is context. Contextual factors are "national and world circumstances and events seemingly unrelated to the issue area under consideration."[73] The importance of context is that such factors often do impact the institutional bargaining process and play a major role in the formation of international regimes. In the case of the ICC there are at least five contextual factors that impacted the negotiation process: the end of the Cold War, the rise in conflicts of independence and/or civil wars, the formation of the ad hoc tribunals in Yugoslavia and Rwanda, US domestic policy, and the emergence of new governance structures in the global arena.[74]

End of the Cold War

The first and most important contextual factor is the end of the Cold War. The impact of the Cold War was first felt in the early 1950s. It was at this point in time that the ILC completed a draft statute for an international criminal court and brought it before the UN General Assembly. The statute was met with little enthusiasm, despite the fact that less than a decade earlier the international community had undertaken various activities that upheld a sense of international

72 Young, "Political Leadership, Regime Formation," 302-305.

73 Young and Osherenko, "Testing Theories," 251.

74 This is not a comprehensive list of contextual factors that have influenced the formation of the ICC, but I believe that the five factors that I have listed have had the greatest influence on the regime formation process. My historical analysis, chapter two, discussed many of these factors in greater detail.

humanitarian justice.[75] According to many scholars of the ICC, the primary reason for this failed attempt was the onset of the Cold War.[76] The initiation of this War led to a revitalized notion of state sovereignty, a lack of cooperation on non-security related issues, and a sense of international justice that revolved around the opinions of the two superpowers. As one scholar described this era: "[D]uring the Cold War, violations of human rights by the Enemy went unpunished because of its power, while violations by Friends were excused or justified on essentially strategic-diplomatic grounds."[77]

With the end of the Cold War many actors in the global community feel an increased sense of freedom and possibility. The construct of global society is no longer predicated on the action of two global superpowers. The global political context of the 1990s had the feel of an international community in which cooperation through regime formation was not only plausible, but also desirable. The end of the Cold War left the once bipolar structure of global politics searching for new forms of political organization institutions for problem solving and conflict management.[78] The formation of new international regimes was one possible solution to this problem. International regimes are "devices that groups of actors create to avoid or ameliorate these collective-action problems."[79] One such post-Cold War problem was the desire of once suppressed polities to gain their independence.

Independence Movements and Civil War

This brings us to the second contextual issue, the rise in independence movements and/or civil wars. The end of the Cold War, in many ways, had the consequence of re-awakening old polities. Ethnic, tribal, and religious polities were now challenging the traditional Westphalian states, which dominated the international landscape throughout the Cold War.[80] With this rejuvenation of once dormant

---

75 Such activities included the following: The formation of the IMT and IMTFE, and the signing of the Universal Declaration Human Rights, the Genocide Convention, and the Geneva Conventions.

76 One example is Leila Nadya Sadat, "The Evolution of the ICC: From The Hague to Rome and Back Again," in *The United States and the International Criminal Court: National Security and International Law,* ed. Sarah B. Sewall and Carl Kaysen (Lanham, MD: Rowman & Littlefield Publishers, Inc., 2000), 38. Sadat states that, "The Cold War rendered action on the…ICC virtually impossible."

77 Chris Brown, "Universal Human Rights: A Critique," in *Human Rights in Global Politics,* ed. Time Dunne and Nicholas J. Wheeler (Cambridge: Cambridge University Press, 1999), 115-116.

78 Rosenau, *Domestic-Foreign Frontier,* 153.

79 Young, *Governance in World Affairs,* 24.

80 Ferguson and Mansbach, *Polities,* 413-417; and Ferguson and Mansbach, "Global Politics at the Turn of the Millennium."

polities, the international community also received a new wave of independence movements and struggles for authority from these awakening polities. In places like the former Yugoslavia, the former Soviet Union, Rwanda, Quebec, Mexico, Sierra Leone, East Timor and many others, there have been struggles between competing identities for authority and the right to govern. Such struggles did exist prior to the Cold War, but the intensity and sheer number of these movements has undeniably increased over the past decade.[81] This new form of conflict has increased the need for an international criminal justice system that goes beyond traditional interstate violence. Thus, the contextual factor concerning increased independence movements, increased intra-state violence, and failed states, makes the necessity of establishing an international court that much greater.

Ad Hoc Tribunals

As a result of the lack of international justice institutions in place, and the rise in ethnic and tribal violence within Westphalian states, the international community responded with the establishment of the first ad hoc tribunals since the immediate post-World War II period. The International Criminal Tribunal for the Former Yugoslavia (ICTY) and the International Criminal Tribunal for Rwanda (ICTR) are important contextual factors in the ICC formation process. The formation of these ad hoc tribunals demonstrated the international communities desire to end impunity.[82]

The community of states undertook a concerted effort to bring those individuals responsible for war crimes, crimes against humanity, and genocide to justice and end the Cold War norm that placed state sovereignty above international justice.[83] These two courts represent a major step forward in the fight for a permanent ICC and scholars must consider them when analyzing the contextual influences on the negotiating process.[84]

However, the formation of these ad hoc tribunals did not simply impact the negotiation process because of their positive attributes. In many ways, it was the negative aspects of these tribunals that had the greatest impact on the negotiating process. The ad hoc tribunals encountered numerous problems. First, they were difficult to establish, resulting in slow start up times. They also encountered numerous personnel problems, financial difficulties, and management problems. They also took a long time to actually bring suspects to trial, due to both

---

81 The Commission on Global Governance, *Our Global Neighborhood,* 15-17.

82 The ICTY and the ICTR are not the only post-Cold War ad hoc tribunals however, they are the most successful. It is still not clear whether the Special Courts for Cambodia, East Timor, Iraq, and Sierra Leone will enjoy such success.

83 Nevertheless, this is still state sovereignty as defined by the term juridical sovereignty. These states still abide by the norm of empirical state sovereignty. Leonard, "Seeking Sovereignty," provides a detailed discussion of these terms.

84 Bassiouni, *Statute of the ICC,* 18-19.

enforcement difficulties and infrastructure dilemmas. Finally, these courts failed to implement a codified form of universal justice. In other words, the international community did not establish ad hoc tribunals in all instances of genocide, war crimes, and crimes against humanity. Thus, many scholars have concluded that these ad hoc tribunals are simply selective justice and not an objective form of universal justice.[85]

These problems led many actors in the international community to the conclusion that ad hoc tribunals were not the answer to the world's future humanitarian law issues. In order to rectify these problems, a large portion of the international community began to rally around the idea of a permanent international criminal court. Their argument was that a permanent ICC would alleviate many of the problems associated with ad hoc justice, while overcoming the future need for new ad hoc courts.[86]

American Domestic Context

Thus far the contextual factors all seem to enhance the prospects of an International Criminal Court. The global community has abandoned the Cold War mentality, the need for a new form of international justice is gaining acceptance, and the ad hoc tribunals made the norm of international courts of justice more palatable, while still showing the need for further rectification. But not every contextual factor was as beneficial to the formation process. In particular, the US domestic environment on this issue was far from supportive. Prior to the Rome Conference, the Senate Foreign Relations Committee, chaired by Jessie Helms, had publicly stated that any treaty emerging from Rome that had even a hint that an American could be tried by the ICC would be "dead on arrival" in his committee.[87] This type of domestic environment literally handcuffed the US delegation in Rome. The only way that David Scheffer and the US delegation could have approved a statute is if there were a clause that excluded US servicemen and citizens from prosecution by the ICC or the United Nation's Security Council retained veto power over all prosecutions. Helms' statement rang of "American

[85] Ball, *Prosecuting War Crimes,* 194, and Richard J. Goldstone and Gary Jonathan Bass, "Lessons from the International Criminal Tribunals," in *The United States and the International Criminal Court: National Security and International Law,* ed. Sarah B. Sewell and Carl Kaysen (Lanham, MD: Rowman & Littlefield Publishers, Inc., 2000), 51-60.

[86] Since the establishment of the ICTY and the ICTR, the UN Secretariat has called for the establishment of three other ad hoc tribunals in Cambodia, East Timor, and Sierra Leone. The establishment of a permanent ICC could prevent the need for future ad hoc tribunals and institutionalize a more permanent and universal norm concerning humanitarian law.

[87] Weschler, "Exceptional Cases in Rome," 91.

exceptionalism" and the desire by the US to have control over international institutions and yet, be excluded from their jurisdiction.[88]

Despite this anti-ICC domestic environment, the other participants at the Conference did not immediately dismiss the possibility of US approval. As discussed earlier, several concessions were made in an attempt to negotiate a position that would be acceptable to both the US and the pro-ICC states, such as the Like-Minded Group. Despite a strengthening of the complementarity clause and the establishment of a role for the Security Council, the US was still not willing to approve the Rome Statute. One of the primary reasons for this disapproval was the domestic environment that Scheffer would have to return to.[89] In fact, because of his disapproval of the Rome Statute, Scheffer returned a hero to Helms and many on the Foreign Relations Committee.[90]

Helms' rhetoric on the ICC did not slacken after the Rome Conference and in fact, has become complementary to the Bush administration's position on the ICC. In a speech to the United Nations Security Council, Senator Helms stated that:

> Americans distrust concepts like the International Criminal Court and claims by the United Nations to be the sole source of legitimacy for the use of force because Americans have a profound distrust of accumulated power…There is only one source of legitimacy of the American government's policies, and that is the consent of the American people.[91]

Helms continued his attack on the ICC following Clinton's last minute signing of the Statute on December 31, 2000. In response to Clinton's action, Helms stated that: "[He] will make reversing this decision, and protecting America's fighting men and women from the jurisdiction of this international kangaroo court, one of my highest priorities in the new Congress."[92]

---

88 Edward C. Luck, *Mixed Messages: American Politics and International Organization 1919-1999* (Washington, DC: Brookings Institution Press, 1999), 15-40, explains the premise "American Exceptionalism."

89 During the question and answer period at American University, David Scheffer said that the Helms statement was not a reason for US disapproval. In fact, Scheffer stated that the US would have approved a statute had several factors been incorporated into the text and the delegation would have been given more time to analyze the text. But judging by Scheffer's statements on what the US wants in the ICC, it is safe to say that Scheffer's wishes definitely parallel Helms' wishes.

90 Weschler, "Exceptional Cases in Rome," 110-111.

91 Senator Jessie Helms, "A Lack of Gratitude" (speech delivered to the United Nations Security Council, January 2000).

92 Christophe de Roquefeuil, "US Unlikely to Ratify Permanent International Criminal Tribunal," *Agence France Presse,* January 1, 2001.

Helms also introduced the *American Servicemembers' Protection Act of 2000* (ASPA) in the US Senate.[93] According to Helms and other US Congressmen, the purpose of this act is to protect US troops from unlawful prosecution. In fact, this bill attempts to prohibit any form of US cooperation with the ICC and its signatory states. The bill includes the following provisions:

- No governmental entity in the United States, including any court, may cooperate with the International Criminal Court in matters such as arrest and extradition of suspect execution of searches and seizures, taking of evidence, seizure of assets, and similar matters.
- The U.S. must secure permanent immunity for American personnel from ICC jurisdiction before the U.S. can participate in any assessed United Nations peacekeeping operation (or other arrangements must be in effect protecting such U.S. personnel from extradition to the Court).
- No classified national security information can be transferred directly or indirectly to the ICC.
- No country that has ratified the treaty establishing the Court can receive U.S. military assistance. (Exemption for NATO member countries and "major non-NATO allies," cited in the bill as Australia, Egypt, Israel, Japan, the Republic of Korea and New Zealand).
- The President may waive this restriction for countries that ratify the treaty but then enter into an agreement with the United States protecting U.S. personnel from extradition to the Court.
- The President is authorized to use all means necessary and appropriate to bring about the release from captivity of U.S. or Allied personnel detained or imprisoned against their will by or on behalf of the Court.
- The President is directed to analyze U.S. status-of-forces agreements and alliance command arrangements, and develop plans to achieve enlarged protection for U.S. military personnel from the ICC.[94]

As a result of this action, the US domestic environment continues to be a contextual factor that must be taken into account when attempting to understand the negotiation process. Senator Helms had a great impact on the US position and this has in turn had a great impact on the ICC formation process.

Global Governance

The final contextual factor brings together the first three factors that I discussed above. This factor is simply the new form of governance that appears to be

[93] Jessie Helms (R-NC) introduced the Senate bill (S. 2726) and Tom Delay (R-22nd TX) introduced the House bill (H.R. 4654) on June 14, 2000. The Bill passed the US Congress in August 2002.

[94] This summary comes from the World Federalist Association website: <http://www.wfa.org/icc.htm>.

pervading all issue-areas of world politics. The ICC is not the only regime the international community currently is or has recently formed that appears to transcend the sovereignty of states and involves multiple non-state actors in the formation process. In the emerging post-Westphalian order, arguably, the location of governance and authority is shifting to entities other than nation-states.[95] This relocation of authority has provided the international community with an environment that is much more conducive to regime formation and the ceding of authority, or at least sharing of authority, from states to transnational entities. One example would be the formation of the World Trade Organization in 1995, another is the ICC.

What this more open and fluid society has provided international actors with is an environment that is more amiable towards a permanent international criminal court. It is now acceptable for non-state entities to embody the attributes of governance and evoke some form of authority. Thus, the ICC is simply another attempt to form such an institution.[96]

Institutional Bargaining and Advocacy Networks

I have now discussed the five factors that have a bearing on regime formation within a multivariate model. One can see the culmination of these factors in the institutional bargaining process. It is within this institutional bargaining process that all of the aforementioned factors must come together and interplay to either form an international institution or fail in their attempt. Young and Osherenko admit that their model of institutional bargaining is still quite basic. It lacks a logical set of propositions that address the interrelationship between the direct and indirect factors of regime formation.[97] In an attempt to better understand the interplay between these different factors, and the actors that determine the influence of these factors, I would suggest employing an amended version of Margaret Keck and Kathryn Sikkink's discussion of transnational advocacy networks.[98]

Keck and Sikkink define transnational advocacy networks as follows:

---

95 This is not to say that states have lost their authority, but that the exclusivity of their authority has been undermined. In the current world order, authority can be found in numerous actors, including non-state entities.

96 The next chapter will discuss the premise of governance beyond states in much greater detail. I will also be using this perspective to understand the ICC and its implications on world politics in chapter nine.

97 Young and Osherenko, "Testing Theories," 244-245.

98 Margaret E. Keck and Kathryn Sikkink, *Activists Beyond Borders: Advocacy Networks in International Politics* (Ithaca, NY: Cornell University Press, 1998).

> relevant actors working internationally on an issue, who are bound together by shared values, a common discourse, and dense exchanges of information and services…they are organized to promote causes, principled ideas, and norms, and they often involve individuals advocating policy changes that cannot be easily linked to a rationalist understanding of their "interests."[99]

Before proceeding to apply this term, it is important to note the distinction between transnational advocacy networks and epistemic communities. According to Keck and Sikkink, both groups use information to further their cause, but TANs interpret information in order to influence policy-makers, whereas epistemic communities rely on hard data accumulated by natural scientists to convince policy-makers.[100] This is due to the fact that Keck and Sikkink define epistemic communities as primarily constructed of natural scientists. But as discussed earlier, Peter Haas does not make such a distinction.

According to Haas, epistemic communities can be constructed of either natural scientists or social scientists employing the methodology that is accepted for their discipline. Therefore, counter to Keck and Sikkink's definition, Haas, states that epistemic communities must have, "a shared set of *normative and principles beliefs*, which provide a *value-based rationale* for the social action of community members;"[101] and the information that they provide is "neither guesses or 'raw' data; it is the product of human interpretations of social and physical phenomena."[102]

A transnational advocacy network undertakes campaigns whose primary goal is to influence state decision-making policies in an attempt to implement a solution for that issue-area, often in the form of an international regime. According to Keck and Sikkink, the major actors in transnational advocacy networks are nongovernmental organizations, local social movements, foundations, the media, religious organizations, trade unions, consumer organizations, intellectuals, regional or intergovernmental organizations, and parts of national governments.[103] One shortcoming of this model is the failure to provide any role for states. This is where the amendment of their model may be useful for my analysis.

I believe that states, acting in their best interest, can be part of these advocacy networks. Keck and Sikkink's distinction between states and governmental parliaments and/or executives is not necessary. In many instances, states will take up the plight of a particular issue and pursue this issue in an attempt to influence the policies of other states. In the case of the ICC, it is obvious that the Like-Minded states acted in this capacity. If we analyze their role in conjunction with

---

99 Keck and Sikkink, *Activists Beyond Borders,* 2 and 8-9.

100 Keck and Sikkink, *Activists Beyond Borders,* 30.

101 P. Haas, "Introduction to Epistemic Communities," 3. Emphasis added.

102 P. Haas, "Introduction to Epistemic Communities," 4.

103 Keck and Sikkink, *Activists Beyond Borders,* 9.

the role of particular leaders and NGOs, I feel that the resulting discussion will center on the formation of a transnational advocacy network.

Young and Osherenko are looking for an understanding of the relationship between the influencing factors of a multivariate regime. Transnational advocacy networks may provide us with that understanding. In the case of the ICC negotiations, we see the interplay between several different actors who are all attempting to implement the same solution—a strong, fair, and independent ICC. It can be hypothesized that at the outset of the negotiating process, during the PrepCom meetings, there was a group of actors that would take the form of a transnational advocacy. This group would include: the Like-Minded Group of States, the members of the CICC, and the leadership of the negotiating process. These actors rallied together in an effort to achieve a successful campaign, which would involve the formation of an international criminal court. What bound this group together was a set of shared values and a common discourse, and throughout this negotiating process there was a tremendous amount of information exchange between these three sets of actors. They attempted to influence other state actors' interests on this issue, in particular those outside of the Like-Minded Group, and for the most part they were successful.

We can quantify the success of the transnational advocacy group for the ICC by looking at the number of states that joined the group, approved the Statute at Rome, and/or signed the Statute.[104] At the time of their formation, the Like-Minded Group was composed of approximately one dozen states. By the time the Rome Conference ended, this group numbered over sixty;[105] when the final vote was taken in Rome, one hundred and twenty nations voted in favor of the Statute; and at this point in time, the number of states that have signed the Rome Statute is one hundred and ninety-six.[106] This is clear evidence that the transnational advocacy group for the ICC was a successful one. Numerous states either changed policy or simply adopted this group's policy (because they lacked any real policy on this issue) and the support for this campaign continues to expand.

This discussion of transnational advocacy groups relates to the multivariate model of regime formation because it shows the links between many of the influencing factors. Interest-based factors, knowledge-based factors, and leadership factors all tie together around the formation of this transnational advocacy network. The states with a shared interest also have a common discourse with the knowledge-based actors and the individual leadership. The bond that exists among these actors is not only a shared discourse, but also a shared value system and a

---

[104] I do not include the number of NGOs that joined the CICC because the primary goal of a transnational advocacy group is to influence state policy, not the policies of non-state actors. But due to the increased membership in the CICC, one could also assert that the membership in this transnational advocacy group also grew tremendously.

[105] Bendetti and Washburn, "Drafting the ICC," 20 and 30.

[106] As of March 31, 2005.

common ideational construct. The two factors that are not prevalent in this advocacy group also influenced its formation. Power-based factors, especially those found in the hegemonic status of the US, influenced this process by making it necessary to form an advocacy group in an attempt to combat the US position on the ICC. Context is also a factor in the formation of this group because it is the contextual factors that were discussed that make the success of this advocacy group's goal plausible. Therefore, the formation of a transnational advocacy group is a way to view the linkages that exists between these different factors, and it is the success of this group that often determines the success of the regime formation process.

Conclusion

This chapter employed a multivariate model of regime formation in an attempt to better understand the ICC negotiation process. Previous analysis of the ICC, using a neoliberal institutionalist model, proved elementary and lacking in its conclusions. Many unanswered questions remained after such an analysis, but Young and Osherenko's model seems to have clarified most of those flaws.

The multivariate model is a very complex analysis of regime formation. It analyzes the regime formation process by engaging several different factors and the impact that these factors have on the formation process. In terms of the ICC negotiations, this model proved extremely beneficial because of its complexity. The formation of the Rome Statute and the ensuing International Criminal Court was not a simplistic process that engaged relatively few actors. Instead, what this analysis concluded was that the regime formation process was very complex, both in terms of the number of actors involved and the influences that affected the negotiations.

First, the multivariate model looked at the direct effect of the three traditional bivariate models of regime formation. In essence, because of the use of an interest-based perspective in this model, this analysis has subsumed the neoliberal perspective discussed in chapter five. However, the premise behind the use of a multivariate model is that any attempt at such a simplistic, parsimonious theory will probably fall short.[107] In this case that conclusion was true. By engaging only one school of thought, the analysis of the ICC lacked understanding. Maybe we would understand the role of states, *or* the role of the US, *or* the role of the CICC, but we would never understand the complex nature of the formation process unless we understood *all* of these factors. The multivariate model allows precisely that. This chapter was able to assess the impact of participating nation-states, hegemonic support (or lack of in this case), and epistemic communities or NGOs.

---

[107] Young and Osherenko, "Testing Theories," 238-240.

Along with assessing the impact of these direct factors, the multivariate model also analyzes two cross-cutting or indirect factors—leadership and context. Both of these factors had a tremendous influence on the ICC negotiation process. The type of leadership that was initiated at both the PrepCom meetings and the Rome Conference was crucial to a successful negotiation process. Without the leadership that was in place, the formation of an ICC would not have been as plausible, if possible at all. This aspect of the negotiations was a key component to the international community's approving of the Rome Statute. Context also played an influential role. Such factors as the end of the Cold War, the rise in independence movements, the formation of two ad hoc tribunals, the domestic environment within the US, and the emergence of a new governance structure in global politics all played a part in the formation of the ICC.

What is now apparent is that the ICC formation process was neither an easy process nor a simplistic one. Multiple actors, including non-state actors, had an impact on the Rome Statute. Multiple contextual factors also played a role in this process. Therefore, although this analysis appears to have encompassed a large number of factors, it is clear that any other type of conceptual analysis would have been failed to adequately understand the ICC and its complex nature.

This chapter also succeeded in addressing one of the shortcomings of the multivariate model. By applying the term transnational advocacy network to the final coalition that supported the ICC, I have recognized a primary link between the influencing factors of the multivariate model. The establishment of this TAN allowed for a successful negotiation process and provides an understanding of the relationship between the seemingly detached factors.

Young and Osherenko's multivariate model was extremely useful in understanding the formation of the ICC, but that was not the only goal of this text. The second goal of this text was to draw some conclusions, concerning world politics, from the novel features of the ICC case. It is clear that states, along with the CICC, individual leadership, and context all played a major role in the negotiations. It is also clear that a purely interest-based analysis of the ICC is inadequate. Knowledge factors played a crucial part in this process and even power factors, in the form of US opposition, impacted the negotiations. We also know that much of the reason for the formation of an ICC in 1998, and not in the early 1950s, is contextual. But this conclusion is not entirely clear. In order to properly address this issue we need to look beyond the ICC to the global environment. The next two chapters will discuss the analytical perspective global governance and then use this perspective to understand the impact and implications of the ICC's formation on the larger realm of international relations.

Chapter 8

What is Global Governance?

> The "tribes" of academe are notoriously subject to fads. We invent new words to show our uniqueness, as well as to overcome what we regard as the inadequacies of exiting languages to express what we mean... We should ask ourselves, then, is the phrase "global governance" just another such fad? With all of the literature on international organizations, regimes, and other multilateral institutions, what does the phrase "global governance" connote that these other terms do not? Or, is it just today's catchphrase among the up-to-date aspiring cognoscenti?
>
> Margaret P. Karns[1]

Introduction

As Margaret Karns notes, within the field of international relations there always seems to be a fad arising. These fads usually manifest themselves in the construction of new terminology and/or a new language for discussing global politics. The goal of their supporters is to overcome the perceived inadequacies of past perspectives of world politics. Scholars who see the previously "accepted" or mainstream paradigms as stagnant and lacking explanatory value try to introduce new paradigmatic language that they believe captures the nature of current global politics better. Sometimes the field enthusiastically accepts these fads and other times they fade into the distance and are only referred to in obscure journals.

Many international relations scholars view the current global governance literature as a fad. These scholars see this literature as embodying an ambiguous concept whose definition and usage lacks clarity. Therefore, in order to provide the field with a new tool of analysis, global governance scholars must define this concept more clearly. Only upon ascertaining a foundational definition of the condition of global governance can it serve as an analytical tool for understanding events in our global environment.

However, this task is not an easy one. This is primarily due to the fact that, as Lawrence Finkelstein stated, "global governance appears to be virtually anything."[2] It encompasses the actions of a multiplicity of actors, but does not involve government. Thus, scholars often perceive global governance as an

---

1 Margaret P. Karns, "Postinternational Politics and the Growing Glomerations of Global Governance," in *Pondering Postinternationalism: A Paradigm for the Twenty-first Century?* ed. Heidi H. Hobbs (Albany, NY: State University of New York Press, 2000), 40.

2 Lawrence S. Finkelstein, "What is Global Governance?" *Global Governance* 1 (1995), 368.

activity that encompasses all aspects of steering or guidance in world politics. While this may be true, such a description does not assist us in our endeavor to understand world politics. The broad nature of global governance theory only breeds confusion. It is this ambiguity that scholars must deal with before the discipline of international politics will accept this concept as a viable analytical tool. Therefore, the necessity to both define and understand this concept is crucial to any study of current global politics including this analysis of the ICC.

An Analytical Perspective

If global governance is to be considered a viable analytical perspective, then what is the foundation of this perspective?[3] What is its epistemological basis? What does it provide us in terms of our ontological understanding of the world? What are its primary units of analysis? In other words, what is the basic framework of this analytical perspective?

This is certainly not an easy question; therefore my readers should consider this attempt to address these queries preliminary and open to future alteration.[4] However, with this caveat in mind, if international relations scholars are to employ global governance as an analytical perspective, then they must first construct a toolbox that will hold this perspective. This toolbox will assist us in understanding the changing nature of global politics in a more fundamental manner than previous international relations theories. The importance of this endeavor lies in the fact that the field currently has only a "depleted tool shed" to assist in our understanding of the world.[5] An understanding of the condition of global governance may contain the necessary equipment to improve our knowledge and broaden our understanding of global politics.

Analytical Foundations

The first premise that our toolbox must contain is that the world is not static. Ontologically speaking, it is imperative that when employing a global governance

---

[3] I use the term "analytical perspective" instead of "theory" because I do not believe that there is currently a formal theory of global governance. One of the goals of this chapter is to bring the field closer to an understanding of global governance and the possible use of this concept as an analytical perspective.

[4] It is important to note that the intention of this brief foray into constructing an analytical perspective surrounding global governance is not to act as a comprehensive theory building exercise. Such an endeavor would take a tremendous amount of future analysis and research. What I intended to accomplish is to simply lay the foundation for future work.

[5] James N. Rosenau, "Toward an Ontology of Global Governance," in *Approaches to Global Governance Theory,* ed. Martin Hewson and Timothy J. Sinclair (Albany, NY: State University of New York Press, 1999), 287.

perspective that we view the international community as ever changing and transforming; and understand that this alteration leads to new relevant actors and new forms of authority.[6] In other words, the world and the change that occurs within it are all part of a socially constructed process. Knowledge and ideas play a central role in understanding the dynamic nature of global politics therefore, when we attempt to understand the foundational component of global society we must keep in mind that change is always possible.[7]

If we cannot consider the set of intersubjective meanings that define reality as static then a global governance perspective must attempt to understand shifts in ontology.[8] This is the main underlying assumption of a global governance perspective—that reality is always in flux. One can ascertain a clearer understanding of change (in the form of ontological shifts, global order change, and emerging governance structures) if they adhere to this main principle.

With an initial assessment of ontology in place, I must now turn attention to a discussion of the units of analysis that global governance scholars focus on. I believe that it is safe to assert that no single entity can hold its primacy throughout time. For example, if one were analyzing global relations in a Westphalian dominated era, then the primary units of analysis would have to be states and the relations between these states.[9] During this era, states were the rule-makers or the constitutive element of reality; therefore, analysis of their actions was crucial if scholars were to understand the Westphalian order. However, in the current post-Westphalian order, the influx of new international actors has complicated the ability of states to exercise their authority. Many non-state actors are now emerging as claimants of authority and it is their interactions, not only amongst

6 James N. Rosenau, "Toward an Ontology of Global Governance," 289, defines ontology as "the broad assumptions that people make about the nature of reality." Ontology attempts to understand what the world is like by explaining its base or foundational level and understanding the transformations that occur at this level.

7 Note that knowledge and ideas are not the only constitutive forces of global society. Material-structural forces also impact the formation of global orders thus initiating a co-constitutive relationship among these forces. For further discussion of this issue see: Robert W. Cox, "Social Forces, States and World Orders: Beyond International Relations Theory," reprinted in *Neorealism and its Critics,* ed. Robert Keohane (Princeton, NJ: Princeton University Press, 1986), 218.

8 Robert W. Cox, "Critical Political Economy," in *International Political Economy: Understanding Global Disorder,* ed. Bjorn Hettne (London: Zen Books, 1995), 34, defines ontology as "the configuration of intersubjectively constituted entities…[which] are not arbitrary constructions; they are the specification of the common sense of an epoch."

9 Following Bjorn Hettne, "Introduction: The International Political Economy of Transformation," in *International Political Economy,* ed. Bjorn Hettne (London: Zen Books, 1995), 12, one can attribute the Westphalian era to "the peace of Westphalian… the sovereign independence of states; each state being motivated in its international behavior by a consistent national interest; the inter-state system regulated by a balance of power among the principle powers."

themselves but also with states, which IR scholars must analyze. Thus, when employing a perspective that centers its analysis on the dynamic nature of global politics, what units should we be analyzing?

The answer lies in the common denominator between states and non-state units—spheres of authority (SOAs).[10] In the Westphalian order, scholars asserted that the primary sphere of authority revolved around the interaction amongst states. They saw states as the primary determinant concerning what norms and rules guide and influence the actions of international actors. With the emergence of a new order, a post-Westphalian order, a new group of scholars is declaring that a shift is occurring within the global governance pattern, and that shift includes a rise in the authority of many non-state actors.[11] This new primary sphere of authority entails a mixture of state and non-state units, whose interactions entail working collectively to achieve solutions to the rising number of transnational problems.[12] Therefore, when addressing the question of what is the world like and what is its furniture (ontology), global governance scholars reply that the world's natural reality is one of change and that the furniture that we see in it entails an analysis of spheres of authority.

With an ontological perspective complete, we can now turn to the question of epistemology. The basis for our knowledge of the world, or global governance's epistemology, resides with both an empirical analysis of our surroundings, in particular a historical analysis of global change, and also with an understanding of the crucial role that knowledge and an actor's ideational perspective play. As Hewson and Sinclair point out, a historicist's epistemology is crucial to understanding change.[13] This type of epistemology is clearly a rejection of positivism due to the fact that positivism, by its very nature, cannot explain structural change.[14] Historicism, on the other hand, looks at "human institutions [as being] made by people—not by the individual gestures of 'actors' but by

---

10 Rosenau, "Ontology for Global Governance,"295-297, explains the idea that the world is comprised of spheres of authority and that these spheres are what global governance scholars should be analyzing. Rosenau, *Domestic-Foreign Frontier,* 156-172, discusses four different types of SOAs in his work. These four forms of SOAs impact the current governance system, but because of the nature of the ICC, this analysis is primarily concerned with "accomodative SOAs." I will discuss this concept at greater length later in this chapter.

11 Heidi H. Hobbs, ed., *Pondering Postinternationalism: A Paradigm for the Twenty-First Century?* (Albany, NY: State University of New York Press, 2000), is an example of this new post-Westphalian literature.

12 Rosenau, *Domestic-Foreign Frontier,* 159-168, refers to these SOAs as "accomodative SOAs." The use of the term collective does not connote an absence of conflict. Instead, it refers to the action of conflict management through multilateral means.

13 Hewson and Sinclair, "Emergence of Global Governance Theory," 17-18.

14 Cox, "Social Forces, States and World Orders," 242-249, discusses the shortcomings of positivism versus the benefits of historicism.

collective responses to a collectively perceived problematic that produces certain practices. Institutions and practices are therefore to be understood through the changing mental processes of their makers."[15]

Acknowledgment of change is endemic in this epistemology. As stated above, Robert Cox understands that no historical structure will endure forever and that change comes about through both material transformation and/or ideational transformation. Both constitute the existing world order and therefore, when examining the change in ontology and order, scholars must acknowledge both.[16] Simplistically speaking then, what a global governance perspective entails is an analysis of shifting ontology, global order change, and the material and ideational forces that helped shape that change. Such an analysis allows us to examine and understand the emerging spheres of authority that constitute the new global governance structure.

Ontological Shift

Global governance is often thought to have emerged as a result of considerable global change.[17] Events within the last fifteen years have resulted in a drastic transformation of world politics: from the rise to prominence of non-state actors, to the increased formation of both IGOs and NGOs, to the shifting of authority away from, but not excluding, the Westphalian state.[18] The global governance perspective originated in these turbulent times and as a result, one could assert that the primary function of this analytical perspective is to understand change and the accompanying ontological shift.

An ontological shift is a transformation in the shared perception of how we define reality. According to Robert Cox, this transformation occurs as the result of historical structural change.[19] In other words, the system within which we live and the material construct of that system becomes altered. The result is a shift in the

---

15 Cox, "Social Forces, States and World Orders," 242.

16 Robert W. Cox, "Multilateralism and World Order," *Review of International Studies* 18 (1992), 170.

17 Hewson and Sinclair, "Emergence of Global Governance Theory," 3-23, state that global governance theory emerged as a reaction to events like the end of the Cold War and the intensification of the globalization process. Thus, one can consider global governance theory to be a new perspective within the field and assert that its relevance is directly related to the transformative times that existed after the Cold War period ended.

18 The change that global governance theorists are attempting to analyze has been most prevalent over the last decade or so. But the foundations of this change, depending on the issue-area of analysis, may stem back several decades if not centuries. I will discuss the origins of global change within the issue-area of human rights and humanitarian law later in this chapter.

19 Cox, "Towards a Post-Hegemonic Conceptualization," 132-134, discusses the idea of shifting ontologies and the foundations of such transformative moments.

shared set of meanings that people hold about global politics. James Rosenau and others offer a different perspective on the origins of change. According to Rosenau, this alteration can occur in two ways:

> [E]ither the *conditions* of peoples' existence are so profoundly transformed that people are led by the cumulation and normalization of anomalies to alter the way they intersubjectively experience them, or their *awareness* of their existing conditions shifts in response to new technologies that enable them to perceive their prevailing circumstances in a new context.[20]

In the current period of time, both causal factors appear prevalent and the emergence of an analytical perspective predicated on global governance stems from the fact that traditional analytical perspectives of international relations failed to account for the changing global environment. The globalization of national economies, the decline of state sovereignty, the rise of NGO influence, the broadening of IGO mandates, the internationalization of human rights and environmental crises, and the failure of the nation-state community to control the rising tide of transnational problems, have all led to an expansion of governance activities beyond the state and provided an analysis of the world, via global governance, with the opportunity to flourish because of its ability to explain such change.[21]

However, accompanying this material-structural transformation has been a cognitive-ideational shift. As Rosenau explains, without a human awareness of transformations taking place, change is never fully implemented. Therefore, I feel that it is safe to conclude that neither the material-structural forces nor the cognitive-ideational understanding of this process fully explains change. One must understand change as a complex co-constitutive relationship between the two. As a result, the primary goal of this analytical perspective is to analyze change in regards to both world order and ontology, and then use this knowledge to understand the emerging governance pattern and the authority structures that may embody that pattern.

As discussed earlier in this chapter, this statement does not mean that global governance is a new phenomenon. Global governance as a *social condition* has existed for centuries, but global governance, as an *analytical perspective*, is the result of recent global events. Therefore, we should consider this perspective new, but this does not preclude the use of this analytical perspective to understand previous transformative periods. In other words, this perspective may be applicable to more than the alteration between Westphalian and post-Westphalian

---

20 Rosenau, "Ontology for Global Governance," 290. I added the emphasis for this text.

21 Karns, "Postinternational Politics, Global Governance," 44, categorizes the factors contributing to the transformation of global politics' ontology: environmental degradation, global socioeconomic changes, and technological revolutions.

orders. IR scholars may also use it to understand change in global order and governance structures no matter the time period.

Grounding the Perspective

Thus far I have discussed global governance as a perspective from which one can understand change—change in ontology, order, and governance structures. However, if scholars use such a global governance perspective to understand change, what is the definition of global governance as a condition? As stated at the outset of this chapter, some scholars in the field of international relations view global governance as the field's current fad.[22] They see this term as simply the reformulation of the international regime literature, only less tangible because the global governance literature lacks the necessary clarity that could provide it with some staying power in our field. Such criticism appears justifiable considering the lack of cohesion that international relations scholars have had surrounding a definition of this concept.

In attempting to define global governance, one could find a multiplicity of definitions ranging from: the sum of ways in which individuals and institutions manage their common affairs through cooperative action,[23] to the rules, norms, and organizations that address international problems that states cannot solve unilaterally,[24] to collective actions that establish norms and institutions for the purpose of dealing with multilevel problems.[25] Most of the current definitions tend to center around the idea of global cooperation and the establishment of norms and/or institutions through a process of conflict management. Clearly these attributes are a large part of global governance. However, what these definitions often fail to investigate is the basis for these norms and institutions, the actors that impact the type of governance pattern that exists, and the evolutionary nature of the concept. In short, most current definitions of global governance are too simplistic and too ambiguous.

Despite the simplistic and ambiguous nature of the current global governance literature, there is one thing that all definitions do agree on, and that is the fact that governance is not government. Therefore, this analysis will not entail a discussion

---

[22] Karns, "Postinternational Politics, Global Governance," 40-45, discusses the question of whether global governance is a fad or not.

[23] Commission on Global Governance, *Our Global Neighborhood*, 2.

[24] Karen A. Mingst, *Essentials of International Relations* (New York, NY: W.W. Norton & Company, Inc., 1999), 268.

[25] Raimo Vayrynen, "Norms, Compliance, and Enforcement in Global Governance," in *Globalization and Global Governance,* ed. Raimo Vayrynen (Lanham, MD: Rowman & Littlefield Publishers, Inc., 1999), 25. These definitions are only a small example of the numerous definitions that have been posed over the past decade. The importance of these examples is the lack of cohesion surrounding a definition of this concept.

of an emerging, formalized form of global government. Instead, it will center on the notion of governance as it exists outside of formalized governmental institutions. This analysis will engage the concept at the level in which it becomes established in accepted norms and rules, and will attempt to understand the impact of these norms and rules on the broader global system and its governance pattern. Once I have established this point, then I can begin to look at one of the possible results of this order, the formalized institution of the ICC, and examine whether or not this institution is working to stabilize the actors' intersubjectively shared understanding of global governance.[26]

Defining Global Governance

Often times the global governance literature uses the terms governance and authority interchangeably. In order to properly understand the concept of global governance let me begin this analysis with an examination of these two concepts and their relationship to global governance.

The term governance is etymologically tied to the premise of steering or helmsmanship.[27] As James Rosenau describes it, "The process of governance is the process whereby an organization or society steers itself, and the dynamics of communication and control are central to that process."[28] Olav Schram Stokke builds on this foundation to define governance as, "the establishment and operation of a set of rules of conduct that define practices, assign roles, and guide interactions so as to grapple with collective problems."[29] Thus, we can view governance as an accepted set of rules that guide actors' behavior in their endeavor to solve collective problems.

Authority, on the other hand, is often defined as, "the right to command and correlatively, the right to be obeyed."[30] This type of definition tends to view authority as being predicated on a hierarchical structure in which a specific entity or group of entities holds the ability to command the actions of other actors. Governance, at least in an accommodative SOA, does not necessitate such a hierarchical command structure. Governance only requires the existence of control through an intersubjective consensus among actors.[31] Thus, authority can be

---

[26] Cox, "Social Forces, States, and World Orders," 219, discusses the fact that "institutionalization is a means of stabilizing and perpetuating a particular order."

[27] Rosenau, "Governance in the Twenty-First Century," 14, explains that "governance" is derived from the Greek word *kybenan* or *kybernetes* which means to steer or pilot.

[28] Rosenau, *Domestic-Foreign Frontier,* 146.

[29] Stokke, "Regimes as Governance Systems," 28.

[30] R.P. Wolff, "The Conflict Between Authority and Autonomy," in *Authority,* ed. Joseph Raz (Oxford: Basil Blackwell, 1990), 20. *Webster's New World Dictionary* provides a similar definition: "The power or right to command, act, etc."

[31] Rosenau, *Domestic-Foreign Frontier,* 145-149, discusses the fact that hierarchy and command are not prerequisites for governance. This does not mean that hierarchy cannot

viewed as an outcome of governance. Once the establishment of norms and rules is determined and accepted by the relevant actors, governance becomes authority or the right to command and maintain the established rules. It is at the moment in time when a specific governance pattern becomes socially accepted that the terms governance and authority become congruent. This is an important point to emphasize because it shows that the location of authority is central to any discussion of global governance as a condition.

In the emerging global order, which may be termed a post-Westphalian order, there is a newly emerging governance structure. Rosenau describes this emerging governance structure as follows:

> considered in a fragmegrative worldview [a post-Westphalian order], not only have states lost some of their earlier dominance of the governance system, but also the lessening of their ability to evoke compliance and govern effectively is in part due to the growing relevance and potential of control mechanisms sustained by transnational and subnational systems of rule.[32]

This shift in the location of authority appears to be from the Westphalian state to multiple spheres of authority (SOAs), both at the subnational and supranational level.[33] The result of this shift in the location of authority is the emergence of a governance structure that encompasses both state and non-state centric entities, which has, in turn, triggered the initiation of a post-Westphalian order. Rosenau argues that several factors have facilitated this shift in authority: the end of the Cold War, the search for more effective political organizations, the skill revolution, the emergence of subgroupism, continued globalization, and the intensification of interdependence and the issues that now apply to this term.[34] The result is that authority and governance in the post-Westphalian order are derived from the actions of states and non-state actors, sometimes acting independently and other times acting in coordination with one another. Therefore, it is arguable that the emerging global governance structure is centered on the premise of global civil society.[35] Thus, the means of governance appear to be shifting as well, and the result is an altered form of global governance in the post-Cold War world.

---

exist as part of a governance pattern. Rosenau discusses several forms of compliance relationships within SOAs, one of which is command. But the point I wish to establish is that this hierarchy is not necessary for an SOA or governance to exist.

32 Rosenau, *Domestic-Foreign Frontier,* 173.

33 Rosenau, *Domestic-Foreign Frontier,* 39-41.

34 Rosenau, *Domestic-Foreign Frontier,* 153.

35 Young, *Governance in World Affairs,* 9, defines global civil society as a "system that is made up of a variety of nonstate actors, including interest groups, professional associations, and corporations, that operate above the level of the individual but below or apart from the level of any structure of governance."

Means of Global Governance

Just as the condition of global governance is altered with the transformation of global order, so too does the means of global governance become altered with a transformation in the pattern of global governance. The means of governance refers to the mechanisms through which the norms and rules that guide international actors' actions are established.[36] In other words, it is the regimes, in the broadest understanding of the term, or institutions that embody the current governance pattern.[37] As described earlier, the global governance pattern varies. Therefore, with the evolving global governance pattern comes a different means of governance. This logic tends to uphold Finkelstein's critique of this literature that "global governance appears to be virtually anything."[38] Even Rosenau argues that the means of governance can be state-sponsored, non-state sponsored, or jointly sponsored. They can exist within the boundaries of nation-states, in transnational institutions, or in subnational entities.[39] Nevertheless, if we can understand the condition of global governance, as it exists within a particular global order, then one can make certain generalizations about the dominant pattern of governance and the means of governance. As a result, Finkelstein is correct—global governance can be virtually anything, but not everything at any given time. Certain patterns of global governance emerge during certain periods of time, thus allowing international relations scholars the ability to generalize about that particular period.

One way to approach this question of means of governance is to think of the world as being constructed of different "spheres of authority (SOAs)." As stated earlier, Rosenau uses this term to refer to the existence of actors who possess the ability to both command others and require their obedience within a particular sphere.[40] This terminology is used to refer to the loci of global governance existing within a particular period in time; thus, there is no one sphere of authority that embodies the governance patterns across global orders. Instead, new spheres of authority rise to prominence and coexist due to the diverse demand for forms of

[36] Oran R. Young, "Global Governance: Toward a Theory of Decentralized World Order," in *Global Governance: Drawing Insights from the Environmental Experience,* ed. Oran R. Young (Cambridge, MA: The MIT Press, 1997), 275-280, refers to regimes as "sources of governance." The premise means of governance can be thought of in much the same manner.

[37] Krasner, "Structural Causes, Regime Consequences," defines regimes as explicit or implicit norms, rules, and decision-making procedures around which international actors' interests converge within a given issue-area. According to this definition, institutionalization is not a required attribute of a regime. A regime can simply exist around a socially accepted norm that is adhered to by the community of actors. This broad understanding of regimes enables it to be a key aspect of the means of governance.

[38] Finkelstein, "What is Global Governance?" 368.

[39] Rosenau, "Governance in the Twenty-First Century," 20-39.

[40] Rosenau, *Domestic-Foreign Frontier,* 39-41.

governance. As collective choice problems continue to proliferate, the need for more governance arrangements increases. The result is an upsurge in the formation of SOAs or means of governance. This may also result in multiple spheres of authority existing within one pattern of global governance. Nevertheless, within each pattern there exists a more prominent sphere that tends to better capture the norms and rules that are guiding the actions of the international community. This dominant sphere is thought of as the primary means of governance.

Rosenau defines four different types of SOAs. 1) Established SOAs, which refers to the continued dominance of states and state authority when constructing global policies. 2) Accomodative SOAs, in which authority is constructed as part of cooperative relationship between both nation-state governments and other non-state entities.[41] 3) Contested SOAs, in which accommodation is not an option due to the contentious nature of the system. In a contested SOA, international actors consider the use of force a viable option. 4) Transient SOAs, which result from an unclear location of authority due to domestic activities that cause cross-border spillover. If and when actors can resolve the consequences of the spillover, these domestic activities may prove transient.[42]

Now Rosenau considers SOAs as part of governance along the "Frontier." In short, the Frontier refers to a salient locus of global politics. It "points to an epochal transformation…[and] a new way of thinking about how global politics unfolds."[43] Rosenau's understanding of the Frontier is part of the ontological shift that global governance theory attempts to explain. His discussion and categorization of SOAs is referring to the status of SOAs in the current governance pattern, which is "postinternational." For this analysis, I will center my discussion of SOAs as a means of authority on established and accomodative SOAs, and their resulting norms, rules, and institutions. In my opinion, these two broad understandings of SOAs best capture the tension that exists between an order based on the idea of international society and one predicated on global civil society. Thus, these two forms of authority embody the means of global governance within the most recent world orders.

The Westphalian order, or international society, is predicated on the norms and rules put forth by Rosenau's established SOA. In other words, this system of governance was primarily determined by the action of states and the norms and rules that they established, most notably, the state sovereignty norm. It would be hard to argue against the idea that since the formation of international relations as a field of social science, the dominant unit of analysis has been the state. This is due

41 My use of the term cooperation does not connote an absence of conflict. It is cooperative in the sense that both state and non-state actors are working in coordination to manage the conflict that does exist.

42 Rosenau, *Domestic-Foreign Frontier,* 154-172.

43 Rosenau, *Domestic-Foreign Frontier,* 7.

to the fact that throughout this time period the norms and rules that guided global politics were established by these states.[44] But with the end of the Cold War, it became obvious that a new way of thinking about global politics was necessary.[45] No longer could we consider states the sole vessel of authority. The rise to prominence of numerous non-state actors, both transnational and subnational, has necessitated a reformulation of how international relations scholars study global politics. The result is the necessary acknowledgement, by both scholars and policymakers, that a new global order is emerging, and that this new order is based on the idea of global civil society and a new pattern of global governance that more closely accords with Rosenau's accomodative SOA.[46]

Governance is now undertaken by multiple actors working to overcome the world's collective problems. States do not initiate governance structures on their own. They now must account for the ideas and power of numerous non-state actors. In many ways, we can see the formation of the ICC as a classic example of this new governance structure.

World Order

Throughout this discussion of global governance, the term world order has repeatedly arisen. This is due to the fact that world order is an "interactive phenomena" with global governance.[47] Therefore, in order to provide a complete analysis of global governance, I must briefly examine the concept world order in

---

44 Since the formal establishment of the discipline in 1919, state-centered theories have tended to dominate the study of IR. This can be seen as a reflection of a state-centered world and a governance structure that was dominated by the action of these units. But in recent years this basis of our field has come under increased scrutiny. The primacy of the state is under fire and this attack is well documented in a wide array of recent literature. This includes: Martin Hollis and Steve Smith, *Explaining and Understanding International Relations* (Oxford: Clarendon Press, 1990); Smith, "Self-Images of a Discipline"; Strange, *Retreat of the State;* Rosenau, *Domestic-Foreign Frontier;* Ferguson and Mansbach, "Global Politics at the Turn of the Millenium," among numerous others.

45 This is not to say that the end of the Cold War initiated an ontological shift, but that this event was simply part of an evolutionary process, albeit a proverbial watershed. In other words, the origins of this ontological shift are at least decades old. Within the issue-area of humanitarian law, the origin of the ontological shift stems back at least to the Holocaust. It was at this point in time that the international community began to alter their set of shared understandings on human rights. The shift evolved from that point and its culmination resulted in the ratification of the Rome Statute.

46 This does not mean that accomodative SOAs are the only current form of governance or that established SOAs are the only form of governance. Other SOAs exist and there remains a significant amount of contention among these SOAs. But the accomodative SOA appears to be the dominant one in this post-Westphalian order and the established SOA appears to have been the dominant one in the Westphalian order.

47 Rosenau, "Governance, Order, and Change," 8.

order to understand the foundations of the current order, within which the ICC is being formed.

Hedley Bull defines world order as "those patterns or dispositions of human activity that sustain the elementary or primary goals of social life among mankind as a whole."[48] Stephen Gill expands on this definition to construct a more complex notion of world order. According to Gill:

> A world order configuration involves a persistent pattern of international relations—or global social relations—over time. It is a term that helps to define and to outline the conditions of war and peace in a given era. Hence, 'world order' does not necessarily imply stability or a desirable set of international arrangements—it is an analytical phrase that principally seeks to represent the actual configuration of social forces in a given era.[49]

This definition of world order provides us with several crucial elements of this concept. First, it is important to note that world order is not synonymous with stability. World order is simply the underlying pattern of social relations that exist within a particular era of time. Thus, world order may take the form of anarchy, bipolarity, hegemony, etc. World order is simply the basic construct of the global system and its social relations, regardless of whether that construct is "peaceful," "orderly," or "anarchical."

The second crucial component to understanding world order is that it is not a static concept. World order is dynamic, a condition that is constantly evolving, altering, and transforming. Depending on the historical period that one is analyzing, the world order that exists during this era will be unique. So during the "Westphalian era," one form of world order was prevalent; but now that some scholars are asserting a movement towards a post-Westphalian order, it is necessary to discuss a newly emerging world order. This dynamic quality is due to the fact that world order is primarily based on two separate, but interactive forces: material-structural forces and cognitive-ideational forces.[50] These two forces are the foundation of any world order; thus, as these forces are altered and transformed, the world order will change as well. In general, these forces act as the foundational construct of world order and as a result of their dynamic nature

---

48 Bull, *Anarchical Society,* 19.

49 Stephen Gill, "Transformation and Innovation in the Study of World Order," in *Innovation and Transformation in International Studies,"* ed. Stephen Gill and James H. Mittelman (Cambridge: Cambridge University Press, 1997), 15.

50 Rosenau, "Governance, Order, and Change," 14-15, cites three basic levels of activity that sustain global order: ideational, behavioral, and political. In an attempt to simplify this understanding, I have altered Rosenau's conception of global order to encompass the two forces mentioned above. One can view the behavioral component as simply a resulting pattern of these two forces.

we must consider world order a dynamic phenomenon.[51] But what exactly are material-structural and cognitive-ideational forces?

Material-structural forces are basic material capabilities, resources, and actors that control these resources. This would include the primary actors in world politics, the institutions that either exist or are being constructed, and the interplay that exists between these two groups during the formation of norms and rules. Thus, as Robert Cox describes them, the material-structural forces: "In their dynamic form… exist as technological and organizational capabilities, and in their accumulated forms as natural resources which technology can transform, stocks of equipment (for example, industries and armaments), and the wealth which can command these."[52]

It is difficult to define cognitive-ideational forces as objectively. Cognitive-ideational forces are the shared sets of values and belief systems that tend to permeate the international environment.[53] In other words, cognitive-ideational forces serve as the social knowledge that assists in forming the framework for institution building, behavioral action, and rule making within the global order. These forces are grounded in the accepted and adhered to perceptions that international actors have of the international system; therefore, it is this ideational aspect that in many ways establishes the norms and rules that international actors use to construct the world order's international institutions. The accepted cognitive-ideational forces also serve as part of the foundation of the resulting world order, which then forms the foundation for the governance structure. As a result, one can conclude that if there were a shift in these forces, the result would be not only a probable shift in material-structural forces, but also a shift in the world order itself and the resulting governance structure.

This type of logic shows the socially constructed nature of world order and global politics in general. [54] Cognitive-ideational forces act as a primary constitutive element of global order, thus making an understanding of the socially

---

[51] Cox, "Social Forces, States, and World Orders," 217-219, discusses a closely related framework. His framework discusses three categories of force that interact in historical structures: material capabilities, ideas and institutions. The premise of cognitive-ideational and material-structural in many ways parallels Cox's framework with institutions, or the institutionalization of these two, being the outcome of material-structural and cognitive-ideational interaction. It is important to note that once this institutionalization occurs, the resulting institutions do not lose their influence on the co-constituted world order. They now exist as a locus within this world order for the exercise of authority.

[52] Cox, "Social Forces, States, and World Orders," 218.

[53] We can think of cognitive-ideational forces as the prevailing ontology among the global community.

[54] Nicholas Onuf, "Constructivism: A User's Manuel," in *International Relations in a Constructed World,* ed. Vendulka Kubalkova, Nicholas Onuf, and Paul Kowert (Armonk, NY: M.E. Sharpe, Inc., 1999), 58-78, provides a summary overview of constructivism and its applicability to the field of IR.

accepted norms and rules of international society a necessary focus of world politics.[55] This is due to the fact that without an understanding of the collective intentionality that forms the socially accepted norms and rules, one cannot understand the origin of actors' interests and/or actions. We make the world what it is; therefore it is necessary to understand the cognitive-ideational forces that guide international actors because they are the constitutive elements of global society.

However, this does not mean that society does not impact the cognitive-ideational forces of global actors. Society and its material forces also act to construct the ideational positions of people. As a result, one can assert that ideas and society are co-constitutive, thus forming the need to study both cognitive and material forces when analyzing the construct of international institutions (such as the ICC) and world order. It is the interplay between these two factors that results in the establishment of a world order and the attendant international institutions that stabilize, perpetuate, and embody that order.

Another way to think about the concept of world order is in terms of international society versus global civil society.[56] The mainstream understanding of international relations has always asserted that the international social system is an international society. In other words, these scholars believe that the social system is constructed of and by states and the institutions that these states control. All power and authority are bound up in these entities, resulting in a very state-centric approach to the study of international relations.

The construct of global civil society, however, has a membership that is not confined to the community of nation-states. Instead, this society is more inclusive. In general, this perspective claims that any discussion of the world's social system must include not only the nation-states that an international society perspective discusses, but also the plethora of non-state actors that now exist.[57] These actors would include NGOs, multi-national corporations (MNCs), professional associations, social movements, and others.[58] The importance of this more

---

55 John Gerard Ruggie, *Constructing the World Polity: Essays on International Institutionalization* (New York: Routledge, 1999), 32-34, discusses the core components of social constructivism. In Ruggie's analysis, ideational factors are one of the core features of social constructivism.

56 Young, *Governance in World Affairs*, 8-11, discusses the idea of international society versus global civil society. I discuss these terms earlier in this chapter.

57 This does not mean that states are now longer crucial actors to an analysis of world politics. If the world order is predicated on the premise of global civil society then states remain key actors, they are now simply complemented by numerous non-state actors that were not prevalent in international society.

58 Note that this definition of global civil society and the actors that make up this type of system is taken from Paul Wapner, "Governance in Global Civil Society," in *Global Governance: Drawing Insights from the Environmental Experience,* ed. Oran Young (Cambridge, MA: MIT Press, 1997), 65-84, and Young, *Governance in World Affairs,* 9-11.

inclusive perspective is that it expands the discourse on global politics to account for a plethora of actors working to manage the numerous transnational problems that now exist. Instead of the study of world politics remaining tied solely to the nation-state, a global civil society perspective accounts for the influence of non-state actors, while still maintaining the importance, and in many instances primacy, of states. This perspective is simply a more complex and multifaceted lens through which one can view global politics.[59]

This analysis of international society versus global civil society relates to my analysis of world order by invoking two broad forms of recent world order.[60] The first, which is bound up in the idea of international society, is an order that centers on the nation-state and its primacy within global politics. This world order is generally referred to as the Westphalian order. The Westphalian order centers on the importance of the nation-state and the primacy of the norm of state sovereignty.[61] As Stephen Gill explains, "[T]he Westphalia settlement ratified emerging conceptions of sovereignty, and outlined norms and rules for interstate competition… sovereignty, authority, and legitimacy were re-articulated both within and between emerging nation-states.[62]

Thus, one can consider state sovereignty a primary constitutive principle of the Westphalian order and the ontological foundation on which that order rests. It is on this foundation that the Westphalian system is predicated and it is this perception of global politics that has dominated the field of international relations since its inception.[63] So when we talk about a Westphalian world order, what we are discussing is a persistent pattern of global activity that is centered primarily on the state and inter-state relations. Both the material-structural and cognitive-ideational forces of this order regard the state as the primary, and possibly sole, unit of analysis, and any scholarly endeavor to understand the global system was to

---

Some scholars and practitioners would not accept this notion of MNCs as part of global civil society and would actually view them as a problem that global civil society must deal with. But due to the origin of the definition employed, I shall consider all of the aforementioned actors to be part of this type of system.

59 Jean L. Cohen and Andrew Arato, *Civil Society and Political Theory* (Cambridge, MA: The MIT Press, 1992), have a detailed analysis of the evolution of civil society.

60 I use the term "broad forms" because as we will see, within the two orders I discuss there are smaller alterations and transformations that occur. These alterations often have to do with authority and hegemonic title, but an alteration concerning who holds these positions does not always result in a transformation of the broader global order.

61 These social forces include capitalism and property producing state sovereignty. Robert W. Cox, *Production, Power and World Order: Social Forces in the Making of History* (New York: Columbia University Press, 1987).

62 Gill, "Transformation and Innovation in World Order," 16.

63 We can clearly see this in the dominance that state-centered paradigms, such as realism/neorealism and neoliberal institutionalism, have had on the field's mainstream theoretical title.

be formulated through the use of a state-centric paradigm. Thus, the Westphalian order embodies Young's conception of an international social system—that being state-centered and exclusionary.

But as discussed earlier, world order is an evolving and dynamic social condition. The international society that once dominated the field's understanding of world politics is no longer an unquestioned ontological perspective. As I discussed earlier in this chapter, over the past decades some scholars have begun to describe the international system as an increasingly global civil society, or a post-Westphalian order. This type of system differs from the Westphalian order in that it is constructed not only of nation-states, but also non-state actors. Thus, the way scholars perceive the global system becomes not only more open and inclusive, but also more complex.

If international relations scholars are to properly understand the events and phenomenon of world politics, then they must look beyond the territorial boundaries of the state and take into account the actions of a plethora of non-state actors that have now arrived on the scene of global politics.[64] We must account for not only material-structural forces, but also cognitive-ideational forces. It is the interaction and influences of these forces that both shapes the world order and the subsequent governance structure and are shaped by it. The rising acceptance of this type of analysis by an ever-growing number of international relations scholars is proof that an ideational shift is occurring within our field. What these scholars are arguing is that current analysis of the international system is no longer limited to the Westphalian state system, because this type of analysis does not provide us with an accurate understanding of the existing world and its material forces. This type of thinking is prompting both a cognitive-ideational shift and a material-structural shift from an international society perception, to a global civil society perception. As a result, this is also one causal factor related to the current shift in world order from a Westphalian one to a post-Westphalian order.[65]

Conclusion

Global governance is the examination of the existing rules and norms that dominate global society. For the majority of international relations scholars, this

---

[64] The rise in the number of NGOs, social movements, transnational corporations, international regimes and other transnational movements has been well documented over the past decade. This increase in the number of non-state actors can be viewed as an alteration in the material-structural aspect of global order. This material-structural alteration has demanded that a cognitive shift occurs, and the combination of these two forces is causing a shift in global order.

[65] Not all international relations scholars adhere to this cognitive-ideational shift. Many prominent scholars still cling to a state-centric analysis of world politics, but this is slowly changing. Thus, the cognitive-ideational shift is occurring, but it certainly is not complete.

pattern centers on the Westphalian state system and the interaction among nation-states. However, over the past decades, this governance structure appears to be changing. What scholars once defined as an international society now appears to be transforming into a more encompassing global civil society. This type of change brings numerous non-state actors into the forefront of the global arena and necessitates the formation of a new perspective from which international relations scholars analyze world politics. Global governance may be that analytical perspective.

Global governance is a difficult perspective to define. This is because although there is a plethora of literature on global governance as a condition, there is very little literature on its analytical usage. Returning to the earlier definition of the perspective, I determined that global governance is about change—change in the existing ontology, order, the relevant actors, and the governance structure. Therefore, one of the primary goals of global governance as an analytical perspective is to analyze this change in an attempt to understand what the emerging global governance structure looks like. The explosion of writing on this subject is attributable to this very fact—since the end of the Cold War, international relations scholars have been searching for a new analytical lens that will assist them in understanding the transformation that has occurred in global politics and the emerging world order. Global governance may provide the most useful lens for such an endeavor.

Although I employ global governance as an analytical framework for understanding change, not all scholars accept such a position. Let us not forget that global governance remains a highly contested term/condition. Many scholars discuss global governance as a reactionary condition that stems from the need for maintenance in the current world order.[66] According to this perspective, global governance arose as an answer to the growing number of transnational problems, increased interdependence, and the need to reform how the global community initiates international cooperation.[67] Thus, global governance is not necessarily an analytical perspective; it is simply a reactionary condition to the material-structural changes of the past decades.

In terms of the formation of the ICC, this type of conditional perspective views the ICC as a reaction to and an attempt to control (through conflict management) the material-structural changes I have discussed in this chapter. I do not refute the validity of this claim. Material-structural conditions are an integral part of global

---

[66] Mihaly Simai, *The Future of Global Governance: Managing Risk and Change in the International System* (Washington, DC: United States Institute of Peace Press, 1994); Commission on Global Governance, *Our Global Neighborhood;* Weiss and Gordenker, *NGOs, the UN, and Global Governance;* and Young, *Governance in World Affairs,* are all examples of this type of analysis.

[67] According to the Commission on Global Governance, *Our Global Neighborhood,* xiv, this reform will come about through the institutions and processes of global governance.

governance. However, what this chapter its understanding of global governance acknowledges is that although global governance is reactionary, it is reactionary to change. This change need not be monumental, instantaneous change. It might well be evolutionary, step-level change. However, it is change nonetheless and that is what an analytical perspective centered on the condition of global governance is seeking to understand. I also do not refute the fact that global governance is a social condition. However, what this chapter attempted to establish is that IR scholars can also employ global governance as an analytical perspective.

Now if one adheres to the idea that an analytical perspective predicated on global governance is attempting to understand global transformation, what aspect of change is this perspective analyzing? If we recall the original definition of global governance, we see that it encompasses an analysis of the guiding rules and norms within a world order. Therefore, when analyzing the transformation between world orders, global governance must take into account the material-structural and cognitive-ideational causes of change, along with the shifting spheres of authority that occur, or the means of global governance. Such an analytical perspective provides scholars with the tools to understand global change and its origins, but it is important to remember that this type of analysis cannot confine itself to either a structural analysis or an ideational analysis. Both factors contribute to change and it is the interaction between these factors that initiates a shifting of authority. If IR scholars are to understand this change, then a global governance perspective must address both of these factors.

Once this is accomplished, those employing this analytical perspective can then turn their attention to the emerging pattern of governance. This will entail a more detailed investigation of the actors involved in the emerging order and the means of governance that these actors are employing. Obviously such an endeavor is quite complex, but the result is a broader understanding of the global environment and the relations that exist amongst its actors.

With this in mind, I now turn to an examination of the International Criminal Court and how a global governance perspective helps us understand its formation. This endeavor will certainly provide us with a broader, more encompassing perspective on this formation process, and will hopefully address some of the previously unanswered questions.

Chapter 9

The ICC and the Future of Global Governance

> Change means the attrition of established patterns, the lessening of order, and the faltering of governance, until such a time as new patterns can form and get embedded in the routines of world politics. Such is the situation today. One senses that the course of history is at a turning point, a juncture where the opportunities for movement toward peaceful cooperation, expanded human rights, and higher standards of living are hardly less conspicuous than the prospects for intensified group conflicts, deteriorating social systems and worsening environmental conditions. Either set of arrangements—or possibly both—could evolve as leaders and publics get accustomed to the heady realization that some control over the future has been regained as a consequence of all the changes.
>
> James N. Rosenau[1]

Introduction

The primary purpose of a global governance perspective is its attempt to understand change within our global system. This is one reason why international relations scholars have invoked the use of this analytical perspective over recent years. The decade of the 1990s was certainly one that was wrought with global change. One primary, but certainly not exclusive, event that perpetuated this change was the end of the Cold War and the collapse of the world's bipolar system.[2] Among the profound changes that have come about during the past fifteen years are the following: a continued and intensified process of globalization, a rise in intra-state conflicts, an increased number of non-state actors possessing an increased amount of authority, and the formation of a plethora of new intergovernmental organizations (IGOs) to deal with the world's growing number of transnational problems. All of these events, and many more not mentioned, have led international relations scholars to question the dominant paradigms of the Cold War era. As Yale Ferguson tells us:

> There is an urgent need for a postinternational revolution in the study of global politics, broadly conceived as a take-no-prisoners campaign waged by all those from various disciplines who are non-state-centric and yet empirical in their approach(es)...Realists,

---

1 Rosenau, "Governance, Order and Change," 1.

2 The Cold War is not the only reason for global change, instead it is part of an evolutionary process.

> neorealists, institutionalists, neoliberals, statist contructivists, and others are to be commended for trying to analyze the world as it is, but their state-centric blinders make it impossible for them to perceive the full spectrum of political reality.[3]

As a result, one could assert that in recent years there has been a transformation in how international relations scholars perceive global politics. This transformation is most clearly embodied in the movement from an analytical perspective that centered on international society, to one that now contains a more comprehensive conception of international relations as a global civil society. This change has also altered the norms and rules that guide international actors within many issue-areas, including the issue-area of humanitarian law. If we consider humanitarian law from this perspective, one can see that within this issue-area there has been a plethora of changes concerning the role of the state and the location of authority. One example of this change is the formation process surrounding the ICC. Therefore, in this chapter I will examine the formation of the ICC from a global governance perspective. This endeavor will not only provide international relations scholars with a more accurate understanding of why the international community approved the Rome Statute, but more importantly, what this institution means in light of the current change in the global system.

Post-Westphalian Order

In order to understand why the international community approved the Rome Statute by such a wide margin, it is important to first understand the international context in which the Rome Conference and ratification process took place. A global governance perspective is about understanding change and the implications of this change. A transformation in global order is just the type of change that this perspective hopes to understand. The importance of this change stems from the fact that the current global order forms the foundation for a discussion of the emerging global governance pattern, and understanding this pattern allows for a better understanding of the environment within which the formation of the ICC was possible. As described in the preceding chapter, any discussion of global order must begin with its two constitutive forces—material-structural and cognitive-ideational. Let us begin with a discussion of the material-structural forces in world politics and the contribution they have made to the current transformation process.

---

3 Ferguson, "Postinternationalism, Future of IR Theory," 202. It is important to remember that the primary attribute of an international society perspective of world politics is that the state is the central and primary actor. Ferguson is arguing that this form of analysis is no longer, and probably never was, a relevant way to view the world.

Material-Structural Forces

Today's international environment is one constructed on the premise of global civil society. The primary question that a global governance perspective attempts to address is how this type of society is forming and what are the primary factors that have led to this transformation? One of the principle forces in this alteration of international society is the intensification of the globalization process. [4] Martin Shaw defines globalization as: "A complex set of distinct but related processes—economic, cultural, social and also political and military—through which social relations have developed towards a global scale and with global reach, over a long historical period.[5]

Thus, we can view globalization as a boundary eroding process that results in increased interdependence and the increased importance of a more pluralistic group of international actors. These actors include: intergovernmental organizations (IGOs), international non-governmental organizations (INGOs), transnational corporations (TNCs), ethnic groups, religious groups, and other nested polities.[6] The result of this increased globalization process is that any analysis of international relations must now encompass numerous and diverse polities that, as the previous list depicts, include but also goes beyond the Westphalian state. In essence, what the globalization process is causing is an alteration of the material-structural aspect of the Westphalian model. The result is a rise in the relevance of non-state actors and the need for analysis of global order to move beyond the "territorial trap" and become more inclusive.[7]

Recall that the primary actor within the realist/Westphalian paradigm is the nation-state. It was the interaction among these rational, unitary actors that most international relations scholars studied, thus legitimizing the Westphalian global order. There was no question about this type of analysis and therefore, IR scholars

---

[4] As Ferguson and Mansbach, "History's Revenge, Future Shock," 86-88, point out, it is not that this globalization process is new but that over the past couple of decades there has been an increase in the intensification of the globalization process. This intensification has manifested itself in the increase in the transborder flows of goods, services and people, along with a rise in interdependence among states and other international actors.

[5] Martin Shaw, "State of Globalization," 497-513.

[6] This term "nested polities" is taken from Ferguson and Mansbach, "History's Revenge, Future Shock," 197-238. It describes the increased influence of polities that reside within the nation-state or other polities and now are attempting to reassert their identity. It is rare that old polities disappear, so as Ferguson and Mansbach point out, these nested polities are now becoming revitalized and becoming players on the stage of global politics.

[7] "Territorial trap" is a term used by John A. Agnew and Stuart Corbridge, *Mastering Space: Hegemony, Territory and International Political Economy* (London: Routledge, 1995), 78-100. It refers to the unquestioned state-centered analysis that has dominated international relations theory. Agnew and Corbridge see IR theory as caught in a nation-state, territorial trap that does not allow analysis of global politics to move forward.

simply took it as an ontological given that the Westphalian state served as the basic construct of global order. What this chapter is arguing is that this fundamental, material component of the Westphalian order is changing. We can no longer conceive of states as simply the primary actors within international relations because, as Susan Strange tells us, "the world has changed."[8]

The intensification of the globalization process has perpetuated a change in the material-structural forces that make up the global system, and as a result, it is also perpetuating a change in the global order. Thus, one could assert that the globalization process is causing a fundamental shift in the spatial construction of the world and transforming whom is considered an international actor and what their interactions look like.[9] This transformation is also causing an alteration in the governance pattern and the location of authority. Therefore, in order to analyze and understand both the current global order and the emerging global governance structure, IR scholars must look beyond the state, while not excluding it, to a more pluralistic view of the international system. The world has changed and with it so must our understanding of both world order and global governance.[10]

As described above, the broader realm of global politics is changing and as a result, this change has trickled down into particular issue-areas. Within the issue-area of humanitarian law, this change in the material-structural forces of global politics is most clearly seen with the formation of two ad hoc criminal tribunals in the mid-1990s. The first of these tribunals was the International Criminal Tribunal for the Former Yugoslavia (ICTY). The UN Security Council established the ICTY in 1993 "to prosecute persons responsible for serious violations of international humanitarian law committed in the territory of ex-Yugoslavia since 1991."[11] The second tribunal was formed in December of 1994. It was at this time that the United Nations Security Council approved the establishment of the International Criminal Tribunal for Rwanda (ICTR). The Security Council established this tribunal to prosecute persons responsible for genocide and other serious violations of international humanitarian law committed in the territory of Rwanda or by a Rwandan citizen between January 1, 1994 and December 31,

---

8 Susan Strange, "Wake Up, Krasner! The World Has Changed," *Review of International Political Economy* 1 (1994), 209-219. In this article Strange attempts to make this very point to Stephen Krasner and the rest of realist theorists, the world has changed from a Westphalian style system to a more pluralistic and inclusive system.

9 David Held, "Democracy and Globalization," *Global Governance* 3 (199?), 251-267.

10 For a more empirical analysis of the globalization process and its impact on non-state actors, see: Joseph A. Camilleri and Jim Falk, *End of Sovereignty? The Politics of a Shrinking and Fragmenting World* (Brookfield, VT: Edward Elgar Publishing Company, 1992); Strange, *Retreat of the State;* James H. Mittelman, ed. *Globalization: Critical Reflections* (Boulder, CO: Lynne Rienner Publishers, Inc., 1996).

11 Beigbeder, *Judging War Criminals*, 150.

1994.[12] The establishment of these two ad hoc tribunals was the first since the military tribunals following World War II, and they mark the material construction of two entities that embody the idea of global civil society.

The mandate of these ad hoc tribunals provided its participants with the ability to prosecute individuals who violated humanitarian law during an intra-state conflict. Such a mandate clearly clashes with the once unquestioned state sovereignty norm that existed during the Westphalian era.[13] These tribunals were given the ability, via a UN Security Council resolution, to intervene in the affairs of two sovereign states, Yugoslavia and Rwanda, and prosecute their citizenry at an international tribunal held outside of their territorial boundaries by judges of foreign nationality. Such an overt intervention into the affairs of sovereign state entities marks a profound break from the dominant norm of the Westphalian order. Arguably, the establishment of such transnational institutions is a clear example of the material-structural changes that are precipitating the emergence of a post-Westphalian order; and it is these changes that act as a precursor to the formation of a permanent ICC.

Two other material-structural transformations that occurred during the post-Cold War era include: 1) a rise in the number of IGOs being formed; and 2) a rise in the number and influence of international NGOs.[14] As chapter seven described, the global community appears to accept both of these actors as internationally influential. As a result, international relations scholars can no longer simply analyze the interaction amongst nation-states. It is imperative that they also account for the actions of non-state actors, such as NGOs, along with transnational institutions like IGOs. Without acknowledging this aspect of the global community, scholars of world politics will never obtain a true picture of international relations.

Cognitive-Ideational Forces

Material-structural forces are not the only causal factors of global change. Underlying this material-structural change is a new, socially accepted, ideational

---

12 Beigbeder, *Judging War Criminals,* 169-185, gives a detailed description of this tribunal.

13 Nicholas Onuf, "Intervention for the Common Good," in *Beyond Westphalia? State Sovereignty and International Intervention,* ed. Gene M. Lyons and Michael Mastanduno (Baltimore, MD: The Johns Hopkins University Press, 1995), 43, states that the state sovereignty norm "implies freedom from the interference of others." Therefore, a system predicated on this norm would mean that non-interference in others domestic affairs is the dominant rule.

14 Tafe, "Intergovernmental Organizations," discusses the increased number of IGOs and their new role in world politics. Keck and Sikkink, *Activists Beyond Borders,* and Cusimano, Hensman, and Rodrigues, "Private-Sector Transsovereign Actors," discuss the increased number and influence of NGOs.

perspective. This cognitive-ideational force is, in essence, what allows for the construction of new material institutions and what permits the influence of new non-state actors to be felt by the rest of the international community. Without a transformation in the cognitive aspects of international society, there would not be a shift to global civil society.[15] In short, what is occurring is a shift in the intersubjective understanding of the world (by many of the actors involved in global politics) towards a more inclusive understanding of which actors should be allowed to sit at the negotiation table and what type of entities possess authority in the international system.

In other words, a transformation is occurring in the underlying norms and rules of world politics.[16] No longer is state sovereignty the unquestioned, dominant rule in international relations. It is now deemed acceptable to violate this norm because the ideational construct surrounding it has been altered.[17] Thus, one can perceive of the formation of two transnational criminal tribunals that seemingly violate a state's sovereignty as not only acceptable, but necessary. The material construction of such institutions is an example of an alteration in the world's international actors' intersubjective understanding of sovereignty, and as a result, an example of the shift in both global order and the dominant global governance pattern.[18]

This type of alteration (in the underlying norms of society) is possible because of the socially constructed nature of these norms. It is imperative that IR scholars view the natural world as a social world—a social world that is constructed by the shared ideas of international actors. It is from these shared ideas that the establishment of norms and rules occur, thus allowing for the formation of material-structural forces that constitute the current discourse of world politics.[19] Currently, the ideational perspective on world politics is shifting towards a more inclusive understanding of society. I mean inclusive in the sense that one can now

---

15 Gill, "Transformation and Innovation," discusses the importance of cognitive forces on the shifting of global order.

16 Alexander Wendt, *Social Theory of International Politics* (Cambridge: Cambridge University Press, 1999), 24, calls this type of transformation the "constitutive effect of ideas."

17 Ruggie, *Constructing the World Polity,* 16-22, terms this phenomenon "ideational causation."

18 Jens Bartelson, *A Genealogy of Sovereignty* (Cambridge: Cambridge University Press, 1995), 246-248, discusses the alteration in actors' perceptions concerning sovereignty. Bartelson describes sovereignty as a concept that is tied to "the conditions of knowing," and therefore, if that condition changes so does the meaning of sovereignty.

19 Jim George, *Discourses of Global Politics: A Critical (Re)Introduction to International Relations* (Boulder, CO: Lynne Rienner Publishers, 1994), 29-30, defines discourse as the "broader matrix of social practices that gives meaning to the way that people understand themselves and their behavior…[it] generates the categories of meaning by which reality can be understood and explained."

view the construct of society as a global civil society, which allows for the influence of both state and non-state actors on world politics. This intersubjective understanding of the current world order confronts the once dominant norm of state sovereignty and the shared idea concerning world politics that nation-states would choose to undermine their authority, at least in certain instances.[20] As a result, the international communities' shared ideas surrounding state sovereignty have now changed.

No longer is state sovereignty deemed the final arbitrator over international problems. Instead, the authority that once resided in the nation-states' boundaries now exists in newly forming international regimes. In other words, the outcome of such a cognitive shift is a new set of norms and rules that allows for the material construction of new regimes and institutions. These material constructs are the physical embodiment of the international communities shared ideas, and therefore, their existence upholds the new rules, which have allowed for the construction of new regimes.[21] It is this current form of ideational and cognitive transformation that in many ways is allowing for a rise in the previously discussed material-structural forces and institutions.

One such institution is the International Criminal Court and arguably, this newly formed institution is the result of a cognitive-ideational shift and the embodiment of a newly emerging global governance pattern. Thus, by undertaking an analysis of the ICC from a global governance perspective, one can understand the underlying social ideas that currently exist and how these ideas shape our world. What we must now endeavor to understand is how these ideas affect the governance pattern of the current global order.

Emerging Global Governance Pattern

As described earlier, the norms and rules that dominated the global system for the majority of this century centered on the practice of state sovereignty.[22] The

---

[20] Kurt Burch, *"Property" and the Making of the International System* (Boulder, CO: Lynne Rienner Publishers, 1998), 159-160, reminds us that state sovereignty is also a socially constructed practice. As a result, this social practice can be altered, reconceptualized or dismissed. I am not arguing that state sovereignty is being dismissed, but the recent rash of regime formation that tends to undermine state sovereignty shows the diminishing impact of this social practice.

[21] Onuf, "Constructivism: An User's Manual," describes the logic of social construction. He claims that rules make agents and agents make rules, rules form institutions, institutions form societies, and these rules yield a type of rule. Leonard, "Discovering the New Face of Sovereignty," applies this form of social constructivism to the ICC case.

[22] This does not mean that the system has remained static throughout this century. Authority has shifted between multipolar, bipolar and unipolar forms. But those forms of authority have always been bound up in the territorial state and its sovereignty.

construction of regimes and/or institutions during this era usually resulted from the interaction between these sovereign state entities and as a result, was closely controlled by these states. To use Rosenau's terminology, the dominant sphere of authority during this era was "established SOAs."[23] But with the end of the Cold War there appears to have been a shift in the shared ideas surrounding this norm. As a result, in the emerging post-Westphalian order, the global governance pattern appears to be occurring through multiple spheres of authority.[24] The world is now constructed of a complex conglomeration of governance. Depending on the issue-area one is analyzing, the form of governance and the sphere of authority that is established will vary. With this variation in mind, the purpose of this section is to analyze the formation of the ICC using global governance theory. Therefore, my analysis will center on the issue-area of humanitarian law and the shared ideas that exist within this area.

Understanding the Formation of the ICC

Previous chapters have analyzed the formation of the ICC from two different analytical perspectives—neoliberal institutionalism and a multivariate model of regime theory. Through the use of these two perspectives, we have ascertained a full and rich understanding of the formation process. However, one crucial question remains unanswered—why now? Why did the ICC formation process achieve such tremendous success during the 1990s, when it failed to achieve the same success during the early 1950s? A global governance perspective holds the key to that answer in its analysis of change and shifting patterns of governance.

Global governance emphasizes the context within which events are occurring. Therefore, if we want to understand the formation of an international institution from a global governance perspective, then the global environment or, more specifically, the global governance pattern, must have the greatest impact on the formation process. In fact, the global governance pattern influences all of the factors that come into play during the formation process. What we can derive from this is that the multivariate model of regime theory, which was so successful in understanding the ICC formation process, will nest within the global governance pattern and all of its influence. The governance pattern would, in essence, constitute the formation of an international regime.

If we recall the cognitive-ideational shift that is occurring, along with the formation of certain material-structural entities, one can see that the post-Westphalian governance pattern, at least within the issue-area of humanitarian law,

23 Rosenau, *Domestic-Foreign Frontier,* 159.

24 Rosenau, *Domestic-Foreign Frontier,* 154-173, describes four different types of SOAs: established, accomodative, contested, and transient. My analysis of regimes and the ICC as an SOA falls into the accomodative category because of the cooperative interaction amongst both state and non-state actors.

has become based primarily on a greater inclusion of non-state influences and the formation of cooperative arrangements to deal with global problems, such as genocide, crimes against humanity and war crimes. This governance pattern is empirically documented by the formation of two fully functioning international criminal tribunals. One can also cite the Pinochet case and the establishment of other ad hoc tribunals as other examples of the ideational shift that is occurring within this issue-area. The attempt to extradite and try sovereign state leaders for crimes against humanity clearly shows the increased tensions that exist between the state sovereignty norm and the emerging global governance pattern.[25] So when addressing the question of "why now?" one must look to the context and the governance patterns that existed at that time.

The first substantive attempt to establish a permanent international criminal court was in the early 1950s. Between 1951 and 1953, the International Law Commission submitted a series of reports and drafts on the formation of a permanent ICC to the United Nations General Assembly.[26] The global community appeared ready for the establishment of such a court. The immediate post-World War II era was strewn with ad hoc criminal tribunals, human rights treaties, and discussions of ways to prevent future violations of humanitarian law. But upon receiving the 1953 revised statute for an international criminal court, the international community balked. At this moment in time, support for such an institution had subsided and it would be another thirty-six years before discussion of an ICC would re-surface.[27]

The primary reason for this failed formation attempt was the resurgence of a global governance pattern that was explicitly tied to the state sovereignty norm. Although the community of states had "internationalized" the norms of individual human rights and international humanitarian law during the post-World War II era, the state sovereignty norm still held the realization and enforcement of these norms hostage within the nation-state's domestic boundaries.[28] If the international community, most notably the world nation-states, allowed for the formation of an

---

[25] Despite the fact that Pinochet was not extradited to Spain for trial does not diminish the fact that such action upholds the current international distaste for the state sovereignty norm. As Slobodan Milosevic understands, it is no longer acceptable for political leaders to claim non-interference in defending their actions. If a violation of humanitarian law occurs, those responsible will be publicly chastised and in the future, brought to justice. This is the governance pattern that is emerging within this issue-area.

[26] Chapter two discusses these reports at length.

[27] In 1953, the only major world power to support the ILC draft was France. The US was strongly opposed to the formation of an ICC, but couched their opposition around the failure of the ILC to adequately define the crime of aggression.

[28] Jack Donnelly, "The Social Construction of International Human Rights," in *Human Rights in Global Politics,* ed. Tim Dunne and Nicholas J. Wheeler (Cambridge: Cambridge University Press, 1999), 75, discusses the primacy of state sovereignty despite the existence of numerous international conventions on human rights and humanitarian law.

international criminal court, they would be ceding a portion of their authority to this permanent institution, and frankly, the discourse surrounding that moment in time would not allow for such a governance structure to exist. States were determined to maintain a global community that was predicated on the idea of an international society, not a global civil society.

But the world is not static, and the norms and ideas that are shared amongst international actors are also not static. In 1989, the discourse surrounding what global governance is began to change.[29] Within the issue-area of human rights (more specifically humanitarian law), the institutionalization of certain norms once again became a topic of discussion for the international community. In 1989, Trinidad and Tobago resurrected the idea of a permanent international criminal court, and in 1993-1994, The United Nations Security Council established two international ad hoc criminal tribunals that appeared to trump the once dominant state sovereignty norm.

We can view this process of ideational alteration, coupled with the material construction of institutions that uphold the new pattern of governance, and predicated on the notion of global civil society, as part of a "norms cascade."[30] A norms cascade being the process through which norms become internalized by international actors and become an unquestioned quality of their behavior.[31] By the middle of the 1990s, it is clear that an alteration in the guiding norms and rules of humanitarian law was occurring. State sovereignty was no longer an unquestionable norm and as a result, states were becoming more open to non-state influences (NGOs, TANs, etc.) and the formation of institutions that supersede their sovereign rights. The penultimate result of this ideational shift is the success achieved in Rome 1998 and the ensuing ratification process. The new global order (global civil society) gave way to a new global governance pattern, which gave way to the formation of new regimes, which embody the new global governance pattern. The ICC is an example of this process.

Institutionalizing the Global Governance Pattern

Arguably, the new governance structure of the post-Westphalian era is bound up in the formation of international regimes. Oran Young even defines global

---

[29] In many ways, the governance pattern surrounding human rights began to change with the Helsinki process. Refer to Donnelly, *International Human Rights*, 78-82, for a detailed account of this process.

[30] Thomas Risse and Kathryn Sikkink, "The Socialization of International Human Rights Norms into Domestic Practices: Introduction," in *The Power of Human Rights: International Norms and Domestic Change,* ed. Thomas Risse, Stephen C. Ropp, and Kathryn Sikkink (Cambridge: Cambridge University Press, 1999), 21-22.

[31] Cass Sunstein, *Free Markets and Social Justice* (Oxford: Oxford University Press, 1997), has a detailed discussion of norms cascade.

governance as "the combined efforts of international and transnational regimes."[32] If this is the case, then international relations scholars can understand the formation of the ICC as an example of the new global governance pattern. Therefore, global governance's analysis of the formation process not only has to analyze the cognitive-ideational aspects of the process, but also the fact that the ICC is the institutionalization of this emerging pattern.

To begin this analysis, let me reiterate the mainstream definition of an international regime. International relations scholars have traditionally defined an international regime in the following manner: "Regimes can be defined as sets of implicit or explicit principles, norms, rules and decision-making procedures around which actors' expectations converge in a given area of international relations.[33]

This definition may appear to be similar to my previous definition of global governance, but there is one profound difference—the breadth of its analysis. Regime theory entails an analysis of a particular issue area, while global governance constitutes an analysis of the dominant global pattern of authority. But this does not mean that the formation of international regimes is inconsequential to a study of global governance. In fact, international regimes can be viewed as one of the SOAs that are present in the current global governance pattern.[34] As a result, we can view the formation of the International Criminal Court as part of the emerging global governance structure, and the embodiment of that pattern for issues of humanitarian law.

Global governance is defined as the norms and rules that influence and guide the actions of international actors. As discussed above, that pattern of governance has been altered over the past decade and this alteration has given rise to a new form of authority and a new group of relevant actors. One way to understand this transformation is to use a global governance perspective to analyze one issue- area or case study—in this case the formation of the International Criminal Court.

This chapter has established that the emerging global order is one that is conducive to a more transnational form of authority. In other words, the once unquestioned norm of state sovereignty appears to waning in certain issue-areas. The rationale behind such a conclusion is that global civil society (which is the basis for the emerging global order) is not a state-centered society. Instead, it is an inclusive society that finds authority residing in multiple entities. One such entity is the ICC. As a result, we can clearly see that governance, in this emerging order, is embodied in the formation of international regimes. The rapid approval and ratification of the Rome Statute is an example of international regime formation. It is also an example of the new governance pattern in global politics. This becomes evident if one simply analyzes the jurisdiction of the Court.

---

32 Young, *Governance in World Affairs,* 11.

33 Krasner, "Structural Causes, Regime Consequences," 2.

34 This is the central argument of Stokke, "Regimes as Governance Systems."

Governance Beyond State Borders

According to the Rome Statute, the ICC has jurisdiction over crimes committed on the territory of state parties and/or crimes committed by a national of a state party.[35] Any state that ratifies the Rome Statute must automatically accept the jurisdiction of the Court, regardless of their consent at the time of investigation. One could argue that the formation of an International Criminal Court clearly places authority, over the core crimes in humanitarian law, in the hands of this international regime. States that have ratified the Statute have no choice as to whether they consent or not. In fact, even if a state has not ratified the Statute, the nationals of these non-party states can be investigated and tried. This is due to the fact that the Court's jurisdiction extends to all core crimes committed on the territory of state parties, regardless of their nationality.[36]

This shifting of authority, from the territorial boundaries of nation-states to the realm of international institutions, shows the changing nature of global governance in world politics. Transnational institutions, like the ICC, are currently establishing and embodying the norms and rules that guide and influence the actions of today's international actors. In many ways, this is the result of the cognitive-ideational shift that I discussed earlier. This shift has now produced an international consensus on what the governance pattern should look like. At issue is the conflict that exists between the state sovereignty norm that dominated the previous pattern of global governance, and the more inclusive nature of a governance pattern that is predicated on the idea of global civil society. At least within the issue-area of humanitarian law, it appears as if the old pattern of governance is being supplanted by a non-state centered pattern of global governance; and the ICC is an example of this transformation.

Solidifying the New Governance Pattern

As shown in chapter seven, the approval of the Rome Statute resulted from the interaction of numerous international actors. These actors include: groups of nation-states (both pro and anti-ICC), a coalition of NGOs (CICC), and individual leaders who served as chairmen for the PrepCom meetings and the Rome Conference. Although this group of influential actors was very diverse, the majority of them shared one common bond—the desire for the establishment of an

---

35 Rome Statute of the ICC, Article 12 and 13. These crimes include: Genocide, War Crimes, Crimes Against Humanity, and when the state parties agree upon a definition, the Crime of Aggression.

36 Rome Statute of the ICC, Article 12 (a). Michael P. Scharf, "The ICC's Jurisdiction Over the Nationals of Non-Party States," in *The United States and the International Criminal Court: National Security and International Law,* ed. Sarah B. Sewall and Carl Kaysen (Lanham, MD: Rowman & Littlefield Publishers, Inc., 2000), 213-236, explains this premise and its basis in international law.

International Criminal Court. This consensus served as the ideational foundation for this institution. Outside of the United States, no major Western power voted against the Rome Statute or even abstained from the vote. In fact, one hundred and twenty nations voted for the Statute, while only seven voted against it; and the consensus surrounding this regime did not stop with the approval of the Statute. Since the completion of the Rome Conference, one hundred and thirty-nine nation-states have signed the Statute and ninety-nine have ratified it. If we couple this with the fact that currently the NGO Coalition for an International Criminal Court (CICC) has a membership status of over three thousand domestic and international NGOs, it becomes obvious that within this issue-area there has emerged an ideational consensus that has allowed the ICC formation process to move ahead.

So what does the formation of a humanitarian law regime tell us about global governance? First, that the ICC is an example of the emerging governance pattern. Recall that according to Oran Young, global governance is defined as "the combined efforts of international and transnational regimes."[37] If this is true, then scholars can analyze global governance by studying the formation of international regimes. Such an analysis tells us who is involved in the governance structure, how is the governance structure achieved, and how does it affect the larger global system.

Second, if we look at the formation of the ICC, we can empirically address the question concerning relevant actors within the current global governance pattern. According to this case study, both state and non-state actors have assisted in the construction of the current governance pattern. These non-state actors include NGOs, often times acting cooperatively as epistemic communities, and individual leaders who assist in the building of a consensus amongst the other actors.[38] How global governance is achieved is a bit more complex, but for the purpose of this case study, the means of global governance are found in the formation of international regimes. Once again though, this formation process goes back to the cognitive-ideational consensus that exists among a majority of international actors, coupled with the material-structural environment surrounding these actors. In other words, the question of "how" is usually found in a study of the knowledge factors that bring about cooperative, regime formation processes, coupled with an understanding of the material construct of the global order.[39]

The ideational shift amongst international actors from perceiving the world as an international society to a more inclusive perception of it as a global civil society

---

[37] Young, *Governance in World Affairs,* 11.

[38] Often times these two entities, NGOs and individual leadership, combine to form a transnational advocacy network. As chapter seven discusses, that is precisely what happened in this particular case.

[39] This is not to discount other factors such as power, interests, and leadership, but the co-constitutive relationship between cognitive and material forces appears to be the guiding influence in the formation of a global governance pattern. Chapter eight describes this relationship in greater detail.

has meant a shift in global governance patterns and structures. The state is no longer the final arbitrator in questions of authority and the formation of the ICC empirically proves this. Transnational institutions like the ICC now often subsume state authority and although much of the power in these institutions still resides with the state parties, it is possible to conclude that by joining with non-state actors to form these institutions, states have ceded some of their authority to new spheres of authority. Global governance patterns are now bound up in the formation of these transnational institutions, thus confirming the movement to a post-Westphalian era of governance. The jurisdictional issues of the ICC simply confirm this conclusion.

Conclusion

Global governance is a dynamic and complex phenomenon. As an analytical perspective, global governance entails an analysis of global order change and shifting authority structures. By applying this analytical perspective to the case of the ICC, I have encapsulated much of this project's past analysis into a more global understanding of the ICC formation process; thereby broadening the field's understanding of both the ICC formation process and global politics in general.[40]

The application of a global governance perspective on the case of the International Criminal Court was useful in two ways. 1) It allowed us to further our understanding of why the international community approved the Rome Statute for the International Criminal Court. In particular, this perspective addresses the question of why the formation of an international criminal court was so successful at this juncture in time as opposed to past attempts. 2) The case of the International Criminal Court also proved useful in gaining understanding about how the dominant global governance structure has been altered since the end of the Cold War, what actors can be considered part of this transformative process, and where governance now resides. It became apparent through this analysis that IR scholars should view the ICC as both an entity whose formation process is best understood by employing this analytical perspective and as an example of the emerging global governance pattern.

This chapter determined that the once unquestioned state-centered governance pattern, which was once found in the Westphalian order, has now been altered. What has emerged in its place is a post-Westphalian order that is much more inclusive and much more complex. Within the emergence of this new global order, there is also the initiation of a new global governance pattern and as a result, the international community receives the idea of forming an international criminal court with a great deal of enthusiasm.

---

[40] Past analysis meaning the previous two analytical perspectives that this project employed—neoliberal institutionalism and regime theory.

This new pattern of governance, as with any pattern of governance, is predicated on the co-constitutive relationship between cognitive-ideational forces and material-structural forces. The current ideational consensus centers on the interaction of state with non-state actors, and the influence that these two international actors have on each other and on global politics. This ideational foundation also recognizes the need to move beyond the state when forming new governance structures. This would entail the creation of more global forms of authority. Couple this with the material-structural changes that have occurred over the past decades and we can see the shift in governance occurring. In general, this new pattern of governance allows for the construction of new spheres of authority that now reside outside of the state. These new SOAs are often international regimes that the global community has given the authority to uphold the norms and rules that states, non-state entities, and individuals, will have to live by.

Within the issue-area of humanitarian law, the formation of the ICC is representative of this new pattern of global governance. The successful formation of the Rome Statute and the International Criminal Court is the result of multiple actors (both state and non-state) forming an ideational consensus and initiating a cooperative endeavor to institutionalize that consensus. This ideational perspective found a consensus among hundreds of NGOs, individual leaders, and a majority of the world's nation-states. The result was the approval of the Rome Statute, the establishment of a functioning ICC, and the shifting of authority, at least within this issue-area, from states to an international regime. The ICC is an example of the new face of global governance. Its foundations stem from the premise of a world that is predicated on the idea of a global civil society along with the cognitive forces that call for a more inclusive international community. International relations scholars should view the formation of the ICC as a message that the norms and rules that influence and guide international relations are no longer determined solely by states. In other words, the dominant global governance pattern appears to be shifting and as a result, the formation of institutions like the ICC may represent the future global governance structure.

Chapter 10
Conclusion

> First he would find it easiest to look at shadows, next at the reflections of mean and other objects in water, and later on at the objects themselves. After that he would find it easier to observe the heavenly bodies and the sky itself at night, and to look at the light of the moon and stars, rather than at the sun and its light by day. The thing he would be able to do last would be to look directly at the sun itself, and gaze at it without using reflections in water or any other medium, but as it is in itself.
>
> Plato[1]

Incongruities in Interpretations

In the preceding chapters I analyzed the formation process of the International Criminal Court from three different analytical perspectives. As a result, my readers have gained: 1) an understanding of the ICC formation process; and 2) an understanding of the implications of this institution for the issues of authority, governance, and shifting world order interpretations. Let me now summarize the interpretations given in this text and how they interrelate and conflict.

The different perspectives this text employed resulted in different interpretations of why the ICC formed, who were the major actors involved, and how these actors' interests developed. In many ways, this was the primary purpose of this project—to analyze the formation of the Rome Statute using three different perspectives of international relations. If successful, one could break down and analyze the knowledge that was ascertained from these three perspectives in order to gain a fuller understanding of the process. One would accomplish this goal not by attempting to initiate a parsimonious theory of regime formation, but by using diverse interpretations as a foundation for understanding.

Primary Units of Analysis

If we look at the conclusions from each perspective, it is obvious that incongruities exist. Let us begin by looking at the primary units of analysis for each perspective. The narrowest perspective, at least in terms of actors involved, is neoliberal institutionalism. From this perspective the only actors who have a profound impact on the formation of the ICC are states.[2] Therefore, when analyzing the

---

1 Plato, *The Republic,* second edition (London: Penguin Books, 1987), 319.

2 Neoliberalism does acknowledge the presence and influence of some non-state actors, but fails to consider them primary units of analysis. Keohane, *After Hegemony,* and

formation process, neoliberalism centers on states and the interaction amongst these actors. This perspective provided us with a detailed examination of the negotiating positions of the Like-Minded Group, the Non-aligned Movement, and the P-5; and although an examination of these actors and their role in the negotiating process was necessary, it was also incomplete. A neoliberal understanding of the formation process failed to account for the major influence of actors' like the CICC and the individual leadership. Such an incomplete analysis leaves one questioning whether these non-state actors had any real impact at all.

By employing a multivariate model of regime theory, the crucial role of these actors was revealed. According to this model, when analyzing the regime formation process it became necessary to account for both state and non-state actors. The role of NGOs, epistemic communities, individual leadership, and transnational advocacy networks were all crucial components to understanding the formation process. Such an inclusive form of analysis provides an understanding of the impact of all actors involved in the Rome negotiations, regardless of nation-state status. Without the influence of these non-state actors, the Rome Conference and the subsequent signature and ratification process may not have enjoyed such success.[3] As a result of this analysis it is now clear that the CICC and the individual leadership were crucial components of both a successful Conference and a rapid ratification process.

The global governance perspective centers on a different, more complex unit of analysis. From a global governance perspective, the primary unit of analysis is the spheres of authority that constitute the global governance pattern. In this case, the sphere of authority is an accomodative SOA that assists in the formation of an international regime—the ICC.[4] Therefore, from a global governance perspective, the key unit of analysis for understanding international politics is the origin of authority; and despite the fact that the dominant SOA may alter depending on the governance pattern, it is crucial that international relations scholars pinpoint the relevant SOA and analyze the role that they play in the current world order.

Primary Causal Factors

Along with different viewpoints on what scholars consider the central unit of analysis, these three analytical perspectives also differ on what the primary causal mechanism was during the ICC formation process. Neoliberal institutionalism

---

"Institutional Theory, Realist Challenge," both reiterate the state-centered form of analysis that neoliberal institutionalism works within.

[3] I quantify success by the fact that at the conclusion of the Rome Conference one hundred and twenty nations voted in favor of the Statute and only seven voted against it. Since that time, one hundred and thirty-nine nations have signed the Statute and ninety-nine have ratified it (as of 6/1/05).

[4] Rosenau, *Domestic-Foreign Frontier,* 159-168, describes an accomodative SOA as those in which the transformation of authority is accepted by both state and non-state actors.

views states' interests as the primary causal mechanism. According to this perspective, the main reason behind the formation of any international regime is state interest. NLI asserts that a common interest is what binds the actors together and drives them towards cooperation. Without such a common interest, cooperation within an anarchical international system is impossible.

The multivariate model of regimes has a much more complex understanding of why the ICC was formed. The formation of the ICC was, from this perspective, the result of interacting causal effects. It was not simply state interest, or knowledge-factors, or power politics that caused the approval of the Rome Statute. Instead, it was the interaction amongst all of these factors that contributed to the formation process. No one factor can be delineated from the others. Thus, if one is to understand this formation process, then it is crucial that scholars examine all three factors for their causal influence.

A global governance perspective asserts that the primary cause of ICC formation is the emerging global governance pattern. It is the alteration in ontology, transforming global order, and dominant governance pattern that has allowed for the success of the ICC formation process. Within this environment, states and non-state actors are able to realize the need for these types of international regimes to assist them in controlling the plethora of transnational problems. Thus, the governance pattern becomes one based on transnational relations, as opposed to state sovereignty. Global civil society becomes the environment within which actors must exist, and this allows for the growth of a shared understanding that if these collective action problems are to be solved, then authority must move beyond the state sovereignty norm.

But despite the fact that only neoliberalism emphasizes the state as the sole unit of analysis, it is clear that the community of states still played a large role in the formation process, no matter what perspective one is employing. Because of the importance of nation-states to our understanding of the ICC, it is crucial that we understand how state's interests are formed. This analysis is central to understanding the ICC because without this piece of the puzzle, there is no way to understand why the international community approved the Rome Statute. This is due to the fact that states are ultimately the actors that must vote on, amend, and approve the Statute. Without a coalescence of interests around the idea of a permanent international criminal court, there would be no Rome Statute and subsequently, no functioning ICC. With this in mind, how did nation-state interests on the ICC form?

Formation of States' Interests

According to neoliberalism, state interests are exogenously given. In other words, neoliberalism believes that states have a set of *a priori* interests that guides their behavior in an interdependent world. This perspective never questions how these interests are formed or what their origin might be. Such matters are inconsequential to the neoliberal institutionalists. The only thing that neoliberalism accounts for is that cooperation is often times a viable path to achieving self-interests. Therefore, neoliberal institutionalism lacks an understanding of why state interests are formed and this shortcoming necessitates the movement towards another, more complex model of analysis.

A multivariate model of regime theory does not simply accept that state interests exist *a priori.* Scholars applying this perspective question the nature of these interests and how they were formed. In the case of the ICC, state interests were formed primarily, but not exclusively, as a result of cognitive-ideational forces.[5] These knowledge-based factors were articulated most clearly by the CICC, acting in the capacity of an epistemic community. It is through their interaction with the CICC members that some states' interests begin to take shape. The dissemination of information pertaining to the establishment of the International Criminal Court comes primarily from the CICC; thus, when looking at how interests are formed, it is crucial to look at the formation of consensual discourse surrounding the ICC. And when exploring where that consensual discourse sprang from, one has to account for the role of NGOs and individual leadership. These actors helped frame the discourse surrounding this regime formation process and provided the nation-state community with the foundation for a common interest agenda.[6]

Global governance takes a different angle in addressing the question of state interest formation. According to this perspective, state interests resulted from the cognitive-ideational forces of a global order, along with the material-structural forces that are present. These two forces act in a co-constitutive manner to assist in the formation of an international institution. This type of analysis reveals that the formation of state interests is a more complex process than either of the other two perspectives assert. Global governance scholars view the formation of states' interests surrounding the ICC as the result of both the cognitive shift that began during the post-World War II period and the material construction of several functioning ad hoc tribunals. Clearly then, the global governance perspective on state interest formation is a complex one that necessitates a close examination of both ideational and structural factors.

---

5 I emphasize the word "primarily" because this is not the only factor affecting state interest formation—power and context also played a part. However, this case study shows that the primary factor was cognitive forces, such as the epistemic community of NGOs.

6 The CICC acted as a disseminator of information concerning the ICC. Working in conjunction with the Like-Minded Group of states, the CICC was able to provide the international community with a common discourse on this issue and provide an environment in which one hundred and twenty states approved of the Rome Statute. In essence, states' interests were formed, or at least greatly influenced, by the CICC.

Nesting Effect

Despite the incongruities that exist between these three perspectives, there is a relationship that tends to tie them together. I call this link a "nesting effect." The nesting effect centers on the complementary aspects that each of these theories have with one another. If taken as separate perspectives on the ICC formation process, these theories all fall short of a complete and full understanding of this institution and its evolution.[7] However, if taken in conjunction with one another and viewed as complementary perspectives on the ICC, the goal of understanding this institution becomes much more attainable. In other words, it is essential that we think of these perspectives as nesting one within the other.

Let us begin with neoliberal institutionalism. This perspective provided us with a good analysis of state interests and how these interests impacted the negotiation process. This analysis included an understanding of the Like-Minded Groups' strong advocacy of this institution, along with an understanding of why the United States refused to sign or support the Rome Statute. Although necessary to our understanding of the ICC formation process, it was discovered that this perspective was incomplete. It failed to address issues concerning the origins of state interests, the role of non-state actors, and the question of why this institution's formation proceedings were successful in the late 1990s, but not successful in the early 1950s. These questions pushed this examination towards a different, more complex analytical perspective—regime theory.

The multivariate model of regime theory assisted in answering most of the unanswered questions that neoliberalism left behind. Nevertheless, this does not mean that the analysis of the ICC through the lens of neoliberalism was useless. Within the multivariate model of regime theory, neoliberal institutionalism remains a key component. The state-centered, interest-based conception of regime formation plays a major part within the multivariate model. The point is that neoliberalism is only a part of the analysis; however, its lack of understanding necessitates its supplementation with another analytical perspective. Scholars should not discard the analysis of neoliberalism—they need to simply view it as part of a larger analytical framework. In short, neoliberal institutionalism is nested or in this case, subsumed within the multivariate model of regime theory.[8] Its

---

7 In fact, the use of only one of these perspectives to understand regime formation in general may not be adequate. But before such a claim can be considered definitive, there is a need for further testing of this hypothesis through the initiation of a broader set of case studies. I will discuss this issue further later in this chapter.

8 "Nesting" refers to a set of things, each fitting within the next set which is larger, while not losing its own principles despite its congruence with another set of principles. Neoliberal institutionalism does reside within the multivariate model, but it is also part of that model. Thus, the nesting of NLI within the multivariate model is not as crucial as the nesting of the multivariate model within global governance. In this instance, both

interaction with other social driving and cross-cutting factors provides us with a fuller and richer understanding of the ICC. Thus, the knowledge gained from neoliberalism is complemented by that ascertained through the use of a multivariate model of regime theory.

The purest form of the nesting effect is evident when the analysis moves from regime theory to global governance. Regime theory provided an understanding of the actors, both state and non-state, involved, how interests were formed, and the complexity of the process and the regime. What regime theory failed to accomplish was an understanding of how this emerging institution fits into the larger global context.[9] Global governance examines the larger international context and how the global environment acts as a co-constitutive factor with the ICC. This type of analysis directly addresses the question "why now?" and provides us with a clearer understanding of how this regime fits into the transforming global system.

Nevertheless, we must not forget the lessons learned from our use of regime theory. These lessons have provided us with an exemplary understanding of the regime itself, but if one wishes to place the regime into the larger global context, then the use of global governance theory becomes a necessary step. Thus, global governance tends to engulf the regime theory analysis and apply it on a grander scale. This type of analysis allows us to understand that the transforming global governance pattern is what makes the formation of an institution like the ICC possible. A pattern of governance predicated on the norm of state sovereignty was one of the major factors preventing the formation of an ICC in the early 1950s. With the transformation to a global civil society, the idea of forming a transnational court became more realistic. Therefore, the use of each analytical perspective contributed something to our understanding, but none is able to stand on its own.

Complexity Necessitates Complexity

This analysis of the ICC formation process also underscores the fact that the complex nature of regime formation necessitates the need for a more complex model of regime formation. Traditionally, international relations scholars have analyzed regimes through the use of bivariate models of causal effect.[10] Scholars

---

perspectives retain their core principles but complement each other in their understanding of global politics.

[9] Although Young and Osherenko's multivariate model of regime theory does take environmental context into account, this factor is considered a cross-cutting factor. Global governance will place this factor at the forefront of its analysis and examine the implications of this international regime on the global civil society.

[10] Hasenclever, Mayer, and Rittberger, *Theories of International Regimes,* justifies this premise by describing only these three models of regime formation.

hypothesized that regimes formed as a result of power, interest, or knowledge factors. The case of the International Criminal Court undermines such a perspective. What we now understand about the formation of this regime is that no one causal factor is sufficient to understand the negotiations and successful institutional bargaining process that occurred before, during, or after the Rome Conference. The models that scholars have generally employed to understand this phenomenon are to simplistic.

Oran Young and Gail Osherenko provide a model that more accurately depicts the causal factors of regime formation. In their model, all three bivariate factors are brought to bear on the analysis along with the crosscutting factors leadership and context. The significance of this for international relations scholars is that up until this point, most scholars have ignored Young and Osherenko's multivariate model. One is hard pressed to find any analysis of regime formation, since 1993, that employs this model.[11] And yet, the ICC case shows that if one were to employ a bivariate model, their understanding of this case would be incomplete. In short, complexity of the case necessitates complexity in the model. International relations scholars should heed the lessons from this case study and in an attempt to verify this model, apply it to cases in other issue-areas.[12]

Return to States' Interests

As discussed earlier, one important aspect of this analysis is that it examines the importance of states' interest and their formation process. One of the primary problems with a neoliberal institutionalist's perspective was that it failed to account for the origin of states' interests. Neoliberal institutionalists accept that interests are exogenously given and thus, they never investigate the causal factors surrounding the formation of these interests. This type of perspective essentially excludes the role of non-state actors, the impact of ideas or knowledge, and the context in which these interests are being formed. The multivariate model does not exclude such factors and as a result it provides us with an examination of state interest formation.

States are the building blocks of international regimes and organizations. The case of the ICC upholds this claim. In the end, it was states that had to vote on the Rome Statute, it was states that had to sign onto the Statute, and it was states that had to ratify the Statute thus creating a functioning inter-governmental

---

[11] 1993 is the year that Young and Osherenko published their model. Since that time I have not found one example of regime analysis that employs this multivariate model.

[12] Young and Osherenko use this model to understand several cases within the issue-area of environmental politics. This case uses this model to understand regime formation within human rights/humanitarian law. Future research should use this model in other issue-areas in an attempt to either further justify Young and Osherenko's hypothesis or undermine it. This case clearly justifies it.

organization.[13] If one is going to properly understand the causal effects of the formation of this institution, then it would seem logical that you first examine the origin of states' interests. The multivariate model allows us to do just that. This study highlights the fact that state interest formation is also a complex process that must account for a diversity of causal factors and influential actors.

We must begin by understanding that the formation of states' interests is part of a social process. States do not form their interests within a vacuum and once established they are not static. States' interests are constructed through interaction with other actors, both state and non-state, and within the material-structural context of that period in time. In other words, if one is to gain an understanding of the nature of the state interest formation process, they must invoke a constructivist reading of the ICC. As shown throughout this text, such a reading explores what occurred before the neoliberal institutionalist perspective takes hold. It also examines the underlying beliefs that resulted in the overwhelming support of the Rome Statute—such as the dissemination of knowledge, the process of learning, and the formation of consensual knowledge.

As chapter seven explains, ideational causation is a large part of state interest formation in the Rome negotiation process. Most notably, the dissemination of knowledge by the CICC, acting as an epistemic community, greatly influenced the defining of states' interests. Through the diffusion of a common discourse on the ICC, the epistemic community was able to initiate "learning" amongst the international community of states.[14] This process led a large number of states to a common solution (the formation of a permanent International Criminal Court) for a complex problem (how to punish and prevent future acts of genocide, war crimes, and crimes against humanity). However, as Haas explains, epistemic communities can only be successful if they form an alliance with the dominant political coalition.[15] In this case the formation of such an alliance involved the initiation of a transnational advocacy networks.

The ICC formation process was successful because learning occurred amongst a large portion of the nation-state community. Much of the credit for this process has to go to epistemic communities, but epistemic communities working in conjunction with a core group of states (Like-Minded Group) and a strong group of individual leaders. As noted in chapter seven, these entities come together to form

[13] Kelly-Kate S. Pease, *International Organizations: Perspectives on Governance in the Twenty-First Century* (Upper Saddle River, NJ: Prentice Hall, Inc., 2000), 2, defines an inter-governmental organization as "formal institutions whose members are states…governments of nation-states voluntarily join, contribute financing, and make decisions within the organization." This definition clearly shows the primacy of states within the IGO formation and maintenance process.

[14] E. Haas, *When Knowledge is Power,* 23, defines learning as "the process by which consensual knowledge is used to specify causal relationships in new ways so that the result affects the content of public policy."

[15] Haas, *When Knowledge is Power,* 42.

a TAN, and as a result, the dissemination of a common discourse surrounding the ICC occurs and the majority of nation-states' interests coalesce around the formation of this organization. During the negotiation process, the Like-Minded Group grew from just over a dozen nation-states to over sixty. This explosion in membership shows that learning did occur and that the coalition embodied in the TAN assisted in the formation and alteration of states' interests.

Ideational causation is not the only factor that must be considered. Material-structural forces, or institutions and context, also played a large role in the formation of interests. The end of the Cold War, the rise in ethno-political conflict, the genocide in Yugoslavia and Rwanda, and possibly the most important factor, the establishment of several ad hoc tribunals, all influenced the interests of nation-states. In particular, the ad hoc tribunals of the former Yugoslavia and Rwanda are examples of "nested regimes."[16] A nested regime is a linkage between a more restricted regime, in terms of mandate, space, and time, and a broader institutional framework in which one regime is folded into another or nests in the other. The formation of the ICC is the broader linkage into which the international community is folding the ICTY and the ICTR. This broader institution deals with almost the same set of crimes and the same issues only on a broader, more global scale. Often times the formation of these broader regimes have the narrow regimes to thank because they have paved the way. In this case, the ICC is affected by the formation of the ad hoc tribunals and their impact on the interests of the nation-state community.

If we consider both of these forces, we can view the material-structural forces as residing in a co-constitutive relationship with the cognitive-ideational forces. Quantitatively measuring the influence of these forces is problematic therefore, we must regard them as complementary forces acting to constitute state interests. Clearly this further complicates the examination of states interests, but if we are to understand why a large portion of the international community has supported the ICC, then it is necessary to understand state interest formation.

Broader Consequences

This text has succeeded in understanding the formation process surrounding the Rome Statute. It has also shown the need for international relations scholars to re-examine their conception of regime formation and the relevant actors and influences on this process. However, at the outset of this project another goal was set forth—to understand what the formation of an ICC represents in terms of governance in the contemporary world. In short, this text also set out to understand, or at least hypothesize about, the changing nature of world politics.

---

16 Young, *Governance in World Affairs,* 67-68.

One way to examine the case of the ICC within the broader context of global politics is to think of it as an "embedded regime." An embedded regime is an issue-specific regime that is: "Deeply embedded in overarching institutional arrangements in the sense that they assume—ordinarily without saying so explicitly—the operation of a whole suite of broader principles and practices that constitute the deep structure of international society as a whole."[17]

According to Oran Young, the presence of an embedded regime upholds the idea that international politics is constructed of territorial states that exercise their sovereignty over others and refuse to be bound by rules that they have not explicitly consented to. Thus for Young, the examination of embedded regimes only proves the fact that international society is still dominant, not global civil society.[18] However, the case of the ICC may be an example of the opposite. In other words, international relations scholars may be able to point to the case of the ICC as an example of an emerging global civil society and the displacement of international society.

An embedded regime reflects the overarching construct and institutional arrangements in global politics. As the discussion of global governance demonstrated, the underlying construct of global politics (its order) may be changing. We now see movement towards a more inclusive society in the sense that the global order is no longer definable as simply state centric. Non-state actors, such as individuals and non-governmental regimes, are having a tremendous influence on the institutional arrangements of the post-Westphalian order and the ICC is one example of that influence.

The ICC exemplifies the ceding of authority, by states to international regimes. In the case of the ICC, states are willing to give this institution the ability to judge their citizenry and take action to rectify violations of humanitarian law. This case shows the fact that governance is becoming bound up in regimes and their authority structures. The ICC is also a case in which non-state actor influence was crucial to the establishment of the regime. Without the CICC and the individual leadership of the Rome Conference, there is a good chance that the Rome Statute would not have passed or at least been approved by a significantly smaller number of states.[19] If we can consider the ICC as an embedded regime, and I believe that we can, then it is a snapshot of the changes occurring in global politics writ large. Non-state actors are gaining prominence, the state sovereignty norm is diminishing in strength, and the global governance structure is evolving into a more transnational system in which authority is bound up in international regimes and institutions designed for conflict management. Global governance may be

---

[17] Young, *Governance in World Affairs,* 165.

[18] Young, *Governance in World Affairs,* 8-11, has a discussion of the terms "international society" and "global civil society."

[19] As Chayes and Slaughter, "Future of the Global Legal System," 241, state: "Without the NGO community, the ICC might not have been concluded."

evolving into Oran Young's definition, "the combined efforts of international and transnational regimes."[20]

It is important to note that such hypotheses have not been empirically proven. The global system may be transforming but it has not yet transformed. The examination of the ICC case is a first step in understanding the evolution of global politics, but if we are to empirically verify this transformation then future research beyond the boundaries of one narrow issue-area is necessary.

Future Research and Concluding Remarks

In a recent article, Yale Ferguson states: "There is an urgent need for a postinternational revolution in the study of global politics, broadly conceived as a take-no-prisoner campaign waged by all those from various disciplines who are non-state-centric and yet empirical in their approach(es)."[21]

This text is in many ways an attempt to assist in the revolution that Ferguson calls us to. Throughout this discourse I have questioned the Westphalian nature of world politics not from a deductive, theory-driven perspective, but from a more empirically based foundation. This study employed an analytical inductive method in which a case study drove the analysis of international politics and the attempt to understand the nature of the current global system. By studying the formation process surrounding the International Criminal Court, one ascertains an understanding of relevant actors, governance structures, causal factors of regime formation, the origins of states' interests, and numerous other issues. As a result, this text is an example of a "heuristic" case study in that scholars can use this case to learn more about the complexity of the international system and its transforming governance structure.[22]

Does this mean that this case study has sufficiently verified the changing nature of global politics and that the revolution against non-state centric theories is complete? Certainly not! This case study is simply a small step towards verification. We should think of a "heuristic" case study as:

> Part of a "building block approach to the construction and development of theory…a series of heuristic case studies or a simultaneous comparison of two or more cases, if each comprises an instance of the same class of events, can be an excellent research strategy for the cumulative development of theory.[23]

---

[20] Young, *Governance in World Affairs,* 11. Note that I am not touting the demise of the state, but simply calling my readers to view state authority as being complemented by non-state actors.

[21] Ferguson, "Postinternationalism, Future of IR Theory," 202.

[22] For a discussion of "heuristic" case studies, see George, "Case Studies," 51-52.

[23] George, "Case Studies," 52.

Thus, in order to verify some of the hypotheses made about shifting global orders, emerging global governance structures, the onset of global civil society, and the passing of Westphalian norms, there needs to be more empirical research. In taking up Ferguson's call to revolution, scholars should initiate more case study analysis of regime formation. The purpose of this analysis is an attempt to understand the actors involved, the causal factors in the formation process, and the impact it has on governance within that issue-area. This research should then compare these conclusions with the ones from other cases. Are they similar? Does the same class of actors impact the process? Does governance appear to be shifting? Only with such comparative case study analysis can scholars begin to verify the findings of this study.

Despite this less then paradigm shifting conclusion, this text has succeeded in providing an understanding of the Rome Statute's genesis and the subsequent ICC negotiation process. As a result of this analysis, my readers are better able to understand the types of actors that influenced the negotiations, the causal factors that assisted in the state interest formation process, the type of authority that the ICC will wield, and the underlying reasons for why the international community engaged in this type of cooperative endeavor.

As a result of this analysis, it is possible to better hypothesize about the broader impact that this institution and its bargaining process will have on the international community, the possible breaking of the traditional state-centric mold, and the emergence of future governance patterns within world politics. Thus, this text not only provides us with critical knowledge of an emerging international institution, but it also provides us with a window from which to view the transforming nature of global politics. In essence, this text is the starting point for future research endeavors that may ultimately understand the transformative nature of the global governance structure.

Appendix

Rome Statute Signature and Ratification Chart, as of June 1, 2005

139 Signatories and 99 Ratifications
(Alphabetical Order)

Country	Signature	Ratification/ Accession (a)
Afghanistan		02/10/03 (a)
Albania	07/18/98	01/31/03
Algeria	12/28/00	
Andorra	07/18/98	04/30/01
Antigua and Barbuda	10/23/98	06/18/01
Argentina	01/08/99	02/08/01
Armenia	10/01/99	
Australia	12/09/98	07/01/02
Austria	10/07/98	12/28/00
Bahamas	12/29/00	
Bahrain	12/11/00	
Bangladesh	09/16/99	
Barbados	09/08/00	12/10/02
Belgium	09/10/98	06/28/00
Belize	04/05/00	04/05/00
Benin	09/24/99	01/22/02
Bolivia	07/17/98	06/27/02
Bosnia and Herzegovina	07/17/00	04/11/02
Botswana	09/08/00	09/08/00
Brazil	02/07/00	06/20/02
Bulgaria	02/11/99	04/11/02
Burkina Faso	11/30/98	04/16/04
Burundi	01/17/99	09/21/04
Cambodia	10/23/00	04/11/02
Cameroon	07/17/98	
Canada	12/18/98	07/07/00
Cape Verde	12/28/00	
Central African Republic	12/07/99	10/03/01

Chad	10/20/99	
Chile	10/11/98	
Colombia	10/10/98	08/05/02
Comoros	09/22/00	
Congo (Brazzaville)	07/17/98	05/03/04
Costa Rica	10/07/98	06/07/01
Cote d'Ivoire	11/30/98	
Croatia	10/12/98	05/21/01
Cyprus	10/15/98	06/07/02
Czech Republic	04/13/99	
Democratic Republic of Congo	09/08/00	04/11/02
Denmark	09/25/98	06/21/01
Djibouti	10/07/98	11/05/02
Dominica		02/12/01 (a)
Dominican Republic	09/08/00	05/13/05
Ecuador	10/07/98	02/05/02
Egypt	12/26/00	
Eritrea	10/07/98	
Estonia	12/27/99	01/30/02
Fiji	11/29/99	11/29/99
Finland	10/07/98	12/29/00
France	07/18/98	06/09/00
Gabon	12/22/98	09/21/00
Gambia	12/07/98	06/28/02
Germany	12/10/98	12/11/00
Georgia	07/18/98	09/05/03
Ghana	07/18/98	12/20/99
Greece	07/18/98	05/15/02
Guinea	09/08/00	07/14/03
Guinea-Bissau	09/12/00	
Guyana	12/28/00	09/24/04
Haiti	02/26/99	
Honduras	10/07/98	07/01/02
Hungary	12/15/98	11/30/01
Iceland	08/26/98	05/25/00
Iran	12/31/00	
Ireland	10/07/98	04/11/02
Israel*	12/31/00	
Italy	07/18/98	07/26/99
Jamaica	09/08/00	
Jordan	10/07/98	04/11/02

Kenya	0811/99	03/15/05
Kuwait	09/08/00	
Krygyzstan	12/08/98	
Latvia	04/22/99	06/28/02
Lesotho	11/30/98	09/06/00
Liberia	07/17/98	09/22/04
Lichtenstein	07/18/98	10/02/01
Lithuania	12/10/98	05/12/03
Luxembourg	10/13/98	09/08/00
Macedonia (F.Y.R.)	10/07/98	03/06/02
Madagascar	07/18/98	
Malawi	03/03/99	09/19/02
Mali	07/17/98	08/16/00
Malta	07/17/98	11/29/02
Marshall Islands	09/06/00	12/07/00
Mauritius	11/11/98	03/05/02
Mexico	09/07/00	
Monaco	07/18/98	
Mongolia	12/29/00	04/11/02
Morocco	09/08/00	
Mozambique	12/28/00	
Namibia	10/27/98	06/25/02
Nauru	12/13/00	11/12/01
Netherlands	07/18/98	07/17/01
New Zealand	10/07/98	09/07/00
Niger	07/17/98	04/11/02
Nigeria	06/01/00	09/27/01
Norway	08/28/98	02/16/00
Oman	12/20/00	
Panama	07/18/98	03/21/02
Paraguay	10/07/98	05/14/01
Peru	12/07/00	11/10/01
Philippines	12/28/00	
Poland	04/09/99	11/12/01
Portugal	10/07/98	02/05/02
Republic of Korea	03/08/00	11/13/02
Republic of Moldova	09/08/00	
Romania	07/07/99	04/11/02
Russian Federation	09/13/00	
Saint Lucia	08/27/99	
Saint Vincent and the Grenadines		12/03/02 (a)

Samoa	07/17/98	09/16/02
San Marino	07/18/98	05/13/99
Sao Tome and Principe	12/28/00	
Senegal	07/18/98	02/02/99
Serbia and Montenegro	12/19/00	09/06/01
Seychelles	12/28/00	
Sierra Leone	10/17/98	09/15/00
Slovakia	12/23/98	04/11/02
Slovenia	10/07/98	12/31/01
Solomon Islands	12/03/98	
South Africa	07/17/98	11/27/00
Spain	07/18/98	10/25/00
Sudan	09/08/00	
Sweden	10/07/98	06/28/01
Switzerland	07/18/98	10/12/01
Syrian Arab Republic	11/29/00	
Tajikistan	11/30/98	05/05/00
Tanzania (United Republic)	12/29/00	09/20/02
Thailand	10/02/00	
Timor Leste		09/06/02 (a)
Trinidad and Tobago	03/23/99	04/06/99
Uganda	03/17/99	06/14/02
Ukraine	01/20/00	
United Arab Emirates	11/27/00	
United Kingdom	11/30/98	10/04/01
United States of America*	12/31/00	
Uruguay	12/19/00	06/28/02
Venezuela	10/14/98	06/07/00
Yemen	12/28/00	
Zambia	07/17/98	11/13/02
Zimbabwe	07/17/98	

* Despite their formal signature on 12/31/00, Israel and the United States have since withdrawn their signatures.

Bibliography

Abbott, Kenneth W. "International Relations Theory, International Law, and the Regime Governing Atrocities in Internal Conflicts." *The American Journal of International Law* 93 (1999): 361-379.

Adler, Emanuel and Peter M. Haas, "Conclusion: Epistemic Communities, World Order, and Reflective Research Programs." *International Organization* 46 (1992): 367-390.

Agnew, John A. "Timeless Space and State-Centrism: the Geographical Assumptions of International Relations Theory." In *The Global Economy as Political Space*, ed. Stephen J. Rosow, Naeem Inayatullah and Mark Rupert, 87-106. Boulder, CO: Lynne Rienner Publishers, 1994.

Agnew, John A. and Stuart Corbridge. *Mastering Space: Hegemony, Territory and International Political Economy.* London: Routledge, 1995.

Akhavan, Payam. "The Yugoslav Tribunal at a Crossroads: The Dayton Peace Agreement and Beyond." *Human Rights Quarterly* 18 (1996): 259-285.

---"Justice in the Hague, Peace in the Former Yugoslavia? A Commentary on the United Nations War Crimes Tribunal." *Human Rights Quarterly* 20 (1998): 737-816.

Allison, Graham T. Essence of Decision: Explaining the Cuban Missile Crisis. Harper Collins Publishers, 1971.

Andreasan, Scott W. "The International Criminal Court: Does the Constitution Preclude Its Ratification by the United States?" *Iowa Law Review* 85 (2000): 697-733.

Angell, Norman. The Great Illusion: A Study of the Relations of Military Power to National Advantage. London: William Heinemann, 1912.

Appleman, John Alan. *Military Tribunals and International Crimes.* Westport, CT: Greenwood Press, Publishers, 1954.

Arbour, Louise and Morten Bergsmo. "Despite Shortcomings, a Court Deserving Support." *UN Chronicle* 35 (1998): 12-13.

---"Conscious Absence of Jurisdictional Overreach." In *Reflections on the InternationalCriminal Court: Essays in Honour of Adriaan Bos,* ed. Herman A.M. von Hebel, Johan G. Lammers and Jolien Schukking, 129-140. The Hague: T.M.C. Asser Press, 1999.

Arsanjani, Mahnoush H. "The Rome Statute of the International Criminal Court." *The American Journal of International Law* 93 (1999): 22-43.

---"Reflections on Jurisdiction and Trigger Mechanisms." In *Reflections on the International Criminal Court: Essays in Honour of Adriaan Bos,* ed. Hermann

A.M. von Hebel, Johan G. Lammars, and Jolien Schukking, 57-76. The Hague: T.M.C. Asser Press, 1999.

Ashley, Richard K. "Untying the Sovereign State: A Double Reading of the Anarchy Problematique." *Millenium* 17 (1988): 227-262.

Ashworth, Lucian M. Creating International Studies: Angell, Mitrany and the Liberal Tradition. Brookfield, VT: Ashgate Publishing Company, 1999.

Axelrod, Robert and Robert O. Keohane. "Achieving Cooperation Under Anarchy: Strategies and Institutions." *World Politics* 38 (1985): 226-254.

Baldwin, David A., ed. *Neorealism and Neoliberalism: The Contemporary Debate.* New York: Columbia University Press, 1993.

Ball, Howard. *Prosecuting War Crimes and Genocide: The Twentieth-Century Experience.* Lawrence, Kansas: University Press of Kansas, 1999.

Barkin, J. Samuel. "The Evolution of the Constitution of Sovereignty and the Emergence of Human Rights Norms." *Millennium* 27 (1998): 229-252.

Bartelson, Jens. *A Genealogy of Sovereignty.* Cambridge: Cambridge University Press, 1995.

Bassiouni, M. Cherif. *Crimes Against Humanity in International Criminal Law.* Dordrecht, The Netherlands: Martinus Nijhoff Publishers, 1992.

---"From Versailles to Rwanda in Seventy Five Years: The Need to Establish a Permanent International Criminal Court." *Harvard Human Rights Journal* 10 (1997), 11-62.

---*The Statute of the International Criminal Court: A Documentary History.* Ardsley, NY: Transnational Publishers, 1998.

---"Negotiating the Treaty of Rome on the Establishment of an International Criminal Court." *Cornell International Law Journal* 32 (1999): 443-469.

Bassiouni, M. Cherif and Christopher L. Blakesley. "The Need for an International Criminal Court in the New International World Order." *Vanderbilt Journal of Transnational Law* 25 (1992), 151-182.

Beigbeder, Yves. *Judging War Criminals: The Politics of International Justice.* London: MacMillan Press, Ltd., 1999.

Bendetti, Fanny and John L. Washburn. "Drafting the International Criminal Court Treaty: Two Years to Rome and an Afterword on the Rome Diplomatic Conference." *Global Governance* 5 (1999): 1-38.

Berg, Karen. "A Permanent International Criminal Court." *UN Chronicle* 34 (1997): 30-36.

Berman, Sir Franklin. "The Relationship Between the International Criminal Court and the Security Council." In *Reflections on the International Criminal Court: Essays in Honour of Adriaan Bos,* ed. Herman A.M. von Hebel, Johan G. Lammers and Jolien Schukking, 173-180. The Hague: T.M.C. Asser Press, 1999.

Biersteker, Thomas J. "The 'Triumph' of Neoclassical Economics in the Developing World: Policy Convergence and Bases of Governance in the International Economic Order." In *Governance Without Government: Order and Change in World Politics,* ed. James N. Rosenau and Ernst-Otto Czempiel, 102-131. Cambridge: Cambridge University Press, 1992.

Biersteker, Thomas J. and Cynthia Weber, ed. *State Sovereignty as Social Construct.* Cambridge: Cambridge University Press, 1996.

Blakesley, Christopher L. "Obstacles to the Creation of a Permanent War Crimes Tribunal." In *International Law: Classic and Contemporary Readings,* ed. Charlotte Ku and Paul F. Diehl, 281-303. Boulder, CO: Lynne Rienner Publishers, 1998.

Bledsoe, Robert L. and Boleslaw A. Boczak. *The International Law Dictionary.* Santa Barbara, CA: ABC:CLIO, 1987.

Boli, John and George M. Thomas, ed. *Constructing World Culture: International Nongovernmental Organizations Since 1875.* Stanford, CA: Stanford University Press, 1999.

Booth, Ken. "Human Wrongs and International Relations." *International Affairs* 71 (1995): 103-126.

Booth, Ken and Steve Smith, ed. *International Relations Theory Today.* University Park, PA: The Pennsylvania State University Press, 1995.

Bos, Adriaan. "The International Criminal Court: A Perspective." In *The International Criminal Court: The Making of the Rome Statute Issues, Negotiations, Results,* ed. Roy S. Lee, 463-470. The Hague: Kluwer Law International, 1999.

Bosco, David L. "Sovereign Myopia." *The American Prospect* 41 (1998): 24-28.

Broomhall, Bruce. *International Justice and the International Criminal Court: Between Sovereignty and the Rule of Law.* Oxford: Oxford University Press, 2003.

Brown, Bartram S. "The Statute of the ICC: Past, Present, and Future." In *The United States and the International Criminal Court: National Security and International Law,* ed. Sarah B. Sewall and Carl Kaysen, 61-84. Lanham, MD: Rowman & Littlefield Publishers, Inc., 2000.

---"The United States and the Rome Statute: Rejecting the International Criminal Court." Prepared for presentation at the annual International Studies Association conference. Chicago, IL, February 2001.

Brown, Chris. "Universal Human Rights: A Critique." In *Human Rights in Global Politics,* ed. Tim Dunne and Nicholas J. Wheeler 103-127. Cambridge: Cambridge University Press, 1999.

Bull, Hedley. *The Anarchical Society: A Study of Order in WorldPolitics,* 2d ed. New York: Columbia University Press, 1995.

Burch, Kurt. *"Property" and the Making of the International System.* Boulder, CO: Lynne Rienner Publishers, 1998.

---"The Westphalian System and Shifting Forms of Rule," unpublished paper prepared for the International Studies Association annual meeting, Washington DC, 1999.

Buzan, Barry. "The Timeless Wisdom of Realism?" In *International Theory: Positivism and Beyond,* ed. Steve Smith, Ken Booth and Marysia Zalewski, 47-65. Cambridge: Cambridge University Press, 1996.

Camilleri, Joseph A. and Jim Falk. *End of Sovereignty?: The Politics of a Shrinking and Fragmented World.* Brookfield, VT: Elger, 1992.

Campbell, David. "Violent Performances: Identity, Sovereignty, Responsibility." In *The Return of Culture and Identity in IR Theory,* ed. Yosef Lapid and Friedrich Kratochwil, 163-180. Boulder, CO: Lynne Rienner Publishers, 1996.

Cassel, Douglass. "Why We Need the International Criminal Court." *The Christian Century* 116 (1999): 532-539.

Cerny, Philip G. "Globalization and Other Stories: The Search for a New Paradigm for International Relations." *International Journal* 51 (1996): 617-637.

Chang, Iris. *The Rape of Nanking: The Forgotten Holocaust of World War II.* New York: Basic Books, 1997.

Chayes, Abram and Anne-Marie Slaughter. "The ICC and the Future of the Global Legal System." In *The United States and the International Criminal Court: National Security and International Law, ed.* Sarah B. Sewall and Carl Kaysen, 237-248. Lanham, MD: Rowman & Littlefield Publishers, Inc., 2000.

Chimimba, Trevor Pascal. "Establishing an Enforcement Regime." In *The International Criminal Court: The Making of the Rome Statutue Issues, Negotiations, Results,* ed. Roy S. Lee, 345-356. The Hague: Kluwer Law International, 1999.

Clark, Ian. *Globalization and International Relations Theory.* Oxford: Oxford University Press, 1999.

Clark, Roger S. and Madeline Sann, ed. *The Prosecution of International Crimes: A Critical Study of the International Tribunal for the Former Yugoslavia,* Somerset, NJ: Transaction Publishers, 1996.

Cohen, Jean L. and Andrew Arato. *Civil Society and Political Theory.* Cambridge, MA: The MIT Press, 1992.

Commission on Global Governance. *Our Global Neighborhood: The Report of the Commission on Global Governance.* Oxford: Oxford University Press, 1995.

Conso, Giovanni. "Looking to the Future." In *The International Criminal Court: The Making of the Rome Statute—Issues, Negotiations, Results,* ed. Roy S. Lee, 471-477. The Hague: Kluwer Law International, 1999.

Cox, Robert W. "On Thinking About Future World Order." *World Politics,* 28 (1976): 175-196.

---"Social Forces, States and World Orders: Beyond International Relations Theory." Reprinted in *Neorealism and its Critics,* ed. Robert Keohane, 204-255. Princeton, NJ: Princeton University Press, 1986.

---*Production, Power and World Order: Social Forces in the Making of History,* New York: Columbia University Press, 1987.

---"Towards a Post-Hegemonic Conceptualization of World Order: Reflections on the Relevancy of Ibn Khaldun." In *Governance Without Government: Order and Change in World Politics,* ed. James N. Rosenau and Ernst-Otto Czempiel, 132-159. Cambridge: Cambridge University Press, 1992.

---"Multilateralism and World Order." *Review of International Studies* 18 (1992): 161-180.

---"Structural Issues of Global Governance: Implications for Europe." In *Gramsci, Historical Materialism and International Relations,* ed. Stephen Gill, 259-290. Cambridge: Cambridge University Press, 1993.

---"Critical Political Economy." In *International Political Economy: Understanding Global Disorder,* ed. Bjorn Hettne, 31-46. London: Zen Books, 1995.

---"A Perspective on Globalization." In *Globalization: Critical Reflections,* ed. James H. Mittelman, 21-33. Boulder, CO: Lynne Rienner Publishers, 1996.

Crawford, Robert M.A. *Regime Theory in the Post-Cold War World: Rethinking Neoliberal Approaches to International Relations.* Brookfield, VT: Dartmouth Publishing Company, 1996.

Cusimano, Maryann K., ed. *Beyond Sovereignty: Issues for a Global Agenda.* Boston: Bedford/St. Martin's Press, 2000.

Cusimano, Maryann K., Mark Hensman, and Leslie Rodrigues. "Private-Sector Transsovereign Actors—MNCs and NGOs." In *Beyond Sovereignty: Issues for a Global Agenda,* ed. Maryann K. Cusimano, 255-282. Boston: Bedford/St. Martin's Press, 2000.

Dallaire, Romeo. *Shake Hands With the Devil: The Failure of Humanity in Rwanda.* New York: Carroll & Graf, 2003.

Deschenes, Jules. "Toward International Criminal Justice." In *The Prosecution of International Crimes: A Critical Study of the International Tribunal for the Former Yugoslavia,* ed. Roger S. Clark and Madeline Sann, 29-58. Somerset, NJ: Transaction Publishers, 1996.

Destexhe, Alain. "The Third Genocide." *Foreign Policy* 97 (1995): 3-17.

Deudney, Daniel. "Grounded Identity: Nature, Place, and Space in Nationalism." In *The Return of Culture and Identity in IR Theory,* ed. Yosef Lapid and Friedrich Kratochwil, 129-146. Boulder, CO: Lynne Rienner Publishers, 1996.

DiMuccio, Ralph and Eric Drew Cooper. "Turbulence and Tradition in International Relations Theory: Prospects for a Postinternational Revolution." In *Pondering Postinternationalism: A Paradigm for the Twenty-First Century?* ed., Heidi H. Hobbs, 169-196. Albany, NY: State University of New York Press, 2000.

Donnelly, Jack. *International Human Rights*. Boulder, CO: Westview Press, 1998.

---"The Social Construction of International Human Rights." In *Human Rights in Global Politics,* ed. Tim Dunne and Nicholas J. Wheeler, 71-103. Cambridge: Cambridge University Press, 1999.

Dougherty, James E. and Robert L. Pfaltzgraff, Jr. *Contending Theories of International Relations: A Comprehensive Survey,* 4d ed. New York: Addison-Wesley Educational Publishers, 1997.

Duffy, Helen. "Toward Eradicating Impunity: The Establishment of an International Criminal Court." *Social Justice* 26 (1999): 115-124.

Dunne, Tim, Michael Cox and Ken Booth, ed. *The Eighty Years' Crisis: International Relations 1919-1999.* Cambridge: Cambridge University Press, 1998.

---"Introduction: The Eighty Years' Crisis 1919-1999." In *The Eighty Years' Crisis: International Relations 1919-1999,* ed. Tim Dunne, Michael Cox, and Ken Booth, xiii-xx. Cambridge: Cambridge University Press, 1998.

Dunne, Tim and Nicholas J. Wheeler, ed. *Human Rights in Global Politics.* Cambridge: Cambridge University Press, 1999.

Durfee, Mary. "Constituting Complexity: Order and Turbulence in World Politics." In *Pondering Postinternationalism: A Paradigm for the Twenty-First Century?* ed., Heidi H. Hobbs, 137-154. Albany, NY: State University of New York Press, 2000.

Eckstein, Harry. "Case Study and Theory in Political Science." In *Handbook of Political Science,* ed. F. I. Greenstein and Nelson W. Polsby, 79-138. Reading, PA: Addison-Wesley Press, 1975.

Efinger, Manfred and Michael Zurn, "Explaining Conflict Management in East-West Relations: A Quantitative Test of Problem-Structural Typologies." In *International Regimes in East-West Politics,* ed. Volker Rittberger, 64-89. London: Pinter Publishers, 1990.

Elian, George. *The International Court of Justice.* Leiden, The Netherlands: A.W. Sitjthoff International Publishing Company, 1971.

Elshtain, Jean Bethke. "Rethinking Sovereignty." In *Post-Realism: The Rhetorical Turn in International Relations,* ed. Francis A. Beer and Robert Hariman, 171-191. East Lansing, MI: Michigan State University Press, 1996.

Everett, Robinson O. "American Servicemembers and the ICC." In *The United States and the International Criminal Court: National Security and International Law, ed.* Sarah B. Sewall and Carl Kaysen, 137-152. Lanham, MD: Rowman & Littlefield Publishers, Inc., 2000.

Falk, Richard. *On Humane Governance: Toward a New Global Politics.* University Park, PA: The Pennsylvania State University Press, 1995.

---"The Challenges of Genocide and Genocidal Politics in an Era of Globalisation." In *Human Rights in Global Politics,* ed. Tim Dunne and Nicholas J. Wheeler, 177-195. Cambridge: Cambridge Univeristy Press, 1999.

Ferencz, Benjamin. *Defining International Aggression: The Search for World Peace.* Dobbs Ferry, NY: Oceana Publications, Inc., 1975.

---*An International Criminal Court: A Step Towards Peace—A Documentary History and Analysis.* 1980.

---"International Criminal Courts: The Legacy of Nuremberg." *Pace International Law Review* 203 (1998): 22-45.

Ferguson, Yale H. "Postinternationalism and the Future of IR Theory." In *Pondering Postinternationalism: A Paradigm for the Twenty-First Century?* ed. Heidi Hobbs, 197-216. Albany, NY: State University of New York Press, 2000.

Ferguson, Yale H. and Richard W. Mansbach. *The State, Conceptual Chaos, and the Future of International Relations Theory.* Boulder, CO: Lynne Rienner Publishers, 1989.

---"Political Space and Westphalian States in a World of 'Polities': Beyond Inside/Outside." *Global Governance* 2 (1995): 261-287.

---*Polities: Authority, Identities, and Change.* Columbia, SC: University of South Carolina Press, 1996.

---"The Past as Prelude to the Future? Identities and Loyalties in Global Politics." In *The Return of Culture and Identity in IR Theory,* ed. Yosef Lapid and Friedrich Kratochwil, 21-46. Boulder, CO: Lynne Rienner Publishers, 1996.

---"Global Politics at the Turn of the Millennium: Changing Bases of "Us" and Them." *International Studies Review* 2 (1999): 77-108.

---"History's Revenge and Future Shock." In *Approaches to Global Governance,* ed. Martin Hewson and Timothy J. Sinclair, 197-238. Albany, NY: State University of New York Press, 1999.

Fernandez de Guremendi, Silvia A., "The Role of the International Prosecutor." In *The International Criminal Court: The Making of the Rome Statute—Issues, Negotiations, Results,* 175-188. The Hague: Kluwer Law International, 1999.

Finkelstein, Lawrence S. "What is Global Governance?" *Global Governance* 1 (1995): 367-372.

Finnemore, Martha. "Norms, Culture, and World Politics: Insights from Sociology's Institutionalism." *International Organization* 50 (1996): 349-347.

Forsythe, David P. *The Internationalization of Human Rights.* Lexington, MA: Lexington Books, 1991.

---"Politics and the International Tribunal for the Former Yugoslavia." In *The Prosecution of International Crimes: A Critical Study of the International Tribunal for the Former Yugoslavia,* ed. Roger S. Clark and Madeline Sann, 185-207. Somerset, NJ: Transaction Publishers, 1996.

---"The International Court of Justice at Fifty." In *International Court of Justice: Its Future Role After Fifty Years,* ed. Sam Muller, C.D. Rai and Thur Anjzky J.M., 110-123. The Hague, The Netherlands: Kluwer Law International, 1996.

Foucault, Michel. *The Order of Things.* New York, NY: Vintage Books, 1973.

Fried, John H. E. "International Law—Neither Orphan Nor Harlot, Neither Jailer Nor Never-Never Land." In *International Law: Classic and Contemporary Readings,* ed. Charlotte Ku and Paul F. Diehl, 25-51. Boulder, CO: Lynne Rienner Publishers, 1998.

Frost, Mervyn. "A Turn Not Taken: Ethics in IR at the Millenium." In *The Eighty Years' Crisis: International Relations 1919-1999,* ed. Tim Dunne, Michael Cox, and Ken Booth, 119-132. Cambridge: Cambridge University Press, 1998.

Gaer, Felice D. "Reality Check: Human Rights NGOs Confront Governments." In *NGOs, the UN and Global Governance,* ed. Thomas G. Weiss and Leon Gordenker, 51-67. Boulder, CO: Lynne Rienner Publishers, 1996.

George, Alexander L. "Case Studies and Theory Development: The Method of Structured, Focused Comparison." In ed. P.G. Luanan, 43-56. New York: Free Press, 1979.

George, Jim. *Discourses of Global Politics: A Critical (Re)Introduction to International Relations.* Boulder, CO: Lynne Rienner Publishers, 1994.

Gill, Stephen, ed. *Gramsci, Historical Materialism and International Relations,* Cambridge: Cambridge University Press, 1993.

---"Theorizing the Interregnum: The Double Movement and Global Politics in the 1990s." In *International Political Economy,* ed. Bjorn Hettne, 65-99. London: Zen Books, 1995.

---"Transformation and Innovation in the Study of World Order." In *Innovation and Transformation in International Studies,* ed. Stephen Gill and James H. Mittelman, 5-24. Cambridge: Cambridge University Press, 1997.

Gill, Stephen and James H. Mittelman, ed. *Innovation and Transformation in International Studies.* Cambridge: Cambridge University Press, 1997.

Gilpin, Robert. *War and Change in World Politics.* Cambridge: Cambridge University Press, 1981.

Goldstone, Jack A. "Demography, Domestic Conflict, and the International Order." In *International Order and the Future of World Politics,* ed. T.V. Paul and John A. Hall, 352-372. Cambridge: Cambridge University Press, 1999.

Goldstone, Richard J. and Gary Jonathan Bass. "Lessons from the International Criminal Tribunals." In *The United States and the International Criminal Court: National Security and International Law, ed.* Sarah B. Sewall and Carl Kaysen, 51-60. Lanham, MD: Rowman & Littlefield Publishers, Inc., 2000.

Gordenker, Leon and Thomas G. Weiss. "Pluralizing Global Governance: Analytical Approaches and Dimensions." In *NGOs, the UN and Global Governance,* ed. Thomas G. Weiss and Leon Gordenker, 17-51. Boulder, CO: Lynne Rienner Publishers, 1996.

---"NGO Participation in the International Policy Process." In *NGOs, the UN, and Global Governance,* ed. Thomas G. Weiss and Leon Gordenker, 209-223. Boulder, CO: Lynne Rienner Publishers, 1996.

Greppi, Edoardo. "The Evolution of Individual Criminal Responsibility Under International Law." *International Review of the Red Cross* 835 (1999): 531-553.

Grieco, Joseph M. "Anarchy and the Limits of Cooperation: A Realist Critique of the Newest Liberal Internationalism." *International Organization* 42 (1988): 485-507.

---"Understanding the Problem of International Cooperation: The Limits of Neoliberal Institutionalism and the Future of Realist Theory." In *Neorealism and Neoliberalism: The Contemporary Debate,* ed. David A. Baldwin, 301-338. New York: Columbia University Press, 1993.

Gross, Leo. "States as Organs of International Law and the Problems of Auto-Interpretation." In Law and Politics in the World Community: Essays on Hans Kelsen's Pure Theory and Related Problems in International Law, ed. G.A Lipsky, 59-88. Berkeley, CA: University of California Press, 1953.

Haas, Ernst B. *The Uniting of Europe: Political Social and Economic Forces, 1950-1957.* London: Stevens, 1958.

---*Beyond the Nation-State: Functionalism and International Organization.* Stanford, CA: Stanford University Press, 1964.

---"Turbulent Fields and the Theory of Regional Integration." *International Organization* (1975): 173-212.

---"Why Collaborate? Issue-Linkage and International Regimes." *World Politics* 32 (1980): 357-405.

---"Words Can Hurt You: or Who Said What to Whom About Regimes." In *International Regimes,* ed. Stephen D. Krasner, 23-60. Ithaca, NY: Cornell University Press, 1983.

---When Knowledge is Power: Three Models of Change in International Organizations. Berkeley, CA: University of California Press, 1990.

Haas, Peter M. "Do Regimes Matter? Epistemic Communities and Mediterranean Pollution Control." *International Organization* 43 (1989): 377-403.

---"Introduction: Epistemic Communities and International Policy Coordination." *International Organization* 46 (1992): 1-35.

---"Epistemic Communities and the Dynamics of International Environmental Co-operation." In *Regime Theory and International Relations,* ed. Volker Rittberger, 168-201. Oxford: Clarendon Press, 1993.

Haas, Peter M. and Ernst B. Haas. "Learning to Learn: Improving International Governance." *Global Governance* 1 (1995): 255-284.

Hall, Christopher Keith. "The First Proposal For A Permanent International Criminal Court." *International Review of the Red Cross* 322 (1998): 57-74.

Hall, John A. and T.V. Paul. "Introduction." In *International Order and the Future of World Politics,* ed. T.V. Paul and John A. Hall, 1-16. Cambridge: Cambridge University Press, 1999.

---"The State and the Future of World Politics." In *International Order and the Future of World Politics,* ed. T.V. Paul and John A. Hall, 395-408. Cambridge: Cambridge University Press, 1999.

Hasenclever, Andreas, Peter Mayer and Volker Rittberger. *Theories of International Regimes.* Cambridge: Cambridge University Press, 1997.

Held, David. "Democracy and Globalization." *Global Governance* 3 (1996): 251-267.

Held, David and Anthony McGrew. "Globalization and the End of the Old Order." In *The Eighty Years' Crisis: International Relations 1919-1999,* ed. Tim Dunne, Michael Cox, and Ken Booth, 219-244. Cambridge: Cambridge University Press, 1998.

Helms, Jessie. "A Lack of Gratitude." Speech delivered before the United Nations Security Council. January 21, 2000.

Henkin, Louis. "The Future of International Law." In *International Law: Classic and Contemporary Readings,* ed. Charlotte Ku and Paul F. Diehl, 551-568. Boulder, CO: Lynne Rienner Publishers, 1998.

Hettne, Bjorn, ed. *International Political Economy: Understanding Global Disorder.* London: Zen Books, 1995.

---"Introduction: The International Political Economy of Transformation." In *International Political Economy: Understanding Global Disorder,"* ed. Bjorn Hettne, 1-30. London: Zen Books, 1995.

Hewson, Martin and Timothy J. Sinclair, ed. *Approaches to Global Governance Theory.* Albany, NY: State University of New York Press, 1999.

---"The Emergence of Global Governance Theory." In *Approaches to Global Governance Theory,* ed. Martin Hewson and Timothy J. Sinclair, 3-22. Albany, NY: State University of New York Press, 1999.

Hobbes, Thomas. *Leviathan.* New York: Penguin Books USA Inc., 1985. First Published 1651.

Hobbs, Heidi H., ed. *Pondering Postinternationalism: A Paradigm for the Twenty First Century?* Albany, NY: State University of New York Press, 2000.

Hollis, Martin and Steve Smith. *Explaining and Understanding International Relations.* Oxford, England: Clarendon Press, 1990.

Holmes, John T., "The Principle of Complementarity." In *The International Criminal Court: The Making of the Rome Statute—Issues, Negotiations, Results,* ed. Roy S. Lee, 41-78. The Hague: Kluwer Law International, 1999.

Holzner, Burkhart and John H. Marx. *Knowledge Application.* Boston, MA: Allyn & Bacon, 1979.

Human Rights Watch. *Justice in the Balance: Recommendations for an Independent and Effective International Criminal Court.* New York: Human Rights Watch, 1998.

Jackson, Donald W. "Creating a World Criminal Court Is Like Making Sausage Except It Takes Longer." *The Texas Observer,* June 30, 1998.

Janis, Mark W. *International Courts for the Twenty-first Century.* Dordrecht, The Netherlands: Martinus Nijhoff Publishers, 1992.

Jetschke, Anja. "Linking the Unlinkable? International Norms and Nationalism in Indonesia and the Phillipines." In *The Power of Human Rights: International Norms and Domestic Change,* ed. Thomas Risse, Stephen C. Ropp and Kathryn Sikkink, 134-171. Cambridge: Cambridge University Press, 1999.

Johansen, Robert C. "Transnational Politics and Nongovernmental Organizations: Drafting a Treaty to Establish a Permanent International Criminal Court."

Prepared for presentation at the annual International Studies Association conference. Chicago, IL, February 2001.

Jonsson, Christer. "Cognitive Factors in Explaining Regime Dynamics." In *Regime Theory and International Relations,* ed. Volker Rittberger, 202-222. Oxford: Clarendon Press, 1993.

Kahler, Miles. "Inventing International Relations: International Relations Theory After 1945." In *New Thinking in International Relations Theory,* ed. Michael W. Doyle and G. John Ikenberry, 20-53. Boulder, CO: Westview Press, 1997.

Karns, Margaret. "Postinternational Politics and the Growing Glomerations of Global Governance." In *Pondering Postinternationalism: A Paradigm for the Twenty-First Century?* ed. Heidi Hobbs, 39-60. Albany, NY: State University of New York Press, 2000.

Keane, Fergal. *Season of Blood: A Rwandan Journey.* London: Penguin Books, 1995.

Keck, Margaret E. and Kathryn Sikkink. *Activists Beyond Borders: Advocacy Networks in International Politics.* Ithaca, NY: Cornell University Press, 1998.

Kegley, Jr., Charles W., ed. *Controversies in International Relations Theory: Realism and the Neoliberal Challenge.* New York: St. Martin's Press, 1995.

Keohane, Robert. "The Demand for International Regimes." In *International Regimes,* ed. Stephen Krasner, 141-171. Ithaca, NY: Cornell University Press.

---*After Hegemony: Cooperation and Discord in the World Political Economy.* Princeton, NJ: Princeton University Press, 1984.

---ed. *Neorealism and its Critics.* New York: Columbia University Press, 1986.

---ed. *International Institutions and State Power: Essays in International Relations Theory.* Boulder, CO: Westview Press, 1989.

---"Neoliberal Institutionalism: A Perspective on World Politics." In *International Institutions and State Power: Essays in International Relations,* ed. Robert Keohane, 1-20. Boulder: CO: Westview Press, 1989.

---"Institutional Theory and the Realist Challenge After the Cold War." In *Neorealism and Neoliberalism: The Contemporary Debate,* ed. David A. Baldwin, 269-300. New York: Columbia University Press, 1993.

Keohane, Robert and Joseph Nye Jr., ed. *Transnational Relations and World Politics.* Princeton, NJ: Princeton University Press, 1971.

---*Power and Interdependence: World Politics in Transition.* Boston: Little Brown, 1977.

---"Power and Interdependence Revisited." International Organization 41 (1987): 725-753.

Kindleberger, Charles P. "Dominance and Leadership in the International Economy: Exploitation, Public Goods, and Free Rides." *International Studies Quarterly* 25 (1981): 242-254.

---"Hierarchy Versus Inertial Cooperation." *International Organization* 40 (1986): 841-847.

Kirsch, Philippe, Q.C. "Introduction." In *Reflections on the International Criminal Court: Essays in Honour of Adriaan Bos,* ed. Hermann A.M. von Hebel, Johan G. Lammers and Jolien Schukking, 1-10. The Hague: T.M.C. Asser Press, 1999.

---"The Development of the Rome Statute." In *The International Criminal Court: The Making of the Rome Statute—Issues, Negotiations, Results,* ed. Roy S. Lee, 451-461. The Hague: Kluwer Law International, 1999.

Kirsch, Philippe and John T. Holmes. "The Rome Conference on an International Criminal Court: The Negotiating Process." *The American Journal of International Law* 93 (1999): 2-12.

Krasner, Stephen D. *International Regimes.* Ithaca, NY: Cornell University Press, 1983.

---"Structural Causes and Regime Consequences: Regimes as Intervening Variables." In *International Regimes,* ed. Stephen D. Krasner, 1-21. Ithaca, NY: Cornell University Press, 1983.

---"Global Communications and National Power: Life on the Pareto Frontier." In *Neorealism and Neoliberalism: The Contemporary Debate,* ed. David A. Baldwin, 234-249. New York: Columbia University Press, 1993.

---"Sovereignty, Regimes, and Human Rights." In *Regime Theory and International Relations,* ed. Volker Rittberger, 139-168. Oxford: Oxford University Press, 1993.

---*Sovereignty: Organized Hypocrisy.* Princeton, NJ: Princeton University Press, 1999.

Kratochwil, Friedrich. "Of Systems, Boundaries, and Territorality: An Inquiry into the Formation of the State System." *World Politics* 39 (1986): 27-52.

---"Is the Ship of Culture at Sea or Returning?" In *The Return of Culture and Identity in IR Theory,* ed. Yosef Lapid and Friedrich Kratochwil, 201-222. Boulder, CO: Lynne Rienner Publishers, 1996.

Ku, Charlotte and Paul F. Diehl, ed. *International Law: Classic and Contemporary Readings.* Boulder, CO: Lynne Rienner Publishers, 1998.

Kubalkova, Vendulka. "The Twenty Years' Catharsis: E.H. Carr and IR." In *International Relations in a Constructed World,* ed. Vendulka Kubalkova, Nicholas Onuf, and Paul Kowert, 25-57. Armonk, NY: M.E. Sharpe Press, 1998.

Kubalkova, Vendulka, Nicholas Onuf and Paul Kowert, ed. *International Relations in a Constructed World.* Armonk, NY: M.E. Sharpe Press, 1998.

---"Constructing Constructivism." In *International Relations in a Constructed World,* ed. Vendulka Kubalkova, Nicholas Onuf, and Paul Kowert, 3-24. Armonk, NY: M.E. Sharpe Press, 1998.

Lamont, Beth K. "Establishing an International Criminal Court." *The Humanist* (1998): 16-19.

Lapid, Yosef. "Culture's Ship: Returns and Departures in International Relations Theory." In *The Return of Culture and Identity in IR Theory,* ed. Yosef Lapid and Friedrich Kratochwil, 21-46. Boulder, CO: Lynne Rienner Publishers, 1996.

Lapid, Yosef and Fredrich Kratochwil, ed. *The Return of Culture and Identity in IR Theory.* Boulder, CO: Lynne Rienner Publishers, 1996.

Latham, Robert. "Politics in a Floating World: Toward a Critique of Global Governance." In *Approaches to Global Governance Theory,* ed. Martin Hewson and Timothy J. Sinclair, 23-54. Albany, NY: State University of New York Press, 1999.

Lawyers Committtee for Human Rights. *Establishing an International Criminal Court:Major Unresolved Issues in the Draft Statute.* New York, NY: International Criminal Court Briefing Series, 1996.

---*NGO Action Alert on the International Criminal Court.* New York, NY: International Criminal Court Briefing Series, 1998.

---*The Rome Treaty for an International Criminal Court: A Brief Summary of the Main Issues.* New York, NY: International Criminal Court Briefing Series, 1998.

---*Frequently Asked Questions About the International Criminal Court.* New York, NY: International Criminal Court Briefing Series, 1998.

Lee, Roy S., ed. *The International Criminal Court: The Making of the Rome Statute- Issues, Negotiations, Results.* The Hague, The Netherlands: Kluwer Law International, 1999.

---"Creating an International Criminal Court—Of Procedures and Compromises." In *Reflections on the International Criminal Court: Essays in Honour of Adriann Bos,* ed. Herman A.M. von Hebel, Johan G. Lammers, and Jolien Schukking, 141-154. The Hague: T.M.C. Asser Press, 1999.

---"The Rome Conference and its Contributions to International Law." In *The International Criminal Court: The Making of the Rome Statute—Issues, Negotiations, Results,* Roy S. Lee, 1-40. The Hague: Kluwer Law International, 1999.

---"Creating an International Criminal Court—Of Procedures and Compromises." In *Reflections on the International Criminal Court: Essays in Honour of Adriaan Bos,* ed. Herman A.M. von Hebel, Johan G. Lammers and Jolien Schukking, 141-152.

Leonard, Eric K. "Seeking Sovereignty: Gaining Understanding Through Critical Analysis." *New Political Science* 23 (2001): 407-428.

---"Discovering the New Face of Sovereignty: Complementarity and the International Criminal Court." *New Political Science* 27 (2005): 87-104.

Lepgold, Joseph. "An Intellectual Agenda for Students of Postinternational World Politics." In *Pondering Postinternationalism: A Paradigm for the Twenty-First Century?* ed., Heidi H. Hobbs, 155-168. Albany, NY: State University of New York Press, 2000.

Levy, Marc A., Oran R. Young, and Michael Zurn. "The Study of International Regimes." *European Journal of International Relations* 1 (1995): 267-330.

Lipschutz, Ronnie D. "Politics Among People: Global Civil Society Reconsidered." In *Pondering Postinternationalism: A Paradigm for the Twenty-First Century?* ed., Heidi H. Hobbs, 83-98. Albany, NY: State University of New York Press, 2000.

Little, Richard. "The Growing Relevance of Pluralism?" In *International Theory: Positivism and Beyond,* ed. Steve Smith, Ken Booth and Marysia Zalewski, 66-86. Cambridge: Cambridge University Press, 1996.

Luck, Edward C. *Mixed Messages: American Politics and International Organization 1919-1999.* Washington, D.C.: Brookings Institution Press, 1999.

Lynn, Jr., Laurence E. ed. *Knowledge and Policy: The Uncertain Connection.* Washington, D.C.: National Academy of Sciences, 1978.

Mann, Michael. "Has Globalization Ended the Rise and Rise of the Nation-State?" In *International Order and the Future of World Politics,* ed. T.V. Paul and John A. Hall, 237-261. Cambridge: Cambridge University Press, 1999.

Mansbach, Richard W. "Changing Understandings of Global Politics: Preinternationalism, Internationalism, and Postinternationalism." In *Pondering Postinternationalism: A Paradigm for the Twenty-First Century?* ed., Heidi H. Hobbs, 7-24. Albany, NY: State University of New York Press, 2000.

March, James G. and Johan P. Olsen. *Rediscovering Institutions: The Organizational Basis of Politics.* New York: The Free Press, 1989.

Martin, David. *General Amin.* London: Faber and Faber, 1974.

McCorquodale, Robert and Richard Fairbrother. "Globalization and Human Rights." *Human Rights Quarterly* 21 (1999): 735-766.

Meadwell, Hudson. "Stateless Nations and the Emerging International Order." In *International Order and the Future of World Politics,* ed. T.V. Paul and John A. Hall, 262-282. Cambridge: Cambridge University Press, 1999.

Meron, Theodor. "Crimes Under the Jurisdiction of the International Criminal Court." In *Reflections on the International Criminal Court: Essays in Honour of Adriaan Bos,* ed. Herman A.M. von Hebel, Johan G. Lammers and Jolien Schukking, 47-55. The Hague: T.M.C. Asser Press, 1999.

Miller, Lynn H. *Global Order: Values and Power in International Politics.* Boulder, CO: Westview Press, 1994.

Mills, Kurt. *Human Rights in the Emerging Global Order: A New Sovereignty?* New York: St. Martin's Press, 1998.

Mingst, Karen A. "Global Governance: The American Perspective." In *Globalization and Global Governance,* ed. Raimo Vayrynen, 87-105. Lanham, MD: Rowman & Littlefield, 1999.

---*Essentials of International Relations.* New York, NY: W.W. Norton & Company, Inc., 1999.

Mitchell, Ronald B. "Regime Design Matters: Intentional Oil Pollution and Treaty Compliance." *International Organization* 48 (1994): 425-458.

Mitrany, David. *A Working Peace System: An Argument for the Functional Development of International Organization.* London: Royal Institute of International Affairs, 1943.

---"The Functional Approach to World Organization." *International Affairs* 24 (1948): 350-363.

Mittelman, James H., ed. *Globalization: Critical Reflections.* Boulder, CO: Lynne Rienner Publishers, 1996.

---"The Dynamics of Globalization." In *Globalization: Critical Reflections,* ed. James H. Mittleman, 1-20. Boulder, CO: Lynne Rienner Publishers, 1996.

---"How Does Globalization Really Work?" In *Globalization: Critical Reflections,* ed. James H. Mittleman, 229-242. Boulder, CO: Lynne Rienner Publishers, 1996.

Moravcsik, Andrew. "Taking Preferences Seriously: A Liberal Theory of International Politics." *International Organization* 51 (1997): 513-553.

---"The Origins of Human Rights Regimes." *International Organization* 54 (2000): 217-252.

Moreno, Dario. "The Limits of Sovereignty in a Bifurcated World." In *Pondering Postinternationalism: A Paradigm for the Twenty-First Century?* ed. Heidi Hobbs, 25-38. Albany, NY: State University of New York Press, 2000.

Morgenthau, Hans J. *Politics Among Nations: The Struggle for Power and Peace.* New York, NY: McGraw-Hill, 1948.

Morris, Madeline. "Complementarity and Conflict: States, Victims and the ICC." In *The United States and the International Criminal Court: National Security and International Law, ed.* Sarah B. Sewall and Carl Kaysen, 195-212. Lanham, MD: Rowman & Littlefield Publishers, Inc., 2000.

---"High Crimes and Misconceptions: The ICC and Non-party States." *Duke Journal of Comparative and International Law* 63 (2000): 101-151.

Moynier, Gustave. "Draft Convention for the Establishment of an International Judicial Body Suitable for the Prevention and Punishment of Violations of the Geneva Conventions." Reprinted in Christopher Keith Hall, "The First Proposal For A Permanent International Criminal Court." *International Review of the Red Cross* 322 (1998).

Muller, Sam, C.D. Rai and Thur Anjtzky J.M. *International Court of Justice: Its Future Role After Fifty Years.* The Hague: Kluwer International Law, 1996.

Murphy, Cornelius F. Jr. *Theories of World Governance: A Study in the History of Ideas.* Washington, DC: The Catholic University of America Press, 1999.

Murphy, Craig N. *International Organization and Industrial Change: Global Governance Since 1850.* Oxford: Oxford University Press, 1994.

Nanda, Ved P. "The Establishment of a Permanent International Criminal Court: Challenges Ahead." *Human Rights Quarterly* 20 (1998): 413-428.

Nash, William L. "The ICC and the Deployment of US Armed Forces." In *The United States and the International Criminal Court: National Security and International Law, ed.* Sarah B. Sewall and Carl Kaysen, 153-164. Lanham, MD: Rowman & Littlefield Publishers, Inc., 2000.

Neier, Aryeh. "Waiting for Justice: The United States and the International Criminal Court." *World Policy Journal* 15(1998): 33-37.

Neufeld, Mark. *The Restructuring of International Relations Theory.* Cambridge: Cambridge University Press, 1995.

Nolte, Georg. "The United States and the International Criminal Court." In *Unilateralism and U.S. Foreign Policy: International Perspectives, ed.* David M. Malone and Yuen Foong Khong, 71-94. Boulder, CO: Lynne Rienner Publishers, 2003.

Oliver, James K. "The Balance of Power Heritage of Interdependence and Traditionalism." *International Studies Quarterly* 26 (1982): 373-396.

Omestad, Thomas. "The Brief for a World Court." *U.S. News and World Report,* 6 October 1997.

Onuf, Nicholas G. *World of Our Making: Rules and Rule in Social Theory and International Relations.* Columbia, SC: University of South Carolina Press, 1989.

---"Sovereignty: Outline of a Conceptual History." *Alternatives* 16 (1991): 425-446.

---"A Constructivist Manifesto." In *Constituting International Political Economy,* ed. Kurt Burch and Robert A. Denemark, 7-17. Boulder, CO: Lynne Rienner Publishers, 1997.

---"Constructivism: A User's Manuel." In *International Relations in a Constructed World,* ed. Vendulka Kubalkova, Nicholas Onuf and Paul Kowert, 58-79. Armonk, NY: M.E Sharpe Press, 1998.

---The Republican Legacy in International Thought. Cambridge: Cambridge University Press, 1998.

---"Writing Large: Habit, Skills, and Grandiose Theory." In *Pondering Postinternationalism: A Paradigm for the Twenty-First Century?* ed. Heidi H. Hobbs, 99-116. Albany, NY: State University of New York Press, 2000.

Opello, Jr., Walter C and Stephen J. Rosow. *The Nation-state and Global Order: A Historical Introduction to Contemporary Politics.* Boulder, CO: Lynne Rienner Publishers, 1999.

Osiel, Mark J. "Why Prosecute? Critics of Punishment for Mass Atrocities." *Human Rights Quarterly* 22 (2000): 118-147.

Oye, Kenneth A. "Explaining Cooperation Under Anarchy: Hypotheses and Strategies." *World Politics* 38 (1985): 1-24.

Pace, William R. "Globalizing Justice." *Harvard International Review* 20 (1998): 26-30.

---"Relationship Between the International Criminal Court and Non-Governmental Organizations." In *Reflections on the International Criminal Court: Essays in Honour of Adriaan Bos,* ed. Herman A.M. von Hebel, Johan G. Lammers and Jolien Schukking, 189-211. The Hague: T.M.C. Asser Press, 1999.

Pace, William R. and Tanya Karanasios, "Outcome of Preparatory Committee Meeting, March 25- April 12," NGO Coalition for an International Criminal Court, home page: <http://www.igc.apc.org/icc>

Pace, William R. and Mark Thieroff. "Participation of Non-Governmental Organizations." In *The International Criminal Court: The Making of the Rome Statute—Issues, Negotiations, Results,* ed. Roy S. Lee, 391-398. The Hague: Kluwer Law International, 1999.

Palan, Ronen. "Global Governance and Social Closure *or* Who Is to Be Governed in the Era of Global Governance?" In *Approaches to Global Governance Theory,* ed. Martin Hewson and Timothy J. Sinclair, 55-72. Albany, NY: State University of New York Press, 1999.

Panganiban, Rik. "The NGO Coalition for an International Criminal Court." *U.N. Chronicle* 34 (1997): 36.

Paolini, Albert J., Anthony P. Jarvis and Christian Reus-Smit, ed. *Between Sovereignty and Global Governance: The United Nations, the State and Civil Society.* New York: St. Martin's Press, 1998.

Pasic, Sujata Chakrabarti. "Culturing International Relations Theory: A Call for Extension." In *The Return of Culture and Identity in IR Theory,* ed. Yosef Lapid and Friedrich Kratochwil, 85-104. Boulder, CO: Lynne Rienner Publishers, 1996.

Paul, T.V. and John A. Hall, ed. *International Order and the Future of World Politics.* Cambridge: Cambridge University Press, 1999.

---"Introduction." In *International Order and the Future of World Politics,* ed. T.V. Paul and John A. Hall, 1-16. Cambridge: Cambridge University Press, 1999.

Pease, Kelly-Kate S. *International Organizations: Perspectives on Governance in the Twenty-First Century.* Upper Saddle River, NJ: Prentice Hall, Inc., 2000.

Pettman, Ralph. *Commonsense Constructivism: or the Making of World Affairs.* Armonk, NY: M.E. Sharpe, Inc. 2000.

Pejic, Jelena. "The Tribunal and the ICC: Do Precedents Matter?" *Albany Law Review* 60 (1997): 841-860.

Powell, Robert. "Absolute and Relative Gains in International Relations Theory." *American Political Science Review* 85 (1991): 1303-1320.

---"Anarchy in International Relations Theory: The Neorealist—Neoliberal Debate." *International Organization* 48: 313-344.

Prunier, Gerard. *The Rwanda Crisis: History of Genocide.* New York, NY: Columbia University Press, 1995.

Putnam, Robert D. "Diplomacy and Domestic Politics: The Logic of Two-Level Games." *International Organization* 42: 427-460.

Reus-Smit, Christian. "Changing Patterns of Governance: From Absolutism to Global Multilateralism." In *Between Sovereignty and Global Governance: The United Nations, the State and Civil Society,* ed. Albert J. Paolini, Anthony P. Jarvis and Christian Reus-Smit, 3-28. New York: St. Martin's Press, 1998.

Risse, Thomas, Stephen C. Ropp and Kathryn Sikkink, ed. *The Power of Human Rights: International Norms and Domestic Change.* Cambridge: Cambridge University Press, 1999.

Risse, Thomas and Stephen C. Ropp. "International Human Rights Norms and Domestic Change: Conclusions." In *The Power of Human Rights: International Norms and Domestic Change,* ed. Thomas Risse, Stephen C. Ropp and Kathryn Sikkink, 234-278. Cambridge: Cambridge University Press, 1999.

Risse, Thomas and Kathryn Sikkink. "The Socialization of International Human Rights Norms in Domestic Practices: Introduction." In *The Power of Human Rights: International Norms and Domestic Change,* ed. Thomas Risse, Stephen C. Ropp and Kathryn Sikkink, 1-38. Cambridge: Cambridge University Press, 1999.

Rittberger, Volker, ed. *International Regimes in East-West Politics.* London: Pinter Publishers, 1990.

---ed. *Regime Theory and International Relations.* Oxford: Oxford University Press, 1993.

---"Research on International Regimes in Germany: The Adaptive Internalization of an American Social Science Concept." In *Regime Theory and International Relations,* ed. Volker Rittberger, 3-22. Oxford: Clarendon Press, 1993.

Roberge, Marie-Claude. "The New International Criminal Court: A Preliminary Assessment." *International Review of the Red Cross* 325 (1998): 671-691.

Robinson, Darryl. "Defining 'Crimes Against Humanity' at the Rome Conference." *The American Journal of International Law* 93 (1999): 43-57.

Ropp, Stephen C. and Kathryn Sikkink. "International Norms and Domestic Politics in Chile and Guatemala." In *The Power of Human Rights:*

International Norms and Domestic Change, ed. Thomas Risse, Stephen C. Ropp and Kathryn Sikkink, 172-204. Cambridge: Cambridge University Press.

Rosenau, James N. "Governance, Order, and Change in World Politics." In *Governance Without Government: Order and Change in World Politics,* ed. James N. Rosenau and Ernst-Otto Czempiel, 1-29. Cambridge: Cambridge University Press, 1992.

---"Governance in the Twenty-first Century." *Global Governance* 1 (1995): 13-43.

---"Imposing Global Orders: A Synthesised Ontology for a Turbulent Era." In *Innovation and Transformation in International Studies,* ed. Stephen Gill and James H. Mittelman, 220-235. Cambridge: Cambridge University Press, 1997.

---*Along the Domestic-Foreign Frontier: Exploring Governance in a Turbulent World.* Cambridge: Cambridge University Press, 1997.

---"Toward an Ontology for Global Governance." In *Approaches to Global Governance Theory,* ed. Martin Hewson and Timothy J. Sinclair, 287-302. Albany, NY: State University of New York Press.

---"Beyond Postinternationalism." In *Pondering Postinternationalism: A Paradigm for the Twenty-First Century?* ed. Heidi Hobbs, 219-238. Albany, NY: State University of New York Press, 2000.

Rosenau, James N. and Ernst-Otto Czempiel, ed. *Governance Without Government: Order and Change in World Politics.* Cambridge: Cambridge University Press, 1992.

Rubin, Alfred P. "Challenging the Conventional Wisdom: Another View of the International Criminal Court." *Journal of International Affairs* 52 (1999): 783-794.

Ruggie, John Gerard, ed. Constructing the World Polity: Essays on International Institutionalization. New York: Routledge, 1998.

---"The Social Constructivist Challenge." *International Organization* 52 (1998): 855-885.

Rwelamira, Medard R. "Composition and Administration of the Court." In *The International Criminal Court: The Making of the Rome Statute—Issues, Negotiations, Results,* ed. Roy S. Lee, 153-174. The Hague: Kluwer Law International, 1999.

Sadat, Leila Nadya. "The Evolution of the ICC: From The Hague to Rome and Back Again." In *The United States and the International Criminal Court: National Security and International Law, ed.* Sarah B. Sewall and Carl Kaysen, 31-50. Lanham, MD: Rowman & Littlefield Publishers, Inc., 2000.

Schabas, William. "United States Hostility to the International Criminal Court: It's All About the Security Council," *European Journal of International Law* 15 (2004): 701-720

Scharf, Michael P. "The ICC's Jurisdiction over the Nationals of Non-Party States." In The United States and the International Criminal Court: National Security and International Law, ed. Sarah B. Sewall and Carl Kaysen, 213-236. Lanham, MD: Rowman & Littlefield Publishers, Inc., 2000.

Schechter, Michael G. "*Our Global Neighborhood:* Pushing Problem-Solving Theory to its Limits and the Limits of Problem-Solving Theory." In *Approaches to Global Governance Theory,* ed. Martin Hewson and Timothy Sinclair, 239-258. Albany, NY: State University of New York Press, 1999.

Scheffer, David J. "US Policy and the Proposed Permanent International Criminal Court (transcript of a speech at the Carter Center, Atlanta, GA)." *US Department of State Dispatch* 8 (1997): 20-22.

---"Development at the Rome Treaty Conference (transcript of a speech to the Foreign Relations Committee, United States Senate)." *US Department of State Dispatch* 9 (1998): 19-23.

---"The United States and the International Criminal Court," *The American Journal of International Law* 93 (1999): 12-22.

---"The US Perspective on the ICC." In *The United States and the International Criminal Court: National Security and International Law, ed.* Sarah B. Sewall and Carl Kaysen, 115-118. Lanham, MD: Rowman & Littlefield Publishers, Inc., 2000.

---"Evolution of US Policy Towards the International Criminal Court." Address at American University, Washington DC. September 14, 2000.

Schmitz, Hans Peter. "Transnational Activism and Political Change in Kenya and Uganda." In *The Power of Human Rights: International Norms and Domestic Change,* ed. Thomas Risse, Stephen C. Ropp and Kathryn Sikkink, 39-77. Cambridge: Cambridge University Press, 1999.

Scholte, Jan Aart. "Beyond the Buzzword: Toward a Critical Theory of Globalization." In *Globalization: Theory and Practice,* ed. Eleonore Kofmon and Gillian Youngs, 43-57. New York: Pinter, 1996.

Schwarzenberger, G. International Law as Applied by the International Courts and Tribunals, vol II: The Law of Armed Conflict. London: Stevens, 1968.

Sewall, Sarah B. and Carl Kaysen, ed. The United States and the International Criminal Court: National Security and International Law. Lanham, MD: Rowman & Littlefield Publishers, Inc., 2000.

Sewall, Sarah B., Carl Kaysen and Michael P. Scharf. "The United States and the International Criminal Court: An Overview." In *The United States and the International Criminal Court: National Security and International Law, ed.* Sarah B. Sewall and Carl Kaysen, 1-30. Lanham, MD: Rowman & Littlefield Publishers, Inc., 2000.

Shaw, Martin. "The State of Globalization: Towards a Theory of State Transformations." *Review of International Political Economy* 4 (1997): 497-513.

Shotwell, James. "Alternatives for War." *Foreign Affairs* 6 (1928): 459-467.

Simai, Mihaly. The Future of Global Governance: Managing Risk and Change in the International System. Washington, DC: United States Institute of Peace Press, 1994.

Sinclair, Timothy J. "Beyond International Relations Theory: Robert W. Cox and Approaches to World Order." In *Approaches to World Order,* ed. Robert W. Cox and Timothy J. Sinclair, 3-18. Cambridge, England: Cambridge University Press, 1996.

Smith, Steve. "The Self-Images of a Discipline: A Genealogy of International Relations Theory." In *International Relations Theory Today,* ed. Ken Booth and Steve Smith, 1-37. University Park, PA: The Pennsylvania State University Press, 1995.

---"Positivism and Beyond." In *International Theory: Positivism and Beyond,* ed. Steve Smith, Ken Booth, and Marysia Zalewski, 11-46. Cambridge: Cambridge University Press, 1996.

---"Is the Truth Out There? Eight Questions About International Order." In *International Order and the Future of World Politics,* ed. T.V. Paul and John A. Hall, 99-120. Cambridge: Cambridge University Press, 1999.

Smith, Steve, Ken Booth and Marysia Zalewski, ed. *International Theory: Positivism and Beyond,* Cambridge: Cambridge University Press, 1996.

Snidal, Duncan. "The Limits of Hegemonic Stability Theory." *International Organization* 39 (1985): 579-614.

---"Relative Gains and the Pattern of International Cooperation." *American Political Science Review* 85 (1991): 701-726.

Sorensen, Georg. "International Relations Theory After the Cold War." In *The Eighty Years' Crisis: International Relations 1919-1999,* ed. Tim Dunne, Michael Cox, and Ken Booth, 83-100. Cambridge: Cambridge University Press, 1998.

Sterling-Folker, Jennifer. "Competing Paradigms or Birds of a Feather? Constructivism and Neoliberal Institutionalism Compared." *International Studies Quarterly* 44 (2000): 97-120.

Stokke, Olav Schram. "Regimes as Governance Systems." In *Global Governance: Drawing Insights for the Environmental Experience,* ed. Oran R. Young, 27-63. Cambridge, MA: The MIT Press, 1997.

Strange, Susan. "*Cave! Hic Dragones:* A Critique of Regime Analysis." In *International Regimes,* ed. Stephen D. Krasner, 337-355. Ithaca, NY: Cornell University Press.

---"Wake Up, Krasner! The World Has Changed." *Review of International Political Economy* 1 (1994): 209-219.

---*The Retreat of the State: The Diffusion of Power in the World Economy.* Cambridge: Cambridge University Press, 1996.

Sunstein, Cass. *Free Markets and Social Justice.* New York: Oxford University Press, 1997.

Swart, Bert and Goran Sluiter. "The International Criminal Court and International Criminal Co-Operation." In *Reflections on the International Criminal Court: Essays in Honour of Adriaan Bos,* ed. Herman A.M. von Hebel, Johan G. Lammers and Jolien Schukking, 91-127. The Hague: T.M.C. Asser Press, 1999.

Tafe, Ursula C. "Intergovernmental Organizations." In *Beyond Sovereignty: Issues for a Global Agenda,* ed. Maryann K. Cusimano, 221-252. Boston: Bedford/St. Martin's Press, 2000.

Taylor, Paul. "Functionalism: The Approach of David Mitrany." In *Framework for International Cooperation,* ed. A.J.R. Groom and Paul Taylor, 125-138. London: Pintner Publishers, 1990.

Teitelbaum, Alejandro. "Statute of the International Criminal Court: A Critique." *Social Justice* 26 (1999): 107-114.

Thornberry, Cedric. "Saving the War Crimes Tribunal." *Foreign Policy* 104 (1996): 72-86.

Tomuschat, Christian. "International Criminal Prosecution: The Precedent of Nuremberg Confirmed." In *The Prosecution of International Crimes: A Critical Study of the International Tribunal for the Former Yugoslavia,* ed. Roger S. Clark and Madeline Sann, 17-27. Somerset, NJ: Transaction Publishers.

Vayrynen, Raimo, ed. *Globalization and Global Governance,* Lanham, MD: Rowman & Littlefield Publishers, Inc., 1999.

---"Norms, Compliance, and Enforcement in Global Governance." In *Globalization and Global Governance,* ed. Raimo Vayrynen, 25-46. Lanham, MD: Rowman & Littlefield Publishers, Inc., 1999.

Vincent, R.J. *Human Rights and International Relations.* Cambridge: Cambridge University Press, 1997.

Viotti, Paul R. and Mark V. Kauppi, 3rd edition. *International Relations Theory: Realism, Pluralism, Globalism, and Beyond.* Needham Heights, MA: Allyn and Bacon, 1999.

Von Hebel, Herman A.M. "An International Criminal Court—A Historical Perspective." In *Reflections on the International Criminal Court: Essays in Honour of Adriann Bos,* ed. Hermann A.M. von Hebel, Johan G. Lammers and Jolien Schukking, 13-38. The Hague: T.M.C. Asser Press, 1999.

Von Hebel, Herman A.M., Johan G. Lammers and Jolien Schukking, ed. *Reflections on the International Criminal Court: Essays in Honour of Adriaan Bos.* The Hague: T.M.C. Asser Press, 1999.

Von Hebel, Herman and Darryl Robinson. "Crimes Within the Jurisdiction of the Court." In *The International Criminal Court: The Making of the Rome*

Statute—Issues, Negotiations, Results, ed. Roy S. Lee, 79-126. The Hague: Kluwer Law International, 1999.

Waever, Olav. "The Rise and Fall of the Inter-paradigm Debate." In *International Theory: Positivism and Beyond,* ed. Steve Smith, Ken Booth and Marysia Zalewski, 149-185. Cambridge: Cambridge University Press, 1996.

Waltz, Kenneth N. *Theory of International Politics.* New York: McGraw-Hill, 1979.

Wapner, Paul. "The Normative Promise of Nonstate Actors: A Theoretical Account of Global Civil Society." In *Principled Politics: The Challenge of Normative International Relations,* ed. Paul Wapner and Lester Edwin J. Ruiz, 261-274. New York: Rowman & Littlefield, 2000.

Weber, Cynthia. *Simulating Sovereignty: Intervention, the State and Symbolic Exchange.* Cambridge: Cambridge University Press, 1995.

Wedgewood, Ruth. "The Constitution and the ICC." In *The United States and the International Criminal Court: National Security and International Law, ed.* Sarah B. Sewall and Carl Kaysen, 119-136. Lanham, MD: Rowman & Littlefield Publishers, Inc., 2000.

Weiss, Thomas G. "Principles, Politics, and Humanitarian Action," *Ethics & International Affairs* 13 (1999): 1-22.

Weiss, Thomas G. and Leon Gordenker, ed. *NGOs, the UN, and Global Governance.* Boulder, CO: Lynne Rienner Publishers, 1996.

Weiss, Thomas G., David P. Forsythe, and Roger A. Coate, 2nd edition. *United Nations and Changing World Politics.* Boulder, CO: Westview Press, 1997.

Wendt, Alexander. "Anarchy is What States Make of it: The Social Construction of Power Politics." *International Organization* 41 (1992): 335-370.

---"On Constitution and Causation in International Relations." In *The Eighty Years' Crisis: International Relations 1919-1999,* ed. Tim Dunne, Michael Cox, and Ken Booth, 101-118. Cambridge: Cambridge University Press, 1998.

---*Social Theory of International Politics.* Cambridge: Cambridge University Press, 1999.

Weschler, Lawrence. "Exceptional Cases in Rome: The United States and the Struggle for an ICC." In *The United States and the International Criminal Court: National Security and International Law, ed.* Sarah B. Sewall and Carl Kaysen, 85-114. Lanham, MD: Rowman & Littlefield Publishers, Inc., 2000.

Willis, James F. Prologue to Nuremberg: The Politics and Diplomacy of Punishing War Criminals of the First World War. Westport, CT: Greenwood Press, 1982.

Wilmshurst, Elizabeth. "Jurisdiction of the Court." In *The International Criminal Court: The Making of the Rome Statute—Issues, Negotiations, Results,* ed. Roy S. Lee, 127-142. The Hague: Kluwer Law International, 1999.

Wolff, R.P. "The Conflict Between Authority and Autonomy." In *Authority,* ed. Joseph Raz, 20-31. Oxford: Oxford and Basil Blackwell, 1990.

Woods, Ngaire. "Good Governance in International Organizations." *Global Governance* 5 (1999), 39-61.

Woolfe, Leonard. "De Profundis." *Political Quarterly* 10 (1939): 463-476.

---*The War for Peace.* New York, NY: Garland Publishing, Inc., 1972.

Yee, Lionel. "The International Criminal Court and the Security Council." In *The International Criminal Court: The Making of the Rome Statute—Issues, Negotiations, Results,* ed. Roy S. Lee, 143-152. The Hague: Kluwer Law International, 1999.

Young, Oran R. "International Regimes: Problems of Concept Formation." *World Politics* 32 (1980): 331-356.

---"International Regimes: Toward a New Theory of Institutions." *World Politics* 39 (1986): 104-122.

---"Political Leadership and Regime Formation: On the Development of Institutions in International Society." *International Organization* 45 (1991): 281-308.

---ed. *Global Governance: Drawing Insights from the Environmental Experience,* Cambridge, MA: The MIT Press, 1997.

---"Rights, Rules, and Resources in World Affairs." In *Global Governance: Drawing Insights from the Environmental Experience,* ed. Oran R. Young, 1-23. Cambridge, MA: The MIT Press, 1997.

---"Global Governance: Toward a Theory of Decentralized World Order." In *Global Governance: Drawing Insights from the Environmental Experience,* ed. Oran R. Young, 273-299. Cambridge, MA: The MIT Press, 1997.

---*Governance in World Affairs.* Ithaca, NY: Cornell University Press, 1999.

Young, Oran R. and Gail Osherenko. "Testing Theories of Regime Formation: Findings from a Large Collaborative Research Program." In *Regime Theory and International Relations,* ed. Volker Rittberger, 223-251. Oxford: Oxford University Press, 1993.

Zacher, Mark W. "The Decaying Pillars of the Westphalian Temple: Implications for International Order and Governance." In *Governance Without Government: Order and Change in World Politics,* ed. James N. Rosenau and Ernst-Otto Czempiel, 58-101. Cambridge: Cambridge University Press, 1992.

---"Uniting Nations: Global Regimes and the United Nations System." In *Globalization and Global Governance,* ed. Raimo Vayrynen, 47-65. Lanham, MD: Rowman & Littlefield, 1999.

Zalewski, Marysia. "All These Theories Yet the Bodies Keep Piling Up': Theories, Theorists, Theorising." In *International Theory: Positivism and Beyond,* ed. Steve Smith, Ken Booth, and Marysia Zalewski, 340-353. Cambridge: Cambridge University Press, 1996.

Zimmern, Alfred. "Organize the Peace World," *Political Quarterly* 5 (1934): 153-166.

---*The League of Nations and the Rule of Law: 1918-1935.* London: Macmillan, 1945.

Index